'As Eugene Peterson said [...] ...ual life, just your life." *Reimagining th[e ...]* ...ains how developing a robust inner life of self-awa[reness ...] build deeper God-awareness, which flows into healthy, mature and long-lasting outward acts of service: at home, at church and at work. Using practical tools rooted in ancient wisdom, Charles and Mary help us to see how our experiences and assumptions have informed the maps we use to make sense of our lives – and encourage us to be cartographers who navigate the world with skill, empathy and grace.'
Tim Yearsley, Head of Innovation, LICC

'This is the ideal guide to read as part of your spiritual journey. Charles and Mary have an amazing knack of unsettling us both kindly and knowingly to offer resources that help us at every twist and turn. You're safe in their hands whichever route you take through the easy and tough times. I particularly appreciated how they shared so openly from their own experience, and I would heartily recommend that you make room for this wonderful resource in your backpack.'
The Revd Dr Chris Sheehan, Pioneer Distinctive Deacon, Worcester Diocese

'As I read *Reimagining the Landscape of Faith*, it was as if two wonderfully gifted spiritual directors were guiding me along the past, present and future of my own faith journey. This is a refreshing and profound exploration of spirituality, brilliantly combining insights from scripture, theology, psychology and, of course, cartography. I have never been particularly good at reading actual maps but as a result of reading *Reimagining*, I feel much more able to make sense of my journey towards God.'
The Revd Dr Simon Steer, Chaplain, Abingdon School, and former Principal at Redcliffe College, Gloucester and The London School of Theology

'In my role supporting Christian colleagues to grow and develop as they work in an international charity supporting children in challenging circumstances, I can see that this book will enable those I work with to open a space for a deeper relationship with God, and a sense of working together with God in the world. *Reimagining the Landscape of Faith* will help activists and those who are engaged in social justice to recognise that their action can be even more powerful when it is grounded in deeper self-awareness.'
Kezia M'Clelland, Director for People and Organisation, Viva

'Charles and Mary have been faithful companions on my spiritual journey for many years and I can't wait to introduce them to others through this book! Their material hangs together well with a penetrating coherence, managing to make contributions from historical Christians and contemplatives much more accessible. In these pages they also vulnerably share their path through life and in doing so, undoubtedly equip others to find their own. Given today's shifting and disorientating landscape of faith this is an incredibly timely book which offers fresh perspective on both ancient paths and contemporary thinking. I'm certain it will provoke courage to enable next steps in discovering the presence of God in unexpected places.'
Simon Shaw, Chair of Intercultural Churches, Derby City Vision and Jacob's Well, Derby

'As an African Pentecostal marrying an Anglo-French Catholic with a Dominican priest for a brother, my life – and understanding of God – has expanded far beyond the narrow boundaries I once set for myself. Much of this transformation I owe to the spiritual tools outlined in this book and the insights of its authors. Like me, you may have experienced profound loss, which fuels a deeper yearning for more. Mary and Charles guide us on this pursuit, challenging us to let go of rigid assumptions and unexamined certainty, to embrace critical reflection and humility. This book will guide you further and deeper on your spiritual pilgrimage.'
Amoge Ukaegbu, anti-trafficking and modern slavery professional

Mary and Charles Hippsley

Reimagining the Landscape of Faith

Essential pathways for spiritual growth

 Ministries

15 The Chambers, Vineyard
Abingdon OX14 3FE
+44 (0)1865 319700 | brf.org.uk

Bible Reading Fellowship (BRF) is a charity (233280)
and company limited by guarantee (301324),
registered in England and Wales

ISBN 978 1 80039 271 7
First published 2025
10 9 8 7 6 5 4 3 2 1 0
All rights reserved

Text © Mary Hippsley and Charles Hippsley 2025
This edition © Bible Reading Fellowship 2025
Map on p. 24 © World History Archive / Alamy Stock Photo; p. 35 © PhotoStock-Israel / Alamy Stock Photo; p. 212 © Colin Waters / Alamy Stock Photo
Cover and inside illustrations by Ben Bloxham

The authors assert the moral right to be identified as the authors of this work

Unless otherwise stated, scripture quotations are taken from The Holy Bible,
New International Version (Anglicised edition) copyright © 1979, 1984, 2011
by Biblica. Used by permission of Hodder & Stoughton Publishers, an Hachette UK
company. All rights reserved. 'NIV' is a registered trademark of Biblica.
UK trademark number 1448790.

Scripture quotations marked KJV are taken from The Authorised Version of the
Bible (The King James Bible), the rights in which are vested in the Crown, and are
reproduced by permission of the Crown's Patentee, Cambridge University Press.

Scripture quotation marked ESV is taken from The Holy Bible, English Standard
Version, published by HarperCollins Publishers, © 2001 Crossway Bibles, a division
of Good News Publishers. Used by permission. All rights reserved.

'It Is Time' from *Rumours of Light* by Gideon Heugh is copyright © 2021 Gideon
Heugh. Used by permission. **gideonheugh.com**

Every effort has been made to trace and contact copyright owners for material
used in this resource. We apologise for any inadvertent omissions or errors, and
would ask those concerned to contact us so that full acknowledgement can be
made in the future.

A catalogue record for this book is available from the British Library

Printed and bound by CPI Group, Croydon CR0 4YY

With love and thanks to all those who travel alongside us on our spiritual pilgrimage – for your companionship, which brings rich wisdom, fresh insights and so much joy.

Photocopying for churches

Please report to CLA Church Licence any photocopy you make from this publication.
Your church administrator or secretary will know who manages your CLA Church Licence.

The information you need to provide to your CLA Church Licence administrator is as follows:

Title, Author, Publisher and ISBN

If your church doesn't hold a CLA Church Licence, information about obtaining one can be found at **uk.ccli.com**

Contents

Introduction 9

PART I   IDENTIFYING YOUR MAP

1. How are you finding your way? 16
2. Where has your map come from? 31
3. Where are you starting from? 63

PART II   ENLARGING YOUR MAP

4. Where are you on your journey? 92
5. What happens when your map runs out? 120
6. Where is your centre of gravity? 150
7. How do you navigate from a new perspective? 177
8. How does 'looking beyond' change how you live? 202

Epilogue 232

Appendix 1   Some key contributors to spiritual formation 235

Appendix 2   Sketching out your faith journey 239

Appendix 3   Spiritual practices 240

Further resources 248

Notes 251

It is time

Turn your gaze upon your soul, for it is time.
Look past the shadows, look between the light;
it has been waiting –

waiting for you to step back
from the endless undertakings,
to take your leave from the busyness of existence,
to release (let us say it) the obligations,

to realise that you are here.

Turn your gaze upon the world, for it is time.
Reach out to it, afraid or otherwise;
it has been waiting –

waiting for you to wake up,
to open your heart entirely to wonder, to beauty,
to the divine (that is, to the abundance
and generosity of reality).

Do not delay; let us bow to the surge of grace
that comes with each breath; let us embrace the gift
that is each singular and heaven-scented moment.

My friend, my good and worthy friend –
it is time.

Gideon Heugh, from *Rumours of Light* (2021). **gideonheugh.com**

Introduction

How do you feel about your journey of faith? Do you feel confident, sure-footed, that you know where you're going? Or perhaps you're a little uncertain, disappointed at where the path has taken you, or even lost. Maybe it would have been handy to have had a 'faith map', so that you could have planned your course and recognised some key landmarks as you travelled.

We all carry a kind of mental map of our spiritual journey, even if you are not aware that you do. As you delve deeper into this book, our hope is that you will learn not just how to recognise that map, but also how to critically evaluate it and begin to make choices based on a much deeper understanding of yourself and the nature of your map as you continue to journey with God.

But even when we *are* aware of having a map to hand, some of us still aren't sure how to read one or even which way up it should be! In my (Charles) many years of walking in the beautiful Lake District, the hardest part always seemed to be choosing the right direction to head out of the car park.

How are you reading your map, and what kind of faith landscape does it show?

Your map probably depicts familiar landmarks by which you navigate and measure progress on your faith pilgrimage. Symbolising the fundamentals of faith – such as orthodox beliefs and doctrines; regular personal and communal times of worship, prayer and sacraments; acts of evangelism, mission or social action – we consider our landmarks or milestones as being there to keep us on the 'right path', ever pointing towards God.

But here's a question to consider: are these common landmarks the *only* ones? They may seem fundamental, creating familiar rhythms of Christian life, but is there a possibility that your map is not yet complete? If you turned to the next page of your map, might you notice landmarks you haven't seen before, or could you even reimagine some old landmarks from time to time, sparked by changes in your experience or understanding? Might there be there some benefit in looking *beyond* your familiar routes to identify some even deeper and more significant pathways?

So, how might this book help you?

This book arises out of our experience as trained spiritual directors.[1] While this is a well-established historical ministry, the art of spiritual direction may be less familiar within some Christian traditions. It's a different way of listening that helps people to notice what may lie beneath the surface of what's going on in their lives, to discern and interpret how God might be working towards their spiritual growth. We encourage people to ask themselves good questions, to take intentional notice of the landscape through which they are travelling and to pay attention to the feelings which arise. A key part of this process is to encourage the active use of their God-given imagination as they explore the roots of their beliefs and expectations, facilitating both better self-awareness and God-awareness.

We find this approach to be helpful because having had many conversations with people who are wrestling with their faith, we noticed that they tend to be strongly influenced by both recognised and unrecognised expectations for their spiritual journey. These expectations often colour our perceptions of what's happening along the way. Philip Yancey helpfully summarises some common hopes for the life of faith saying:

> I want God to… overcome my doubts with certainty, give final proofs of his existence and his concern. I want quick and spectacular answers to prayers, healing for my diseases, protection, and safety for my loved ones.[2]

So it won't be a surprise to learn that we will be inviting you as a reader to become more conscious of your secret hopes and often hidden inner world, activate your imagination, identify your feelings and participate in asking yourself some good questions. But rather than leave all those questions until the end of each chapter, we will weave them into key ideas, inviting you to reflect on how what we're sharing applies to your own faith journey as we go.

We're also exploring how a variety of disciplines must work in coordination if we are to fully grasp the contours of our maps of faith, especially if we want to grow spiritually. These include theology, spirituality, psychology and epistemology (how truth is pursued and perceived). When these aspects of our faith come together, it can be hugely enriching (see Appendix 1 for further discussion of how these disciplines relate to our formation).

Realising that we are not experts in all these disciplines, we have drawn on a range of those who are, many of whom you can find referenced in the endnotes and suggested reading list at the back of the book. But our overall aim is to highlight and integrate an awareness of where our Christian beliefs have come from together with an understanding of the humanity (heart, mind, body and spirit) with which we engage those beliefs.

Overview of content

In part 1, 'Identifying your map', we will look at the map as a concept and as a useful metaphor for our journey of faith. We'll explore the cultural and Christian assumptions that have shaped the faith landscape we perceive ourselves to be travelling through and look at how our human make-up as map-readers can affect the ways in which we perceive our journey.

Part 2, 'Enlarging your map', tackles the stages of our journey, helping us to work out where we are now. We face up to what happens when we run into rough terrain, and how consequential challenges can stimulate equally significant spiritual growth if we allow ourselves to be trained by them. All this leads to some pivotal changes of perspective as we wrestle with what it really means to put off our old self and put on the new. And we offer some practical steps towards that. We end by exploring what living from a different perspective looks like in our daily interactions with God, others and ourselves and how looking beyond this current existence towards life after our physical death can affect the perspective with which we live in the present.

You may be wondering how two authors co-write a book without there being confusion about who is 'speaking' at any given time. Perhaps unusually within a partnership like this, we have chosen to use just one voice in presenting our material, i.e. using the first person 'I'. We only default to one or the other as we tell specific personal stories or introduce friends of ours. Thus, although each chapter has been developed and written by both of us, a name appears at the head of every chapter to bring clarity as to whose voice is being used for the majority of personal reflections or stories within that chapter. If a story from the other pops up, it is so labelled in brackets – e.g. 'I (Charles)…'

You may or may not belong to a formal Christian community or always feel comfortable with how God is presented in church circles, either in gendered terms or in familial images used. You may feel there is no map which could adequately explain your past or direct you in a faith-related future. We may not even pose the questions that most frequently bother you or address them in the way you desire. But our sincere hope is that you will still be able to successfully steer a path through the landscape we have out laid out because this book is for *all* pilgrims making their way in life, all adventurers, wanderers and wonderers, wherever they find themselves and whatever their Christian background.

Our aim is to give you space to reflect on the map you may be consciously or unconsciously using to find your way, even if there have been some unexpected twists to the journey you originally anticipated. You may even allow yourself the freedom to reimagine seminal landmarks and milestones you've perhaps taken for granted or, alternatively, found quite baffling. To that end we introduce approaches and tools to help you recognise and understand your map better – where it came from, where it's leading you and how to use it more intentionally so you can travel with greater confidence and purpose.

Part I
Identifying your map

1
How are you finding your way?

Charles

We are all pilgrims on the same journey – but some pilgrims have better road maps.

NELSON DEMILLE

It's a bleak November day in Cambridge. A cold wind is blowing across the fens as my 18-year-old self jogs down the tow-path in an attempt to get fit for an upcoming rowing race. I'm a slow jogger, so there's plenty of time to think. It's been three years since I responded to an invitation to come to Christ at my local church's mission. But what's bothering me is that nothing much seems to have changed since then. Yes, I've picked up the disciplines of the Christian faith – regular church, lots of Bible study and prayer – but I don't feel *I've* changed. Well, not significantly anyway.

After about three miles I stop running, look back from where I've just come from and ask myself, 'How did I get here? Is this all there is?' And I'm not referring simply to the tow-path. I couldn't quite imagine what it might be, but I felt there had to be more to Christian life than what I was currently experiencing.

Twenty years later, I'm married, have two kids, a busy job… and lots of leadership responsibilities at church. As I listen to the morning sermon, it strikes me I've heard those same truths and themes expounded many times before. Or at least something similar. In fact, I've probably spoken about them myself in different Christian contexts. I feel like I've explored these same landmarks many times.

And then I'm in my 50s, and I find myself wondering what it is I have invested my time in so far. The jigsaw pieces of life seem to have fallen apart in the last couple of years: I've stepped down from leadership roles at work and in the church; my children have left home; and we have moved to a different area. I'm not sure anymore where this journey of faith is taking me, and that same old question keeps cropping up: 'How on earth did I get here and is this all there is?'

Sometimes questions come back periodically to haunt us like that – causing us to stop and evaluate *where* we are in life, to consider what's happened to shape *who* we are, and to wonder *how* we are.

I wonder what questions you ask yourself? Or perhaps have asked God?

I'm not sure I was waiting for God to actually answer my question. Rather, I think it took that long for me to realise what that question meant and why I kept asking it. And I've since worked out that it's the sort of question God seems to delight in answering – but in God's own unique way. Every time I've asked that kind of question, unexpected experiences crop up: events or revelations that seem to shift the tectonic plates of my life. It's like God is just waiting, impatient almost, for me to realise that the picture of life in Christ I have at any given time is far too limited and doesn't allow for 'the unknown', at least what's unknown to me! And, what's more, I'd not been in the habit of stepping back to evaluate any of it.

It seems that God carries such a strong desire for us his children that he works through all the aspects of our lives to draw us closer, to help us realise who we truly are created to be. But it's not always obvious what's going on. Wouldn't it be handy if there was a map we could be following, with recommended routes that might help us to arrive at that place?

In my current work as a spiritual director, I travel alongside other pilgrims and try to help them listen to their life. We reflect on where they sense God might be in the twists and turns of their story and look for perspective and wisdom so they are better equipped to discern how these life experiences might be part of God's loving formative purposes.

I also have someone to do the same with me, to walk alongside me in my own faith journey, and I'm convinced that mentoring or spiritual accompaniment promotes a kind of self-understanding and spiritual growth which is hard to discover otherwise. Something I've observed within this sort of spiritual accompaniment is that I can often be blind to where I've got to on my own faith journey. I need the help of a wise friend to recognise when God may be carefully unfolding another page, signposting that which lies beyond my present understanding towards a far greater vista.

'Ah… I see… there's more to understand, there's always more terrain to explore than I originally thought or imagined. My life isn't necessarily what I assumed it would be and the person of God isn't either…'

Life can be like that. We become so preoccupied with *doing* life – with all its busyness, demands, stress and excitement – that we travel on for years before we realise that our vision really hasn't grown much. And when something happens that cuts across our expectations, we can find that we are just not equipped to respond well. Often our mental image of the journey is actually quite limited, though we're blissfully unaware of this, and it lacks the depth of maturity to help us with anything that falls beyond the narrow boundaries of our hidden assumptions.

It's a bit like using a satnav. We glance periodically at a small portion of our journey, just the bit we are on at the time. But, of course, we are missing the big picture. And there are so many salutary stories of people who trusted their satnav to get them to a certain destination but found themselves ending up in a place of the same name in a different county. By contrast, maps of old, real physical maps, were made to show us the whole journey and to help us choose a route: to set out the way points, landmarks and terrain we'd expect to encounter on the way.

The connection between maps and our journey of faith was brought home to me recently when Mary and I visited an exhibition at the Bodleian Library in Oxford.[3] On the surface, the exhibition simply led us through the history of maps by displaying various designs on a timeline. In reality, it turned out to be a ride through the worlds of history, philosophy and even epistemology (how truth is pursued and perceived). The aim of the exhibition was to help me as the viewer to step back and consider what a map actually represents, the fact that every map tells a story. We might only think of them as mere route-finding devices, and while they do usually get you from A to B, people have used maps throughout history to understand not just *where* they are, but *who* they are.

What I was doing on that tow-path was essentially to question the map of faith I seemed to be holding:

- Where was I on my faith map?
- Where was I hoping to get to?
- And where had this 'map' come from? How had it been formed?

In this first chapter, we'll be exploring how our understanding of physical maps and the ways in which they are created and operate can help us to reflect on and expand the faith maps we carry. But to do that, we first need to delve a little deeper into what maps really are and what they represent.

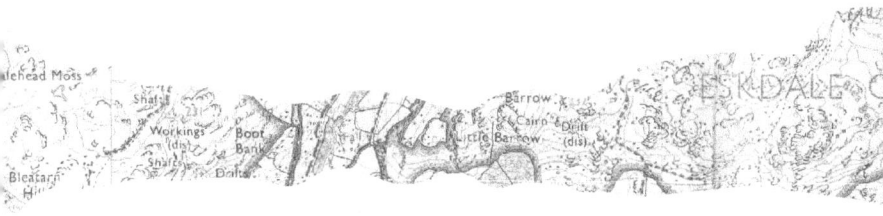

A brief excursion through the nature of maps

When you think about the concept of a map, I wonder what picture comes to mind. Is it an Ordnance Survey (OS) map you might take with you to walk the South West Coast Path? Is it your satnav app that helps you navigate when driving through unfamiliar territory? Maybe it's the Mercator projection map of the world, so familiar from your geography studies at school.

In truth, there are many types of maps and many forms of coded information which qualify as some sort of a map. We're probably all so familiar with using maps in their different forms that we may never have considered the nature of the cartography that lies behind them. So, before we go any further, it may be helpful to define what a map is, in its most general sense. According to the Bodleian exhibition:

> A map is a spatial model which attempts to represent aspects of reality, within certain recognised limitations thereby recognising potential for distortions. In war and peace, on land and on seas, maps have enabled people to build empires, discover new worlds, and plan military campaigns. We use them to construct our cities and understand our place in them. They are key tools in defining the boundaries between nations and administering the states in which we live. Maps are not just instruments of scientific communication or political ideology, they are proposals about our world. Artists and writers have always understood the powerful illusion of reality that maps offer their users.[4]

From these descriptions we learn that maps, at base level, are 'storied vehicles',[5] representing how humanity has evolved through changing eras of geography, philosophy, politics and history.

Not all maps are the same. They differ in their purpose, construction, scale, precision and level of detail. One would not expect the average

AA road map, which looks at travel from the motorist's viewpoint, to provide the same sort of detail as an OS map, which helps the hiker to navigate the contours of a Lakeland Fell. There are maps for navigating rivers or canals and tourist maps, which omit some minor roads and rivers, because their primary purpose is to highlight points of interest like castles, National Trust properties or famous gardens for the typical holiday-maker.

Ancient mariners used astronomical 'maps' (the changing position of stars in the sky and their arrangement in constellations) to navigate their way, and without access to modern computers or other instruments, some still do. But reading the stars also depends on where you are, as those in the northern and southern hemispheres see different constellations. And in fact, we're really looking at the past since by the time we see that light, it can be decades, centuries, even millennia out of date.

We understand the intrinsic differences between each of these types of maps and therefore realise in advance that the average city tourist map, for example, will be unlikely to provide enough information to help us find the nearest motorway, let alone identify all the service stations along the way.

In recent times we have also begun to extend the conventional idea of mapping to other activities, such as constructing a mind-map or spider-map to help with thinking through a set of ideas or concepts. This sort of map enables a wealth of information to be seen at a glance, establishing the relationship between ideas, events and facts. Like all maps, these kinds of exercises help the human brain to make sense of big unmanageable concepts by breaking them down into smaller parts, often so that they can be classified and categorised.

Any family tree or photo album represents this kind of map, because more than simply depicting a bunch of random snapshots of the past, they tell the story of how a family may have evolved and who they are today. And it's interesting to note that different members of the same family may well construct entirely different versions of exactly the same material or data because their recollections and even their purpose in constructing such a map may vary enormously.

Maps are rarely what they seem on the surface.

And this leads us to ask how cartography actually works. Surely most maps are just documenting ways to get us from where we are to where we want to go, aren't they?

Well, yes, and no.

Map-makers (cartographers) tend to assemble their material to fulfil a specific brief or agenda. In other words, they fashion their material to tell a particular kind of story, often to suit their intended target audience or market. This will inform their selection, emphasis and composition of the information, eliminating less relevant data and simplifying more complex data in order to portray significant features or represent patterns of information.

This same sort of process informs how the evening news bulletin will be put together or how we self-edit the stories of our own lives when we tell them to others. But we might not realise that the common thread running through the drawing of all maps is that they too are also subject to bias and are only representations of reality, someone's unique interpretation and documentation of that reality. If we expect cartography to be a wholly objective, dispassionate and exact recording of the nature and reality of landscapes, geography and travel routes, we are misled. In fact, maps of any description are the end product of a very specific process of 'selection and emphasis'. In addition, the cartographer's own cultural, political, geometrical and even theological presuppositions will influence *how* their maps will be drawn and *why* they are map-making in the first place!

A prime example of this is the 'standard' Mercator projection world map we are used to seeing today. Great Britain is located at the centre because in a meeting of 25 countries in 1884, it was decided that the prime meridian, ground zero for measuring latitude, should run through Greenwich in London. It's moved since then, but only by 102.5 metres to the east, when the international reference meridian was established 100 years later.[6] Furthermore, countries closer to the north and south poles, like Greenland, look somewhat bloated relative to those at the equator because of the philosophy Mercator adopted in projecting a 3D world on to a 2D map.

If I had asked you to picture a 'map of the world' in your mind, there is a strong possibility that you would immediately imagine the Mercator projection. More recently other projections, such as that proposed by cartographer Oswald Winkel in 1921, give a more accurate representation of the relative areas, directions and distances between different countries. This illustrates how something as seemingly intractable as our idea of how the world looks can merely be the product of someone else's imagination, and so can change.

The influences of cartography on our interpretation of maps

But why am I flagging up these different practices in the somewhat obscure world of cartography? For the simple reason that most map-readers remain completely oblivious of such conscious or unconscious bias when embracing the finished map-product. They are unaware that very basic decisions have been made even at the initial stages of cartographical formation. And bias, however slight, changes the way truth is both presented and perceived.

That's significant for us as faith pilgrims – bear with me! Take the Mappa Mundi, which lies in Hereford Cathedral, for example. Created in the 14th century, a time when religious views were very significant, this map is centred on Jerusalem and oriented with east at the top rather than north. It was drawn with east at the top, because that's the direction that the sun rises, symbolising light and life, and it relegated west to the bottom, because that was seen as the direction of the setting sun and darkness or night. The need for maps to assist with navigating the high seas using a compass or the Pole Star (in the northern hemisphere) meant that over time north became the most important direction and the orientation of our maps changed. So, to modern eyes, it's hard to interpret the Mappa Mundi without turning it 90 degrees clockwise.[7]

Engraving depicting the central section of the Mappa Mundi

But it's not just the cartographers' operating and assumptive framework that affect what we see. Conscious or unconscious biases also influence the lens through which we, the map readers, perceive and utilise maps. All maps demand a surprisingly high degree of interpretation, and when more than one person is doing the interpreting, inevitably there will be differences of opinion, as friends or spouses travelling in the same car will attest. And a satnav doesn't always help, because some of us even argue with the route the satnav has chosen!

When I go walking with friends, they usually possess their own OS map and have their unique ways of reading that map. Many is the time there have been arguments over whether that dotted line represents a footpath or a parish boundary, because none of us has bothered to read the map's key that explains what all its symbols mean. The actual information printed on that map seems as if it should be straightforward, but because it is often represented by symbols, it may not tell the traveller everything they need to know at first glance. It must be interpreted, and any act of interpretation will be coloured by a whole host of factors: previous experience, accumulated wisdom, expectations or desires for the journey ahead, and of course paying attention to the map key, to name a few.

But what has all of this got to do with your faith map?

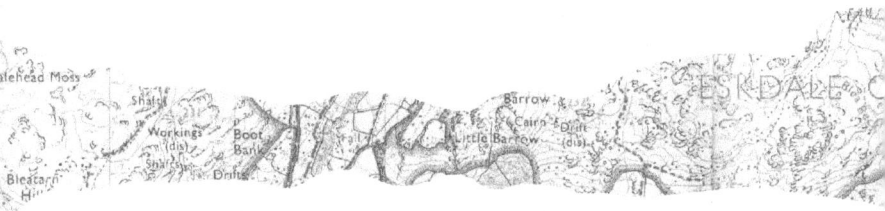

Examining your faith map

At some point on the human journey, we became aware of our spiritual nature as we connected with someone that transcends our human experience, someone we came to know as God or Jesus. At that point our life map started to overlap with our map of Christian faith. Few of us step back to look at the course our spiritual walk has taken, but it can be highly instructive.

Perhaps now is an opportunity to do just that.

Describing your journey so far

Pause here and sketch out the journey of your faith walk so far to see how it maps on to the overall journey of your life. Imagine you are going to describe your faith map to a trusted friend, and ask yourself these questions as you prepare:

- How and where did your Christian journey begin?
- What were some noteworthy landmarks or milestones, representing significant events, encounters, revelations or insights?
- How would you describe and depict times where your journey felt 'mountaintop' exciting, times of boredom, times where you felt you were walking in thick mist or making slow progress, times where you felt you ended up in a cul-de-sac or had inadvertently taken a long detour?
- Can you identify any habits, practices, situations or conditions which seem to have accelerated or inhibited your growth as a Christian?

On the facing page is an example to help you get started.

With this visual reminder in mind, you might ponder a couple more questions:

- Who contributed to making your map look like it does?
- What sources of authority or key influences would you identify in your faith journey?

This might be a living person, an oft-read author long dead, a lifelong friend or a mentor you've just met. Each Christian pilgrim makes their own journey, but most faith journeys bear common features, including moments of new discovery and difficult stumbling blocks to overcome, so it's good to notice and name them.

How are you finding your way? 27

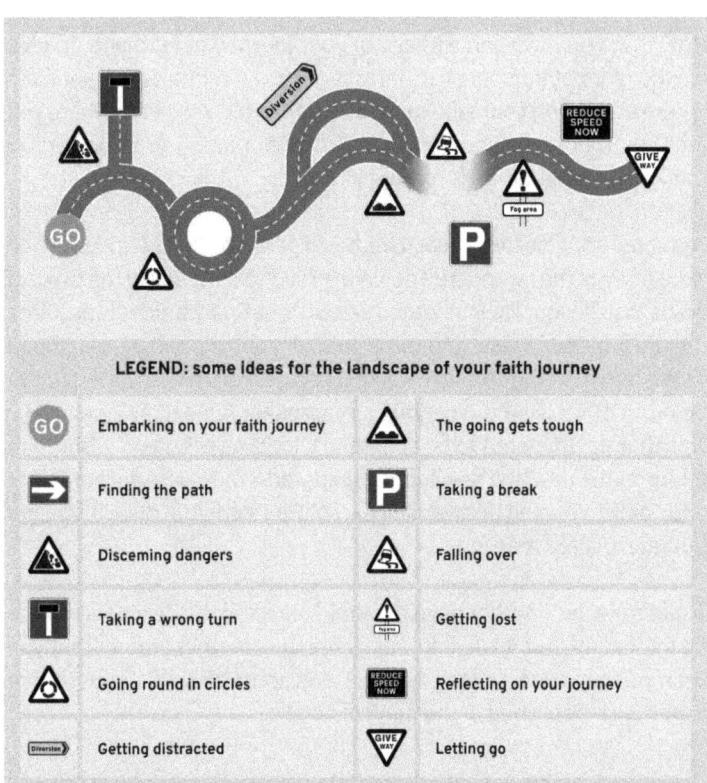

But now the crucial cartographical questions: How did you go about 'shaping' the story you might tell? How aware were you of your own assumptive frameworks and tendency towards 'selection and emphasis' in how you composed your faith map? How did you decide what to keep in or leave out? How did you identify the significant events and landmark features?

Inevitably you will have made choices based on some sort of selection and emphasis, causing a certain amount of distortion in conflating facts for easy consumption. What your map leaves out is possibly just as significant as what it includes.

Now that you have some image of your journey of faith and an idea of who or what influenced its formation, you might also ask yourself: Where are you on your faith map today? How did you get to where you are? What more are you hoping for from your journey? What part do think your imagination is playing in this?

You could imagine these questions being posed by the disciples we find in Luke 24 as they wandered down the road to Emmaus in the wake of Jesus' crucifixion. Their inherited Jewish 'map' had suddenly acquired the most bizarre twists and turns. In their confusion, they were blind to the reality of the stranger walking beside them, who turned out to be none other than the definitive mapmaker himself. All they knew was that he appeared to be someone with the vision and wisdom to interpret the new and bewildering landmarks they were encountering and confirm that all this was still part of God's original plan, his bigger but unexpected map.

There's always another page to unfold and explore, Jesus seemed to be indicating, but it will perhaps demand something more from you than you had expected to give. Just look at the disciples' subsequent experience described in the book of Acts!

If you think about it, the very person of Jesus, the way he acted and what he taught must have blown most people's prevailing maps apart – changing their expectations about what was important in life, what God was like and what kind of life God-followers could expect to lead. As the story progresses from the gospels through the book of Acts, the earliest disciples, like Peter, Paul, James and John, had to navigate their way through uncharted territory. A predominantly Jewish community, with a very specific Messianic expectation of triumph over the prevailing political and social order, slowly had to transition into a multicultural fledgling community whose job was to proclaim God's startling new kingdom.

Interestingly, these earliest Christ-followers were known as 'people of the Way' (Acts 9:2); not people of the book (which is how the Jewish people were known) or people of 'right beliefs' or people of orthodox behaviours, but a travelling people who were on their way somewhere, somewhere new. I like that description, because it allows for faith to be perceived as a lifelong journey – one of pilgrims who are asking questions, seeking to grow, enlarge their vision and expand their horizons without the pressure of having to appear as though they have already arrived with all the definitive answers.

Are you open to God expanding the faith map with which you're most familiar? Perhaps it's time for a change of perspective, like moving projections from the Mappa Mundi to the Mercator or Winkel forms?

Whether or not we can embrace that kind of paradigm shift, in common with those early disciples, we are not just mapmakers but also map-readers – people trying to discover their way forward while simultaneously figuring out how to interpret our maps. We are hoping that they lead us into fruitful living as followers of Christ and point the way towards our ultimate God-intended destination. Knowing more about basic cartographical principles can alert us to times when our internal bias is at play, driving us to cling on to prevailing systems of thought and sometimes blinding us to the next page of the map God wishes to open.

To do that, however, we need to understand much more about who we are as map-readers, what basic questions we ask ourselves as human navigators, and how the maps or snippets of map we inherit from a huge variety of sources inform how we perceive the meaning and significance of our spiritual journeys. As that exhibition at the Bodleian Library declared:

> Today maps are essential tools to help us play, plan travel, or even understand climate change. Maps are changing but they persist in telling us powerful stories about our rapidly evolving global world. At the same time, we are always receiving and constructing our own maps but it's up to us to decide if we accept the stories they represent or not.

Looking back on those moments in life when I have found myself asking, 'How did I get here and is this all there is?', I realise something important about the faith maps I have constructed and the one I carry today: my map is never complete. Not just because I am still journeying, but because like Jesus' disciples, I sense that I will never possess a completely definitive understanding of what the journey will be or is meant to be or even what it is really for. Is the purpose to arrive at my destination or to be transformed along the way? Pilgrims through the centuries were fairly certain that the purpose of pilgrimage included both.[8]

As I learn to survey and interpret the landscape I am in today, and help others do the same, I sense that carrying a partial map is okay as long as I'm aware that it is incomplete and keep allowing God to unfold more of it with me. And as I travel, one of my tasks is to understand myself more, to become more aware of the many desires and drivers which subtly inform how I perceive and interpret the symbols, ideas and constructs that I have accumulated to help me navigate this journey of faith. I learn to ask good questions of myself so that I can evaluate my own motives and the influences on my faith map better. Have the ideas and constructs become a substitute for the actual experience of walking my path? How might I perceive or imagine my progress in embracing the depth and mystery of my relationship with God and everything he creates?

As for those moments of deep questioning that might strike you in life, learn to notice them, and allow them to become a crucial wake-up call, a reminder to stop and take stock of the faith map you have accumulated: is it accurate, where have you got to and how might you travel onwards?

Is this all there is? I certainly don't think so! But with God's help, I hope to keep exploring new territories and landscapes with an open heart and mind. And maybe you're up for that journey too. If so, read on!

2
Where has your map come from?

Mary

What you see and what you hear depends a great deal on where you are standing. It also depends on what sort of person you are.

C.S. LEWIS[9]

Cartography is a demanding business. Keeping the documentation of any given physical landscape up to date with a comprehensive degree of accuracy is a never-ending task. Because, of course, topography is never static. A kaleidoscope of features is subject to all sorts of human intervention, as we build new roads or demolish office blocks, never mind the longer-term changes that the environment can induce.

But what about us? How aware are we of the forces that shape the landscapes of our lives? In our case, these forces reflect the often unexamined but very real assumptions which frequently lurk below the waterline of our consciousness about the world, ourselves and even God.

I was blissfully ignorant of holding any kind of faith map, or indeed being in the possession of the cultural, religious or social assumptions which composed its landscape, until they were all turned upside down one warm September day in the 1970s. I had left my family and homeland as a fresh-faced American to come and settle in Britain. Up until then, many of my most basic cultural assumptions of what constituted 'normal life', together with my religious assumptions about what Christianity looked like, remained hidden from my consciousness and almost entirely unchallenged. Like most people who have never moved away from their country of birth, I had no idea of the mountains I would have to climb to understand and embrace the contours of a completely new cultural, political, religious and even geographical landscape.

At first it seemed like an exciting adventure: new sights, different foods, unintelligible accents and inexplicable customs. But inevitably, the effort of cultural adaptation took its toll, and I began to suffer from what is now labelled 'culture fatigue'. Because when we're confronted with beliefs and assumptions so different from our own, it forces us to continually re-examine our own back story, how we came to acquire our original beliefs. And figuring out how all that maps onto a new landscape feels exhausting.

But that wasn't the only difficulty to contend with. Oh no.

God seemed to have changed overnight as well! In our ignorance, we can all assume that Christianity, or indeed any religion, will be perceived and practised in more or less the same way in every country or context, but I was quickly disabused of this notion. As has become more evident in recent years, the Christian faith I had seen modelled in my home country tends to blur the lines between social, political and religious spheres, as its pledge of allegiance declares: 'One nation, under God, indivisible, with liberty and justice for all.' And although my adopted country also came with a long history of Christian heritage connected to monarchy, the way this was understood and expressed in everyday life was completely different. For one thing, I quickly found out that flag-displaying, so integral to American patriotism and national identity, was not so prominent or frequent a tendency in the UK, being generally reserved for celebrating royal events or the last night of the Proms. Same type of symbol, slightly different significance.

From these and a plethora of other cultural icons, I had begun to understand that behind the belief systems from which we operate, there are always back stories which form a much wider landscape. But these don't tend to come into focus until something challenges the assumptions on which they rest. And so it is with the composition of our faith maps. We like to think that we hold to our religious beliefs primarily because they are right and 'true', self-evidently so. But I wonder if you've ever considered precisely how your map of faith came into being. How was it formed and who or what contributed to the set of beliefs, attitudes and behaviours that you hold today?

What has shaped your faith map?

In an ideal world, we would be given a guidebook which explained the various beliefs, customs and practices into which we are slowly being inculcated as we travel alongside the pilgrims within our own Christian faith traditions. In practice, of course, we are given nothing of the sort. And it can take years to tease out the threads of our chosen or inherited faith community, trying to distinguish the major doctrines from lesser beliefs, mixed in with many idiosyncrasies. Some of these may well have grown up without much conscious thought about origin and meaning or their long-term implications. 'Why do you emphasise that or do things in this way?' was my frequent question about all sorts of expressions of the Christian faith into which I had suddenly been plunged. 'Because that's how they've always been done' was the frequent but extremely unsatisfying answer.

This is where asking good questions of yourself really comes into its own. Why was my initial reaction to unfamiliar faith customs, vocabulary and emphases generally so negative? Was it because I subconsciously believed there to be only one definitive plumbline against which all other patterns should be judged? In a way, my personal experience reflected the wider reality that we all hold a worldview, whether we know it or not. A worldview represents a collection of beliefs and aspirations from which people in all cultures and generations operate in some way or other. And by definition, these worldviews are often an indistinguishable mixture of religious, cultural, ideological and political assumptions.

The Ebstorf Map, discovered in 1832 at a Benedictine monastery, is a brilliant example of this type of integration. Like many maps drawn in that era, the avowed agenda of this medieval European creation wasn't necessarily to aid pilgrims by helpfully signposting the way to such sacred sites as Canterbury or Jerusalem. Rather, it interwove contemporary religious and cultural images, ideas and beliefs to create a visual encapsulation of the journey of faith as it was thought of at the time. To achieve this splendid effect, the person of Christ is drawn in such a way that his head is situated at the top of the map, his hands and arms splayed out appearing to grasp the whole world from east to west (with Jerusalem situated at his navel) and his legs and feet are placed at the bottom to complete the picture of Christ as being 'over all' (see image opposite).

Perhaps this quintessential religious statement was meant to act as an illustration of Colossians 1:16–17: 'All things have been created through him and for him... and in him all things hold together.' Or perhaps it simply provides a window into a typical medieval European mindset, in which every route and human action related to Christ and was to be perceived through the lens of Christian theology. Interestingly for historians, the Ebstorf Map also acts as a sort of visual encyclopedia of the knowledge of that part of the world at the time, covering theology, geography, biology, secular history, iconography and the history of salvation, as well as mythology.

Although there is some topography in the Ebstorf Map, with the inclusion of important cities and other landmarks, as with the Mappa Mundi, we find it hard to relate to these primary images in the 21st century. If

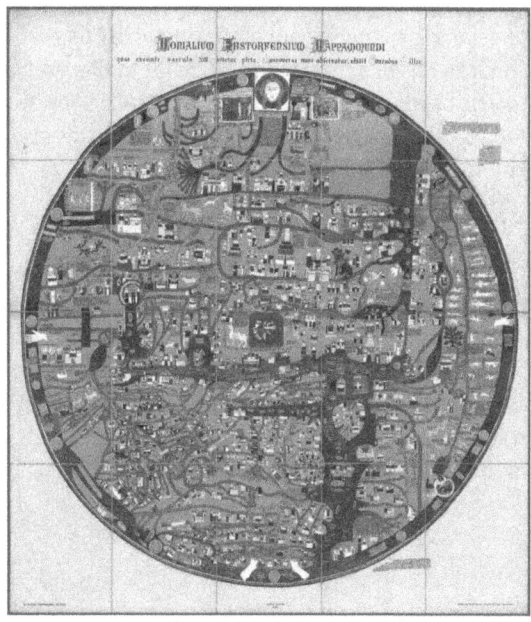

17th-century reproduction of the 13th-century Ebstorf Map

the same cartographical task was left to us today we'd of course make very different 'selection and emphasis' design decisions, choosing landmarks and points of interest that would be more meaningful to us today. But the main value of engaging with such a map is to show how it demonstrates the overlapping nature of a range of the prevailing cultural and religious worldviews, so much so that it is hard to notice where one begins and another finishes.

You might be wondering what all this has to do with the formation of your personal faith map. How might your understanding have been shaped by today's cultural and relgious worldviews, as the Ebstorf Map was by those of its period?

Let's start with this: what were your aims in choosing to follow Christ in the first place? Paul is in no doubt as to God's intent in this. He describes

God in Ephesians 2 as having such great love for us that he acted through Christ to raise us from spiritual death to life. And that great love of God acts beyond our spiritual rebirth to call us towards growth and maturity, to become like Christ. Paul describes this elsewhere as a process of 'being transformed into his image with ever-increasing glory' (2 Corinthians 3:18).

But we are still left with questions, like: How do I respond to such great love beyond that initial 'yes' to God's call? And how exactly do I grow spiritually within my Christian community? To address those questions, we also need to ask ourselves: how has my faith tradition or community evolved? What is the story behind the landmarks and milestones that feature on the faith map I have received? And how do I really know that I'm on the right path to become like Christ?

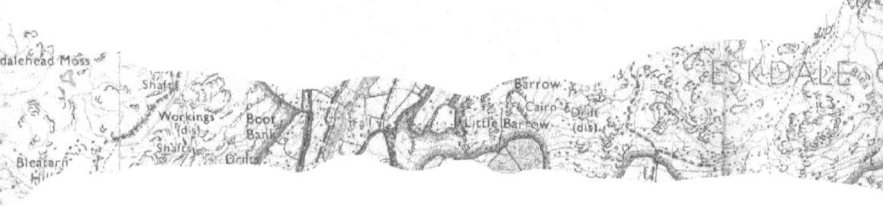

Cultural assumptions and Christian assumptions

What we've discovered so far is that two of the most powerful forces shaping our faith maps are our cultural assumptions and our Christian assumptions (or tradition). A third, but usually unidentified, force is us. *We* are the lens through which we perceive and respond to these forces, so we need to include a third influence, the nature of our human self (see diagram opposite).

What I'd not realised before I'd settled into a new adopted country was that Christian and cultural assumptions come to us, often unknowingly, from a variety of external sources, such as parents, teachers, preachers, our interpretations of popular culture, religious texts like

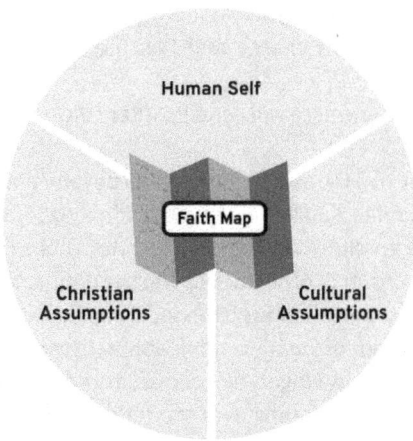

Forces shaping our faith map

the Bible or just through observing the society in which we live. So, we'll address these in the current chapter before looking at how our human self influences our faith map in chapter 3.

We've already noted that every map is a storied vehicle. And the internal map we carry consolidates the story of our lives as we perceive it – a particular interpretation of the path we have travelled so far and our expectations and hopes for the future. But how do we begin to notice that map and become more aware of how it is influencing the choices we make? A good first step is to recognise some of the fundamental questions humans are asking that drive that story. Philosophers, religious thinkers and psychologists through the ages have noted that all humans – and therefore human thought systems, including religions – tackle some core questions that tend to include the following:

- *origin:* where did I come from?
- *purpose:* why am I here?
- *significance:* how do I connect to others?
- *identity:* how do I derive a meaningful sense of self?

- *morality:* how do I establish what is right and what is wrong?
- *authority:* who is in charge and has the power to judge what humans do?
- *ultimate destiny:* where will I end up after I die?

While not many of us consider ourselves to be lofty philosophers, like Aristotle or Socrates, and few of us would admit to consciously asking ourselves these erudite-sounding questions, let's not write them off too quickly. In some form or other they lurk in the depths of our souls, and how they are encountered and processed throughout our faith journey informs an awful lot of what we think about, dream about and work towards. Without knowing it, as I endeavoured to get to grips with British culture, I was tripping over the tendrils of these roots every day as I was forced to evaluate and re-evaluate how to make sense of my life in this new context. And this kind of process parallels the art of cartography, which as we've seen tends to begin with an agenda and then uses selection and emphasis to make sense of and depict that agenda. In other words, how we make sense or find meaning in and through our lives is informed by how we are seeking to answer these questions (whether knowingly or not), and this is what in turn informs our worldview.

How do we acquire cultural assumptions as we grow up?

A measure of curiosity might help us in this endeavour. And this is why I like old-fashioned paper maps. You can spread out the whole map and examine both macro and micro perspectives, both of which are useful in gaining a comprehensive understanding. If you sketched out a depiction of your faith journey after reading chapter 1, you might try revisiting it now. Take a minute to consider how those who taught you in both formal and informal ways helped shaped your map.

I've suggested this because we often receive aspects of our personal worldview unknowingly. This is especially so if we are introduced to it at a young age and pay little attention to where it came from or the informal shaping that is happening. Children often learn from parents, family members and teachers without enquiring about the legitimacy or prior assumptions of those sources or having sufficient knowledge of the world to critically evaluate what they're being told. All these unconscious 'non-decisions' in a person's life contribute to shaping their worldview.

One of my first memories as a child living in the deep south of the United States was being slapped by a little white girl because I was happily playing with a black friend. She had been told by her mother that playing with black children was forbidden and despicable. Neither I nor this other little girl had any idea how that prejudiced worldview reflected the world around us nor the social 'map' such a view represented in 1960s America. We were simply recipients of and participants in a cultural map drawn by others.

As we mature, we usually become more conscious of our worldview, perhaps as we begin to articulate it, often to our parents or teachers or when we find we disagree with them or others at school, church or university. We may even be asked in an academic context to formally compare a variety of equally valid viewpoints. But by this point many of our default perspectives have already been established.

Not only do the communities we find ourselves in throughout our lives influence what we believe to be true, but we are also driven by a desire to fit in and be validated by significant others within those communities. This is what sociologists call tribalism, the desire to belong or cohere with any given group's overt or underlying philosophy. Belonging to a tribe that thinks like us or upholds the same standards we have for ourselves feeds our sense of belonging, security and significance in the world. Of course, we see this evidenced in all sorts of ways through political discourse, religious divisions and increasingly through social media.

Our Christian assumptions are mapped on to our cultural assumptions

This leads us on to how worldview formation connects to our faith journey. If we carry cultural expectations for our social journey, whether or not we've mapped them out consciously and concretely, it's not surprising that we also carry a set of ideas that map out what we anticipate our Christian journey should be like. Our faith map will be influenced by our cultural map, because our 'Christian worldview' is overlaid on our pre-existing cultural worldview. We see the historical outcome of this in extreme forms, such as in how Christians justified apartheid, slavery or colonialism. For example, Richard Reddie describes how different parts of the Christian church historically advocated for both enslaver and liberator.[10]

Our Christian worldview in early years of faith will normally have been presented or passed on to us from some authoritative source in our tradition, like a church leader, a Christian friend, a Christian author or a particular interpretation of the Bible. The earlier this map is sown into our consciousness, the more impact it has over the long-term. But again, this influence so often sits just below our level of everyday consciousness and simply becomes the accepted reference point, or 'perceived truth', from which we operate day to day.

Alice was raised in a black Pentecostal tradition which persuaded her to believe that when a member of her church died, they should expect to pray as a Christian community for that person's resurrection. You might think that is an odd perspective or you might think it is a perfectly reasonable one, given that we find such occurrences in scripture, not the least of which are Lazarus or Jesus! But faced with this daunting prospect when her own father passed away, it motivated Alice to ask herself some fundamental questions about the different ways the Bible and spirituality could be interpreted. She wanted to determine the level at which she herself felt comfortable exercising faith. But it wasn't until this moment that Alice's Christian and cultural assumptions became obvious, giving her the opportunity to stand back and evaluate how she had gained them and how she wished to move forward with them.

Alongside the interplay between cultural and Christian assumptions, Alice's story illustrates that how the Bible is handled within our spiritual tradition is central to the set of assumptions we acquire for our Christian life. Depending on how much we know about the Bible and have formally studied its historical roots and construction, it may be that we must begin to reimagine what kind of book the Bible represents and how to engage with it in a more clued-up way. So, it's important to spend some time thinking about this cornerstone of our faith map.

How am I interpreting the Bible?

Let's face it, the Bible can be a pretty challenging book by today's standards. And yet somehow it has the capacity when approached in the right way to hold a mirror up to our lives and open a window for us on to God.

However, the Bible is anything but straightforward. Peter Enns, professor of biblical studies at Eastern University in Pennsylvania, describes it as ancient, ambiguous and extremely diverse, and suggests that if we come to it looking for certainty, we will be disappointed. But if we're looking for wisdom and how to become wise rather than seeking ready-made answers, then that's another matter.[11]

Many Christian traditions hold that the Bible represents one's truest or ultimate source of spiritual authority. If we are to access the wisdom that these ancient writings offer us, we will have to consider at least two important factors. First, that we are reading these diverse and ancient writings through the lens of living in the 21st century. And second, that biblical authors also used selection and emphasis to communicate what was most important to them. Keeping the first factor in mind will help us to understand why we might lean towards one interpretation or another, or how our own personality or unexamined assumptions are influencing the interpretation we choose to accept. And the second factor reminds us that we're compelled to do the work to find out what kind of document the Bible is.

I have an ancient map of Britain hanging on my study wall and, although I can recognise a few of the place names, much of it looks quite strange to my 21st-century eyes, especially the Old English spellings. We might find it odd if someone was to pick up an antiquated map like that to navigate their way around modern Britain today, without taking time to translate its language and symbols into their modern context. Yet my observation is that often this is precisely how we can find ourselves using the Bible, particularly if we are coming to it with an agenda, such as looking for guidance or a quick solution to our problems.

Picture the scene: we're desperate for a quick slice of inspiration that might help us navigate our way through a tricky situation at work or within our family. So we open the Bible, pick a random passage and get frustrated when we don't receive that flash of revelation or word from God after a whole ten minutes of reading! In the expectation that the Bible will be instantly relevant to me exactly where I am in my life today, we can all be guilty of forgetting that these manuscripts are thousands of years old, that they were written by and for people living in the Bronze or early Iron Ages, across a variety of successive dominant cultures from Ancient Egypt to the Roman Empire. And then we wonder why many of the cultural and religious assumptions, like slavery, the status of women and certain religious rituals, do not correspond to 21st-century values.

My concern is that we may be dishonouring the nature of those scripts and cheating ourselves of a deeper spiritual experience if we don't make the effort to delve into the cultural background of the people who wrote those texts and received those texts at the time. After all, we'd surely respect the historicity of much younger documents, like the Magna Carta or the American Constitution, by doing that kind of research.

Alongside a respect for context, we might also bear in mind that an element of selection and emphasis shapes every literary work, including the Bible. For instance, scholars now understand that the first half of the Old Testament was probably written many hundreds of years after the events they were recording, most likely during the time of exile in Babylon, for the purpose of reminding the Hebrew people of their foundational stories and beliefs. Without that basic understanding, it's all too easy to assume that the events of Genesis or Exodus, for instance, were being documented along the way, a bit like an ongoing communal diary.[12]

When these same events, laws or teachings were eventually formally recorded, it's reasonable to believe that certain aspects were selected or emphasised for their religious or symbolic significance – to remind God's people of their unique and God-elected national identity (Deuteronomy 7:7). Elements of selection and emphasis are made even more likely as key events and conversations were passed down the generations through 'oral tradition' well before they ever reached a piece of parchment.

Equally, you may have asked yourself, why are there four gospels instead of just one? For starters, good portraits of people are usually thought to be more complete when viewed from a variety of angles. But also, the four gospels are not biographies in the modern sense, since large portions of Jesus' life are omitted while great significance is attached to the final weeks of his life and death. Working towards a very specific agenda with a different target audience in mind, the subtle and not-so-subtle differences in the way Jesus' life and teachings are presented confirm our now-established cartographical principle of selection and emphasis. For instance, since Matthew is writing to a primarily Jewish audience, he is keen to proclaim that Jesus represents the long-awaited Messiah. While Luke, the only Gentile of the four authors, is writing for a largely Greek audience and therefore focuses on Jesus' humanity, providing details of his human genealogy, birth and a few glimpses of his early life.[13]

What might it look like, then, if we were to read the Bible while actively using a well-researched background knowledge of original language, historical and cultural context, as well as the selection and emphasis literary impulse? Do we fear that acknowledging all these factors might in some way negate or dilute God's inspiration of what was written, especially as it applies to us as readers? Surely we are honouring God's part more emphatically as we seek to receive the wisdom the Bible holds through careful handling of the authors' intent as they fashioned texts to carry and convey that wisdom. Of course, reading the Bible is not solely an intellectual exercise. Its poetic and prophetic language call for our emotional and imaginative involvement as well. And in all of this, we are engaging with the Spirit of God to help us to understand Spirit-inspired words about God and God's dealings with humankind.

The Bible is often described as a roadmap for life, but I wonder whether guidebook or travelogue might be a more helpful analogy because of the way it has been written. The Bible is not an esoteric book of impenetrable philosophy or a required list of rules or routes one must take in life, but an attempt by real people to document their human journey with God, with all the dead ends, seemingly pointless wanderings and unexpected milestones included. It is a perspective on discovering God in the midst of life as well an alternative way of living life.

And so, we hold in tension our understanding of 'divine inspiration' with this earthy reality. It reminds us that biblical authors, although not limited to human perspective alone, perceived their experiences of God from within the parameters of their own cultural and generational assumptions. As do we.

If actively employing this kind of informed approach when engaging with the Bible sounds too much like hard work, let's just acknowledge up front that it is! At times the world of the Bible seems like a distant planet to us, not always relatable, and demanding interpretive attention and skills we don't have or always feel like acquiring. But by avoiding approaching it as a recipe book that we consult simply to find the answers to our problems or a convenient 'thought for the day', we start to engage with how God is trying to help us develop from spiritual children to spiritual adults – learning to grapple, wrestle and face uncertainty or the unknown in the company of so many biblical characters. If we embrace the Bible for what it really is, then it will challenge us with the sorts of questions that lead to deeper understanding of who God is and who we are. And it will also hopefully help us to identify our own set of cultural and religious assumptions along with those that informed its authors.

If you've tried climbing mountains, even the relatively modest ones in the UK, you'll know that just when you get to what looked like the top, a further peak often appears in front of you, which will require expending yet more effort. It can feel a bit like that when we sift through our own cultural and Christian assumptions. So before moving on to the next section, why not take a break, make yourself a cup of tea and ponder a little on how your own faith map reflects some of what we've discussed so far.

Working out what we believe to be true

Our children attended a faith school at primary age, and before our daughter, aged four, had her interview with the headteacher, our son, who was already a student at the school, decided she might need some coaching. When subsequently asked by the headteacher what kinds of books she enjoyed reading, our daughter replied solemnly, 'I only read the Bible!' Trying to hide a smile, the headteacher pressed her further. 'What?' he said. 'Are there really no other books that capture your interest?' 'No', she replied, looking at her brother sitting beside her nodding his approval. 'Only the Bible counts,' she declared triumphantly. 'Does that mean I'm allowed to come here now?' she enquired with a cheeky grin.

We may chuckle at the naivety of a four-year-old, but I wonder if this approach doesn't also represent something of what we would say, or like to be able to say, about the central place the Bible occupies in our lives. The reality of course can be rather different. We look for basic information and helpful advice from all sorts of places. Try asking yourself this: where do I most regularly go to find my way in life? The internet? A daily newspaper or TV broadcast? My church priest or pastor? How about my life coach, friends or family?

Internally, we want to be sure that these sources of knowledge are legitimate, and our brain tends to weigh up every fact, suggestion, piece of advice or pearl of wisdom we receive in life against the store of pre-existing wisdom we have already acquired. We're always adding to, evaluating, recalibrating what we're finding out against that which we think we've already established.

That's not only true for the practicalities of life, like the best way to fix my broadband router or grow tomatoes, but also for our many cultural and Christian assumptions. I wonder how these may have changed over time for you. They may be the same as those you held growing up, but it's unlikely. Life has a habit of challenging our beliefs. And when our cultural or Christian assumptions are challenged, how do we respond? And how might that affect the way we grow – or don't?

As we grew older and encountered a wider, more diverse set of belief systems, cultures and communities, the foundations of our original worldview and (if we had developed one at that stage) our Christian faith were probably challenged in multiple ways. When this happened to us, we might have taken it as an opportunity to enlarge and develop the faith map we carried through questioning the ideas about truth, values, morals and principles we were given as children or even as young adults.

But we might instead have doubled down on our original faith map because we didn't want it to be proved wrong, limited or incomplete. Our investment and desire for certainty often makes us reluctant to consider the merits of potentially new and unfamiliar looking landscapes. For instance, when faced with recent discoveries or evidence in the spheres of medicine or science, some of us may retreat to our original, possibly unexamined Christian worldview, feeling it to be under threat.

I once invited a nurse along to a seminar on stem cell research because she was adamant that she opposed the whole practice in any form. I wondered if understanding the nuances of molecular biology – that is, what it actually involved, as opposed to what she assumed it involved – would be helpful. As the careful Christian lecturer, who was both a molecular biologist and an esteemed theologian, presented a sliding scale of possibilities, distinctions and procedures in dealing with both cells derived from human embryos and those derived from a patient's own tissues, we, the audience, all began to realise how difficult it was to make conclusive decisions as to what was and wasn't morally questionable at different points along that scale. My friend acknowledged afterwards that being exposed to the sheer scope of complexity had opened her eyes somewhat, leading to a subsequent conversation about other controversial ethical subjects over which we both regularly probably judged too quickly and often in ignorance.

Sometimes we can skirt round a challenge to our prevailing worldview, but there are times when we just can't avoid it. Some of life's experiences, especially dramatic or traumatic ones, can force us to confront the map we inherited with all its assumptions, particularly if it doesn't provide adequate answers to help us navigate those situations safely. At these times we start to question some of the things we assumed were axiomatic.

I got my first taste of this in a Christian community to which we belonged as a young married couple. The community was quite focused on signs and wonders, so when one of our young leaders suddenly contracted cancer, praying for God's power to heal seemed to be the only viable response. Unbeknownst to me, a form of selection and emphasis was operating, because there are in fact many valid ways a Christian could have responded to such a situation. But this being the only tool in our communal 'toolkit' at that time meant that when the young man subsequently died, our community were quite unprepared for how to cope with that kind of loss or seeming failure. We also had little idea how to lament in a healthy and restorative way because our collective liturgy and rituals were at that stage solely based on praise and worship. We stumbled our way through, but the experience did make me question some of the assumptions which underpinned our stated beliefs and practices.

This process, by which we interrogate systems of thought and establish what we as individuals believe to be true, is a healthy part of how we grow in maturity. For most of us, when we consult a trusted map, including our faith map, our starting assumption tends to be that it's accurate. It has come to represent to us a form of self-evident reality. But despite our assumptions, and what some teachers or religious leaders may tell us, truth is never utterly self-evident. Just as I discovered when I first came to the UK, foundational beliefs and customs in any form of religion or philosophy are often presented together as simply 'the way things are'. And we can find ourselves accepting them just as we accept the way that roads and landmarks have been depicted on the map we happen to have in our possession, with little thought for the mindset or agenda that has dictated that depiction.

Perhaps our preference is to establish that 'truth is just truth' because we want foundation stones we can put weight on and our trust in them to feel reliable in all situations. But as we've found in our study of cartography, all truth is perceived and acted upon by humans, and is done so through the lens of the limitations of being human.

For example, our core human desires will influence us when we really want something to be true. In my spiritual direction practice, I regularly speak to people who acknowledge that their perceptions of God are often based on who they wish or hope he is. A few have admitted that the reason they don't read the Old Testament, for instance, is because they don't like the God that they find there and much prefer the more acceptable picture of Jesus they say they find in the New Testament. At this point I always want to know if they've even read the piercing words of the sermon on the mount or engaged with the Jesus who seemed prone to unpredictable and sometimes inexplicable declarations or actions! But I understand that, to some degree, we all want God to be who we want him to be – to serve our emotional and psychological needs as we perceive them.

I have no doubt that truth – both material truth, in regard to how the universe operates, and eternal truths – can exceed human perception or comprehension. And that's really the point – we are all flawed and limited receptors of truth. So perhaps the trick here is to learn to hold whatever truth we think we possess at any given moment lightly, with open hands, with humility and an openness to considering new ideas, unfamiliar angles and making unexpected discoveries.

From this brief overview it's clear that the ways in which we come to know truth in our inner being to the extent that we feel able to 'put weight' on those beliefs or declare them to others is a much more complicated process than we might have assumed. Purely rationally, true epistemological pursuit involves acquiring a breadth of knowledge, including viewpoints or information which challenge or differ from our own assumptions. This requires times of reflection on and evaluation of that information through applying logic, reasoning and empirical or sensory experience, to ensure that there is internal coherency within our set of beliefs, that is, that one belief doesn't cancel out or detract from another and so forth.

Of course, we are also compelled to add to this the spiritual dimension of our connection with God, which takes us beyond the capacity of our rationality into the realms of felt experience, awareness of the transcendent, emotional engagement and exercising faith in things unseen (Hebrews 11:1).

But what does all this mean for our faith maps?

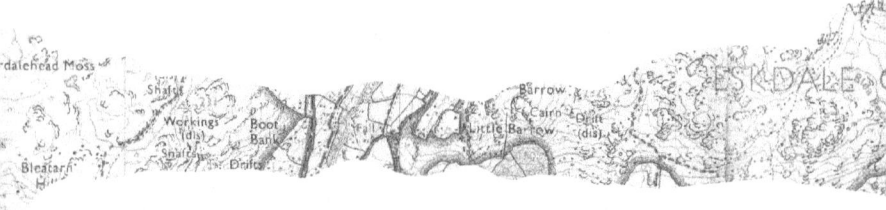

The art of asking ourselves good questions

Resolving to review our faith maps from time-to-time is a healthy practice, especially how they hold up against our unfolding story as humans who are followers of Christ. Does my map cover the ground I find myself walking through today? Will it take me further and help me to grow? In the same way as an interviewer sits down with a celebrity to find out how they've got to where they are by asking questions, so we too can give ourselves permission to make self-interrogation part of our own spiritual growth pattern.

I've noticed for myself and for some of those I accompany that if we don't learn to question ourselves, a kind of partial amnesia can set in. An alarming prospect perhaps to consider that we could fall victim to any kind of amnesia but actually, it turns out to be another example of unintentional 'selection and emphasis'.

Let's take a closer look.

A system of the brain known as the reticular activating system (RAS) essentially personalises the information you take in via a process known as selective attention or perception. This means that your brain filters out information that doesn't immediately align with your core beliefs, often rejecting contradictory information and dismissing or 'forgetting' those experiences that somehow don't match up with your expectations or pre-existing assumptions.[14] In other words, if the reality of your life, such as when you feel depressed, isn't consciously acknowledged or allowed for by your belief system or that of the significant others in your life (which would happen, for example, if you were told that 'Christians don't get depressed'), a sort of subconscious dissonance enters in, which causes inner tension. If it becomes a frequent occurrence, the brain gets used to dismissing that which is causing the conflict, laying tracks for future spiritual and psychological problems.

It is at this point that many seek a spiritual mentor or counsellor to address the fact that things simply aren't stacking up for them internally in a coherent way without really knowing why. But a good way to avert areas of internal discrepancy is to step back on a regular basis, question the roots and shoots of what you believe to be true, and consider how your actual experience bears that out.

And so we come to question-asking in its most valuable form: the arts of reflection and critical evaluation. These are like gold dust! Good questions can be truly transformative in our spiritual journey, as we reflect prayerfully on the cultural and Christian assumptions we have acquired over time. Being curious about our faith map, willing to question and challenge our own thoughts, ideas, senses and assumptions can lead to far deeper understanding. And this in turn influences our judgements and choices.

Reflection lies at the heart of all good learning, as well as mentoring, coaching and spiritual direction, because it represents an invitation to examine oneself, one's own motives, abilities, attitudes and emotions in a regular and consistent way. Self-reflection is essential if we are to become more aware of ourselves, the particulars of who we are, our personality and experience. All these will influence how we perceive or handle our spiritual life – something which we will explore further in the next chapter. And if a friend, family member or mentor is initiating that question process, it's the highest honour that can be ascribed to that relationship. What we're really expressing when we enquire of another is: 'You are deeply interesting, all aspects of you, known or unknown to both me and you, so let's investigate them together to find out who you really are underneath the visible, immediate or obvious.' According to Curt Thompson if we show curiosity about another, it actually causes them to be more curious about themselves. What a gift we will have given them![15]

Facilitating critical thinking is equally fruitful because it invites us to look at our fundamental beliefs and the customs of our Christian tradition or community and ask ourselves why we hold them. When we do this, we move beyond simply accepting our foundations at face value, not to reject them but to ensure they are what we hope they are, allowing our faith to be enriched and develop in depth and maturity.

We may shy away from this sort of approach because we wisely want to avoid falling into some form of error or 'heresy'. Heresy is an interesting label that we might jump towards far too readily, however. In New Testament times, this concept was associated with any sect or division which threatened the unity of the church. Heretical beliefs about Jesus were consistently debated for the first few centuries to establish a mutually agreed set of beliefs considered to be fundamental to Christianity, resulting in the creeds that we continue to quote today.

But, as theologians generally tend to confirm,[16] there is a difference between beliefs which actually denigrate or compromise core truths or doctrines (e.g. Gnosticism or Pelagianism) and those which are merely considered 'errors' of interpretation or practice by one type of Christian in reference to the 'selection and emphasis' made by another. Observing the sacraments in a particular way; ordering your church's form of worship or leadership according to your own Christian tradition; deciding how the work or structures of your Christian community should be prioritised or funded – these are all secondary considerations, which still cause disagreement and debate, but perhaps ought not to erect the high walls between Christians which the Bible so assiduously warns against (1 Corinthians 11:19; Romans 14:1–4; Galatians 2:11–13, to name but a few).

In a spirit of reimagining or enlarging our landscapes of faith, perhaps we could be wary of assuming we are wholly equipped with all the answers or correct opinions in place at any point in our lives to make judgements or draw definitive conclusions which are set in stone for all time. It seems to me that Jesus reserved his harshest comments for those who demonstrated this kind of rigidity (Luke 11:37–53), and I wonder if what pained him the most was a lamentable attitude of heart as much as any error of understanding. I have been consistently surprised at how what I assumed to be immovable landmarks on my own landscape of faith have been shifted or reframed through a change of perspective, either through deeper consideration of biblical texts or exposure to a wider diversity of Christians or Christian traditions. Or perhaps it's just my growing beyond my own sense of hubris!

In fact, my own self-referential stance was first challenged by nothing less than a Peanuts comic strip I saw years ago, when I was still studying at theological college. Snoopy is on top of his doghouse, writing a book, and when asked what he is writing about by Charlie Brown, he replies with great conviction: 'It's a book for theologians, and I have the perfect title… "Has it ever occurred to you that you might be wrong?"' Humorous perhaps, but what an impact it made to my process of education, theological theories and conclusions, as I sought to construct my faith map at that time. I've never forgotten the wisdom of that simple little comic, and it continues to moderate my bias to prioritise my own opinions or conclusions even today, forming part of the motivation for the writing of this book as well!

If I may suggest, the key here is our attitude. Am I open to consider with a spirit of generosity and humility the topics or angles with which I am unfamiliar or that I've never previously thought about? Am I constantly re-examining what I believe to be truth? After all, following an unexamined faith map without question can also be dangerous. And new circumstances frequently arise, which demand careful review and reflection. Take for example those, particularly in the US, who were encouraged by their leaders to assume that God would protect them from Covid-19 and so ignored public health advice on the wearing of masks and social distancing. As a result of this form of selection and emphasis, many caught the virus and spread it to others.

How much better if we were to make a regular practice of looking beyond our well-defined set of assumptions or habit patterns at multiple points in our lives. In other words, I can decide at any time that I don't have to be right and I don't have to hold in contempt people with whom I disagree, on a theological, political or any other level. Instead, we could adopt a more curious posture that might enrich our beliefs with fresh perspectives. Kathleen Dowling Singh puts it this way:

> Maps of new territory expand our paradigms, our worldview. They can pry open some tightly held horizons. We want our paradigms to be porous, our fabrications to be held lightly. Perhaps we've hardened our opinions and beliefs as we've aged, but we've all had the experience of an open mind, eager to expand its horizons. If we have not had that experience often, we can cultivate it.[17]

If you are wondering how to go about this, you don't need to feel that it must be attempted on your own. We all have access to good theological or spiritual literature, online courses and podcasts which can widen the scope of what we know, requiring us to consider new and unfamiliar viewpoints along the way. For many of us, however, we might be inclined to simply consult a friend or Christian leader with theological training to provide the 'right' answer so that we don't 'get it wrong', that is, to do the thinking for us. But what often cultivates better overall growth is to find experienced mentors or spiritual directors who will ask you good questions about what you believe and why, thus helping you to examine your own faith map. And there are also common opportunities to practise in our day-to-day lives.

How can I spot selection and emphasis in the map I hold?

A good place to start is with the Sunday sermon or latest podcast. As we sit listening, how are we reflecting on and critically evaluating what is being presented? Are we aware of the choices the speaker has made or the assumptions they carry as they offer their perspective on that all-too-familiar biblical story or passage? Are we aware of the preferences or desires we ourselves bring to our listening? Can we see how those are shaping our own faith maps? Cartographers are normally making conscious selection and emphasis in composing their maps. But in my experience, as Christians we are not so aware. It goes without saying that we are not advocating a critical mindset here in any kind of superior or destructive way but rather thoughtful and prayerful reflection on what we read or hear. The trick, I suppose, is to be appropriately critical without necessarily criticising!

Consider how in the sermon on the mount (Matthew 5—7) Jesus taught others to critique the two major worldviews in his time of ministry on earth: one imposed by the occupying Roman Empire and the other held and fiercely defended by the religious authorities. In that society, Roman citizens were the elite, projecting power through military might to subjugate and extract wealth and service from those they conquered. And in occupied Palestine, the scribes and Pharisees sought to preserve an underlying spirituality and way of life based on a legalistic interpretation of scripture to protect their positional power.

What both camps had in common at that time was a desire to present the *definitive* map of what was important in life, both spiritually and politically, dictating and defining what was required to live as part of the Roman Empire or within God's kingdom. It's fair to suppose that neither of these 'maps' were what Jesus came to offer. And by pointing out the underlying assumptions of both, he was able to flag up God's true intentions in sending him to earth to save humankind by offering profound inner transformation rather than external political, social or even religious power.

Identifying what has shaped your faith map

Why not take a look now at the map you drew in chapter 1 and reflect on the selection and emphasis that has shaped it? Ask yourself: How have you tackled those seven fundamental questions we posed earlier in this chapter (pp. 37–38)? How aware are you of cultural assumptions and influences you took on board as you were growing up? What were your original key sources of 'truth' and have they changed as you grew older? Have any of your core beliefs been consciously updated or added to since? Understanding what your prominent landmarks of faith are, and why they are significant to you, is crucial.

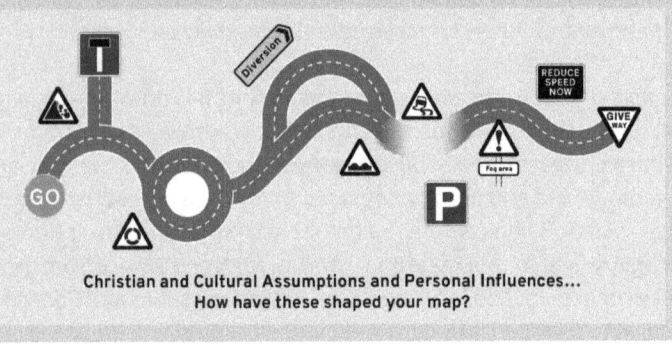

Christian and Cultural Assumptions and Personal Influences...
How have these shaped your map?

Being enriched by maps from other Christian traditions

As we take time to review our faith maps, it's worth remembering that most of us see only a portion of the full landscape that represents the worldwide Christian community. So a final route for us to consider investigating is the story behind the wide range of global Christian traditions, assumptions and denominations, alongside the culture we experience within our own Christian communities. If we ignore the wider picture, the larger map or story of all of God's people over the centuries, it's like only seeing one part of the journey on our satnav at any given moment: relevant for that time or journey as we navigate from a to b but rendering us oblivious to the wider landscape.

I've been going to church now for more than 60 years. I was taken to church while still in my mother's womb and have been a continual attender ever since. It feels like the number of sermons I've sat through, the Christian lectures and talks, seminars and conferences I've attended, never mind the mountains of Christian books I've read alongside hours of studying the Bible are vast. The sheer volume of religious, theological and spiritual investigation and input over those years seems incalculable to me now, especially as all this took place within various Christian denominations or traditions.

But only recently have I noticed the marks of selection and emphasis inherent in each one. Let's back up and discover why this might be the case.

After some successful attempts at unity in the first thousand years of Christianity, by the second millennium the differences between factions of Christians had escalated and become too great to unify, so Christianity found itself divided along some major fault lines: the split between Eastern Orthodoxy and Catholicism (1054) and the Protestant Reformation (1517). And despite the efforts of recent ecumenical movements, the boundaries between what are now considered separate strands of the Christian faith remain quite firm today.

I have realised that the view from whatever strand of Christianity I occupied at any given time lacked valuable perspectives held by others. Picture for a moment a treasure map. The one who knows where the treasure is buried draws a map with only enough information to inform how the treasure may be recovered. In the same way, most denominations or spiritual traditions tend to present their members with only that which they feel is most important while ignoring landmarks they might label less relevant or even heretical. And when we dwell within one community of faith over long periods of time without wider evaluation or self-examination, we are not particularly cognisant of what our 'X marks the spot' emphases are or what those of other traditions may bring or why.

I spent many years within the house-church movement, which tends to emphasise spiritual gifts and the specific types of ministry denoted in 1 Corinthians 12 and Ephesians 4. But one year during Lent, I decided to read the entire New Testament to gain an overview of its themes and thrust. Imagine my surprise when I saw how disproportionately few verses were devoted to those discrete topics. Christian traditions of which I have been a part subsequently have very rarely mentioned those same subjects from the pulpit, tending to focus on the importance of the sacraments or parish ministry instead. Was one tradition right and the other wrong? Not necessarily. It was simply a matter of selection and emphasis.

How about the ways we sense or expect God to be present? Some Christian streams emphasise the presence of Christ in the daily Mass, the ritual of consuming bread and wine, not just to remember him, but to viscerally encounter him. Then there are those who experience an incarnational God within God's created world, as the Celtic Christians or St Francis of Assisi advocated. Some Christians find a sense of God's presence primarily within sung worship, while praying for the miraculous or exercising spiritual gifts, while others sense God most deeply in complete solitude or silence.

Where do you find yourself on this spectrum? How do you perceive God and expect to experience a sense of God's presence? And whose view or 'map' would you most relate to?

And here's an unexpected angle to consider too: you and I would be highly unlikely to recognise or endorse the forms of Christianity that were practised by earnest disciples who lived in the sixth century, the twelfth century or even as recently as the 18th century. Why? Because in those eras or cultures, different emphases, doctrines and practices would have dominated, rendering many aspects of their day-to-day

Christian lives unfamiliar to us living in the 21st century. (For instance, Gordon Smith has written about how the act of 'conversion' has been understood in completely different ways at different times of church history.[18])

We may face the temptation to feel that we must remain loyal to our own community of faith or to dismiss those whose conventions differ from ours as not being 'real' Christians because few of their landmarks match our own.

Would it be fair to suggest therefore that we try to discern how any given Christian tradition might be attempting to faithfully represent different aspects of who they perceive God to be?

The problem arises when any given tradition or denomination assumes that they possess the *definitive* Christian position, a stance which has a long and bloody history within Christendom and has always precluded curiosity and respectful tolerance for other valid and life-enhancing expressions. What if becoming aware or acquainted with other Christians and their faith maps was not dictated by a desire to determine who is right or wrong, but rather had the goal of increasing our knowledge and experience to widen our own frame of epistemological enquiry instead?

Apart from anything else, it would help us to notice and understand the assumptions from which we operate and possibly open our hearts and minds to respect and learn from others who emphasise different aspects of their faith. Showing simple curiosity about Christians who aren't quite like me would be like building a bridge between pilgrims from all traditions while personally offering and receiving wisdom with an open heart. Could demonstrating a spirit of enquiry that recognises and fully embraces the variety of ways that Christians express their spirituality across all ethnicities and cultures create the kind of unity of spirit of which Paul speaks in Ephesians 2:14–18 and 4:2–6? A true outworking of the atonement – or, as Sheldon Sorge observes, an 'at-one-ment'[19] – that overcomes natural divisions?

As part of a theological course that I taught, students were sent out over a series of Sundays to experience the worship of Christian traditions and denominations which were unfamiliar to them in the hope that their horizons would be suitably expanded. Despite some trepidation at having to navigate unfamiliar patterns and emphases, the students always came back greatly enriched by this opportunity to step briefly into another Christian mindset. A few even reported what a humbling experience it had been to have been made so welcome among those 'strange Christians' with whom they had assumed they shared very little. Engaging meaningfully with another spiritual community had caused them to critique some of their own core assumptions about what was fundamental to their faith.

Every religious or spiritual map has been gradually formed, usually over many years. But as we've already seen, all maps are incomplete, being limited to the original cartographer's understanding of the world in relation to God as it was drawn. On the other hand, God is, by definition, infinite, and clearly cannot be fully described by a single 'snapshot'. So, as we explore maps beyond our immediate tradition, the more windows into God's nature and person we encounter, and the larger and richer our perspective grows. We might also consider potential distortions, assumptions and filters that affect how each tradition operates, including those that appear on the map we're currently holding if we are to follow the signposting towards a mature, rounded and robust Christian faith. Richard Foster's book *Streams of Living Water* demonstrates how vital all Christian traditions are to keeping the body of Christ balanced yet rightly diversified in their emphases.[20]

How is my faith map serving me going forwards?

We are grateful for what has been passed on to us over the centuries, but to ensure that our faith maps develop we need to own them for ourselves and travel beyond what is simply provided for us. One way to do this is by asking ourselves epistemological questions to help us decide what is truly reflecting the mystery of God and what is a result of human selection and emphasis – both our own and that of others.

But at the end of the day, we can also acknowledge that there are ultimate truths which transcend all human thinking. All who believe in God are just trying to make some kind of sense of the mystery that our notion or experience of an infinite God has communicated to us. Our interpretation of that – the maps we draw for ourselves and each other – can never be wholly adequate, and in humility we recognise that our understanding will always need to grow, change and be challenged and enlarged.

Seeking truth and exploring other perspectives are not an end in themselves or just an intellectual exercise. They offer us other windows into the nature of God and may also offer us fresh perspectives on ourselves. What God desires is always to call us deeper, often beyond the words and concepts with which we are familiar, and to help us to be transformed towards the likeness of his Son. So, as we close this chapter, and with your carefully curated faith map in hand, take a moment to ask yourself this final but important question: *What kind of a person has your faith map made you to be?*

This isn't a question we consider very often. In our rush to be growing as a Christian, whether that be through being a good Baptist, Anglican, Catholic, contemplative, or no specified tradition or denomination whatsoever, what inner transformation is truthfully happening as a result of the doctrines, beliefs and practices we are adhering to? You might find it tricky to judge this. I know I do.

But perhaps thinking about how we are perceived by those who know us might help. For instance, would I be known for being comfortable in my own spiritual skin and encouraging others to be likewise? Or do I disparage or feel threatened by those who don't believe as I do? Am I known for my love for others, or do I think my friends would say that I am more interested in 'being right'? Is my map leading me towards a more generous or expanded view of other Christian traditions or less so?

I noticed that when someone innocently posted a question online the other day asking for advice over how to navigate a particular controversial ethical issue, he unwittingly sparked a ferocious debate among a group of Christian leaders and theologians that I had known for years. The resulting thread provoked such an intense level of furious vitriol and unnecessary accusation as contributors debated – the kind that sadly has become all too common on social media – that it was painful and quite distressing to read. And the difference for me in this social media example was that these were people I knew and respected.

I therefore ask again: what kind of Christian, indeed, what kind of *person*, has your carefully curated faith map made you to be?

Such a question is central to our journey because 'who we are' is closely tied to what we believe. What we believe on all sorts of levels, not just theologically, is who we become. So next, we will consider who we are as human beings – how we are made and why it matters.

3
Where are you starting from?

Charles

*Isn't it odd that we can only see our outsides,
but nearly everything happens on the inside?*

CHARLIE MACKESY[21]

I don't know about you, but the times when I'm struck by those big questions, like 'Is this all there is?' are rare. I seldom wake up in the morning asking myself, 'Who am I?' or 'What's my life all about?' Normally I'm more interested in 'Where's the coffee?' as I blearily struggle to regain consciousness while those big existential questions remain hidden below the surface. And my days can easily continue in the same vein, taking life as it comes, not pausing to ask why I'm reacting in the ways I do. Just living from day to day.

But those questions – or at least the core desires out of which they arise – are still there, subtly pulling strings behind the scenes of our emotions and influencing our choices and the ways in which we walk with God and others through life. Our faith map may have been shaped by cultural and Christian assumptions, but the way we use it depends on how clearly we perceive it. And to understand that means understanding more about ourselves.

My many years of fell walking in the Lake District have given me the technical skills to navigate an OS map. Because that was the task in front of me – to make my way to our destination without getting lost.

But if I'd noticed more about what happened along the way and learnt how to reflect on those experiences more deeply, I'd have been better equipped to navigate through life as well.

A particular year in the Lakes stands out for me. We were excited to be climbing a peak that we had never attempted before, Pillar Rock. I'd been pouring over my OS map and really wanted to try the more challenging route to the summit. It looked alright on paper, clearly marked, although the stretcher box shown at the base of the narrow Shamrock Traverse we needed to cross should perhaps have given me more pause for thought than it did!

Sitting in a pub the night before, our group was divided on the wisdom of this approach.

'I don't fancy that ledge much,' commented Joe.

'It'll be fine,' I replied. 'Look… my guidebook says there are no dangers if you keep to the path.' I omitted to add that it also said that there were indeed dangers if you deviated from that path, especially on the traverse!

Our disagreement continued the next morning as we climbed the lower slopes of Pillar. It came to a head when we reached the point at which we'd need to turn off if we were going to attempt the traverse.

Finally, Joe put his foot down, 'Sorry, but I'm not going that way.'

But I was determined to have a go. 'Alright,' I said. 'Let's split into two groups. Who'd like to come with me?'

I got my way (against Joe's better judgement) and led my group off across the face of the fell while the rest continued up the shoulder. Something inside me didn't feel right, but I ignored it and carried on. As we followed our path, the voice in my head was working overtime! *Why didn't Joe want to come with me? What's so hard about this path anyway?* I felt frustrated and confused, and if I'm honest a bit guilty about splitting up the group to get what I wanted.

But I didn't know why. I'd never stepped back to evaluate my feelings or why I was feeling them.

In my 20s, I was a devotee of the famous Haynes car manuals, an essential companion during the many hours spent tinkering with my Mk 1 Ford Escort. If only we were issued with something like that – a guidebook which told us in plain and simple language how human beings work! Or maybe a sort of X-ray or CT scan which, instead of telling us information only related to our physical health, also showed us what was going on inside emotionally, mentally and psychologically.

Scripture gives us some great insights into how the thoughts, desires, feelings and attitudes of biblical characters affected their actions or reactions. Jesus masterfully called out the Pharisees for hypocritically hiding behind their tithing rules to skimp on the cost of supporting parents. But he doesn't just say that this was wrong, he pinpoints the inner issue behind their behaviour (quoting Isaiah): 'These people honour me with their lips, but their hearts are far from me' (Matthew 15:3–8). And we can dig deeper into such wisdom using some of the insights that 21st-century psychological and neurological information can now provide to help us to understand more deeply how we work.

James 1 tells us that we can be 'dragged away' from good intentions by our underlying desires (James 1:14–15). That's a vital piece of the puzzle. But without being able to name the actual desires that drive our behaviour (examples of which are shown in the image that follows) and engaging prayerfully in our emotional and spiritual formation, we are often left still subject to them. And we act accordingly.

It was only with hindsight that I realised how much my decisions and actions that day on Pillar were the result of unexamined thoughts and feelings. I'd always spent my life trying to achieve goals I set myself, even if it was only something like crossing that traverse, and had rarely

Some basic human desires

paused to reflect on what was behind the choices I was making. But that 'unexamined' way of living had real implications for my spiritual life. It meant that I'd reached a plateau and, after the initial excitement and steep learning curve of what it meant to follow Jesus, it was clear that I had much work to do in order to grow in emotional and spiritual self-awareness and maturity.

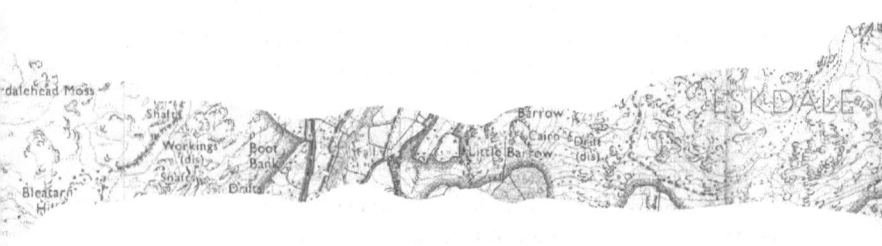

Why do we need to understand ourselves better?

Throughout my Christian life, I have been taught an awful lot about *God*, but not so much about *myself*. And yet, after many years of marriage, I have come to understand that most healthy relationships require each person to understand more about themselves, as well as the other person, in order to relate to them in loving ways. And with respect to loving God, the less I have critically evaluated the assumptions or values attached to my background, cultural context or spiritual tradition, the more I am likely to assume that the God I think I know and love actually *is* God.

Psalm 18:25–26 says: 'To the faithful you show yourself faithful, to the blameless you show yourself blameless, to the pure you show yourself pure, but to the devious you show yourself shrewd.' It's a slightly obscure passage, but it indicates to me that my images and ideas of God may well have been strongly shaped by who I am and what I'm like. I notice that a quite a few biblical characters, e.g. Jacob, Jonah, Job, Saul and Peter, appeared to share this same tendency, at least in the early stages of their relationship with God.

You might be wondering by now whether this emphasis on self-examination is healthy. Why would we ask ourselves these questions? Well, despite the fact that loving God and others is meant to be the point of the Christian journey, we do seem to have a tendency to function at the epicentre of our own faith map. I frequently find myself looking out for *my* concerns, *my* impulses, *my* desires and trying to fulfil *my* agendas. It's like having a faith map with lots of exciting places to go, but only ever being interested in that big red arrow and the accompanying words, 'You are here.'

If we are the lens through which our mental maps of life and faith are interpreted, we are only capable of responding out of the reality of who we are in our inner self. I wonder if that is as unexpected a revelation to you as it was to me. As I read Psalm 139, where the psalmist prays,

'Search me, God, and know my heart… See if there is any offensive way in me' (vv. 23–24; see also Psalm 17:3), he's acknowledging that our outward fruitfulness will always depend on the actual state of our inner self. And this is often quite different from the self that we operate in church or other public contexts, the self we present to the world around us.

This is another unseen example of unconscious selection and emphasis. But whether or not I am conscious of operating these versions of myself, what I often conveniently forget is that we are all humans before we become Christians and, as such, we start reading our new faith map using the same components of human makeup common to everyone else on the planet.

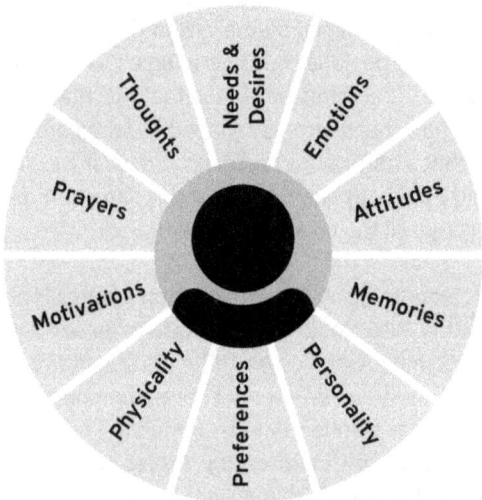

Some components of human makeup

Once we become disciples, we may feel that we are now operating with a completely different Christ-inspired 'map'; but purely as the map-readers, we are no different from those operating a map without this as their key reference. We are trying to follow a new map with our old, untransformed humanity – to impose a 'new self' on top of our 'old self'. In other words, if our natural human tendencies and desires remain unnoticed, unexamined and untransformed, we may wish to be living our lives completely oriented towards God without realising that, in fact, we are still caught up in the gravitational pull of serving ourselves. An effective antidote for this? If Paul is to be believed, it starts with a comprehensive sober self-assessment (Romans 12:3).

And this is what happened as I was trying to reach the Shamrock Traverse on Pillar. It's no surprise perhaps to hear that it turned out to be much more challenging that I'd anticipated. For one thing it sloped downwards and away from the side of the fell towards a sheer drop, and for another it was wet and slippery. Not a good combination.

My group was also a bit taken aback at the prospect. I presented a calm exterior, but inside that voice was beginning to question, *Have you done the right thing here?* And it started to create disaster scenarios, like *What if someone falls off?* and *What will you say to their family – Neville fell off Pillar because I fancied a bit of a challenge?!* With careful steps (and staying rigidly to the path) we made our way across and up to the summit to meet the others. I didn't feel the sense of euphoria I'd anticipated when we joined the others at the top. In fact, I felt ashamed at the peril my eagerness to get what I wanted had placed others in. Yet the spectre of shame at failing to 'bag that peak' drove me on.

Shame seems to lie close to the heart of the human condition, and so we need to explore it further.

How does shame disrupt our faith walk?

Developing a coherent story of who we are, an image of ourselves, is an important part of how we grow up and learn to interact well with the world around us.[22] But to be healthy, this image we develop also needs to be authentic, that is, reflecting who we really are and not just who we feel we ought to be – reflecting something of the image of God that we have been created to carry.

The image we hold of ourselves in adult life is often conformed to the one that we created in those early years as we first ventured out into the world. Formed before we experienced a conscious sense of God's presence, we felt left to our own devices and tried to create a 'public face' that would keep us feeling safe, acceptable, significant and worthy of respect. And this was a necessary process for us to be able to interact successfully with the world in which we found ourselves.

However, over time that self-created public face may often become strongly defended,[23] always trying to ensure that those basic human needs are being met. And so, when we start to follow the ways of Christ, we can end up with a tension between what we might call our self-oriented 'defended-self' and the image of God in which we were made. The image of God we carry is what we aspire to as Christians, but it is often overridden and obscured by the actions of our defended-self.

Sadly, our defended-self is stubbornly persistent! It tends to stay with us for many years and owes a lot of its formation and eventual shape to the action of shame within our heart. Brené Brown and Curt Thompson have both researched and written extensively on shame, because shame is at the core of the story of humankind's fall in Genesis 3.[24]

Hopefully we can agree that God's intent for his children and disciples is to be transformed 'from glory to glory' (2 Corinthians 3:18, KJV). Shame is the very opposite of glory and completely hijacks that intent. Just to be clear, shame is not the same thing as guilt. We feel guilt when we have done something we know to be wrong which dishonours God or harms others or ourselves. But God has given us the means by which we can repent of healthy guilt and be forgiven. So, guilt is associated with actions. And feeling 'ashamed' is sometimes a right response to choosing unwisely, which was exactly my emotion as I reflected on my motivations that day on Pillar.

But shame in its most comprehensive form is not a passing emotion like feeling ashamed; it's an underlying human condition profoundly linked with who we fundamentally believe ourselves to be. As an example:

if I didn't study much and scored badly on an exam at school, I felt guilty and somewhat ashamed. I knew I'd blown it. But I also knew that I could change that outcome by making different choices about my study habits. Shame, on the other hand, is when I believe myself to be pathologically stupid, incapable of being clever or succeeding academically, that I could never live up to either my own or God's expectations of me.

I wonder if shame is something intrinsic to our humanity, born as we are without the conscious assurance of God's unconditional love. Shame can certainly get fanned into flame from an early age. Think back to your early artistic efforts in nursery or primary school. If you were fortunate enough to have an encouraging teacher, even your early scribbles may well have been received as if you were a budding Picasso! And you would have felt a glowing sense of self-worth. But what if your work was disparaged instead? A classmate grabs it and tears it up, laughing. The sense of shame that accompanies that sort of experience can last well into adulthood.

Shame is what I feel now when someone rolls their eyes at something I've said that they find ill-informed or wrong. Shame is what we all feel when somebody comments on something we can't change, like our height or ethnicity, in an unkind way. Shame is rampant in every form of social media, causing enormous emotional and mental anxiety for those whose very identity has come to depend on validation within this arena.

Shame can also be present in Christian contexts because of the compulsion to be seen to be the best 'Christian self' we can appear to be. We dislike feeling shame or indeed any kind of pain so much that we will do whatever it takes to numb that pain and distract ourselves from it.

Biblically, shame has its roots in humankind's response to desire and is graphically illustrated by Eve and Adam's interactions with the serpent. From Genesis 1—2 we see that God's agenda for Adam and Eve was to create a place of security and belonging, in which they could flourish and be fruitful. Naked and unashamed is how Adam and Eve saw themselves and each other in Genesis 2:25.

Let's pause for a moment and savour this scenario.

Although it turned out to be short-lived, it shows us God's heart for the human contexts and interactions that would follow. To know and to be known. To own a rock-solid sense of identity. To know who you belong to and why. To understand your purpose and thrive alongside others in it. Your whole and true God-imaged-self engaged in loving relationship as a reflection of the community that's at the heart of the Trinity – a community I like to see as reflecting unity within diversity, mutual giving and acceptance. Essentially, a family unit that always makes space for one another.

Within his very nature, and within Eden, God created a model and a context for humans to flourish, providing the means by which all our basic needs can be met.

And yet, as Curt Thompson suggests, perhaps the real deception of 'the Fall' was that Eve was persuaded to think that God was withholding something from her that she deserved, the opportunity to be like God or to have what God had (Genesis 3:1–6).[25] In other words, the serpent was suggesting that Adam and Eve were not good enough as they were, not important enough for God to share his nature and his community of perfect love with them.

Thompson rightly points out that all this could have been cleared up in an instant had they thought to discuss this with God, so that he could remind them of all that he had provided and that his imprint was already at their core. But instead, their innate FOMO (fear of missing out) took over and they chose to embrace the false narrative about God and themselves that they had been offered.

And so, the shame and hiding began, despite God coming to look for them, continuing to desire relationship with them, an intimacy that they were now no longer able to enjoy. It becomes fairly evident in looking at the way our stories tend to run that shame can cause any human being to want to hide who they really are from those they feel intimidated or threatened by. This includes God, other people and even the idealised version of themselves that they cling to.

Spotting shame's action

It's one thing to understand what shame is in theory, but another to be able to spot it when it pops up unexpectedly in daily life. The key is noticing when you put on a particular 'face' for a given context, because shame will shape the person we present to others if we let it. Whatever it is that is valued in any given community gives me the criteria for the shape of the person I need to adopt to avoid shame. And my defended-self leaps into action to make it so!

I wonder what sort of faces we present in our church communities, in the office, with our neighbours, doing the weekly shop or playing with the kids.

I'm ashamed to admit that I've noticed what I call the 'competitive Christian face', the version of me that compares myself to others within my Christian community to measure how well I am doing relative to others in my tribe. Subtly, I vie to be perceived to be the best Christian, usually based on the idealised version that my tradition or tribe has presented as the ultimate goal to aim for. You know – the most passionate evangelist or the one who spends the longest time in prayer or is most active on the mission field or working at the local food bank.

What's driving all this masking? Perhaps fear of being found out or exposed as a fraud? Maybe it's imposter syndrome. Our strongly defended-self finds that revealing its perceived weaknesses, fear of shame or pain, is very threatening and will take all sorts of measures to avoid it. That's why we can end up stuck in Romans 7, as Paul seems to suggest, bemoaning the fact that, 'I do not understand what I do. For what I want to do I do not do, but what I hate I do' (Romans 7:15).

Theologically, we probably know that our true identity is 'hidden with Christ in God' (Colossians 3:3), but to our less-than-20:20 vision, it can be so hidden that we cannot access who we want to be or who we are created to be. Somehow, we find that this person we aspire to be as followers of God, that God intends us to be, feels out of reach. Paul addresses this problem in Ephesians 4 when he talks about taking off the 'old self' and reclothing ourselves with the 'new self' in Christ (Ephesians 4:22–24).

How often have you heard that instruction?

How far have you been able to put it into practice?

Although we often recite these verses, we seldom know what to do in response. Most people come to me as a spiritual director hoping to resolve some aspect of this gap between who they are and who they feel they should be or wish to be in order that they might come to know God more meaningfully. And along the way we might consider the deep connection between shame and sin as was first described in Eden. Personally, I don't think that sin is simply 'doing bad things that God doesn't approve of'. That is sin's outcome. I sense that sin comes about because we desire to meet our own needs, whether emotional, psychological, physical or material, in our own way, according to what we think will deliver what we feel we need. Just like Adam and Eve.

Take a look at the ten commandments and review them through this lens. God appears to be addressing our tendency to worship other gods (presumably ones we feel meet our needs more directly and to our specifications), dishonour our parents (because we think we know better), commit adultery or covet what someone else enjoys (because we look to those 'out of reach' entities to provide the emotional stimulus that we feel we lack) and so on. God is suggesting that there is a better way because sin isn't just disobeying him, it's disagreeing with God about how our needs and desires are most fruitfully met. This is our old defended-self still in control.

Here's something to consider: the goal of creating or operating the 'Christian face' in us all is that we desire to appear well in front of others in our community. We focus on external appearance, but this can hijack spiritual transformation because we're not starting with the truth of who we are. If we want to be consistently like Christ, then we can't just try to mimic Christ because, 'The Lord does not look at the things people look at. People look at the outward appearance, but the Lord looks at the heart' (1 Samuel 16:7).

With God's help, we are invited to genuinely become like Christ, to be formed into Christ (or, as Paul says, to have 'the mind of Christ', 1 Corinthians 2:16). This requires digging beneath the surface to understand why we still choose to sin even when we know what the Christ-like response could or should be. Otherwise, we're simply overlaying a Christian veneer on an untransformed self and we end up with that 'Christian face'. Even when we want to want what Christ wants for us, somehow, our 'old self' remains in charge, and we still end up choosing unwisely much of the time.

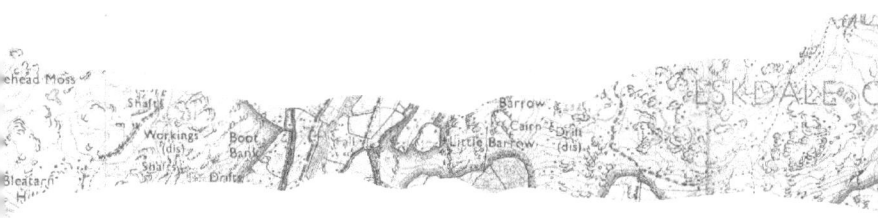

What do I need to understand about myself?

That's what was troubling me after that trek up Pillar. I began to interrogate myself. Why did I feel so compelled to try this route and drag others along with me? What was driving the fear of failing? If only I had known then that my strong achievement orientation was ingrained from long years of highly competitive education, but at the time in my unexamined state I really had no idea. I was walking around with the proverbial plank in my eye (Matthew 7:3).

And so, I resolved to look into my human 'operating system'. And because I could recall the way Jesus summarised the greatest commandment as loving God with our whole beings – heart, mind, soul and strength – I began there, with the heart.

Physically, the heart is central to life itself, and it is well hidden and protected within our rib cage. Perhaps that's why it also used in the Bible to connote the centre of our emotional, intellectual and moral activity, which is also central to how we conduct our lives. All that activity can largely remain hidden away within us. It's in the heart in this sense that we make choices about what we say or do. And so, if we can become more actively aware of this interplay between emotion, reason and our moral compass, we might begin to understand why we do some of the things we do.

Emotions

As I examined my heart, I realised (as someone who spends much of life 'in my head') that I needed to notice and understand my feelings more often and more accurately. Because they normally lie just below the surface of my day-to-day life, only occasionally do I become aware of how feelings bubble up and show themselves.

Some Christians are naturally suspicious of too much emphasis on emotion, and I probably fit into that category, being a middle-aged

British male! But biblically God presents himself as a feeling God, unapologetically experiencing a wide range of emotions, such as tender love and passion for his beloved people and anger and hurt when they rejected him. Jesus – 'the pioneer and perfecter of faith' (Hebrews 12:2) – was angry in the temple courts, sad as he looked out over Jerusalem and felt compassion for the many lost and sick people he encountered.

Despite what we might think, in many aspects we do take after the God who made us. We all have feelings, but some of us are very aware of them, while others aren't so much. Some may think that admitting feelings is a sign of weakness, and others don't think they can handle their feelings even if they were to admit to them. Keeping a good British stiff upper lip, for example, doesn't mean feelings aren't actively influencing our lives and decisions, and almost certainly the quality of our relationships as well.

Some Christians have been brought up to think that the important thing about faith is the objective truth that underpins it and that we must not be influenced by how we feel about it. But perhaps it would also be good to acknowledge that recognising and validating emotions are not the same things as making them the final or definitive determiner of truth. If we pause to notice and evaluate our feelings, we can start to understand where they come from, why we are feeling what we are and which underlying desires they might be signposting.

So, let's do that…

Noticing and sharing your feelings with God

Pause for a moment to reflect. I wonder if you have taken notice of your feelings today. Are you aware of how often have they changed in the last few hours? Are you able to notice any discernible patterns? More importantly, how are you talking to God about your feelings? Have you ever talked to God about them – especially the ones that seem less acceptable to you? Maybe this is the first time you've allowed yourself to admit that you might be feeling things like that. Is God interested in helping you notice and deal with what you feel?

How are you feeling, for example, about where you find yourself on your spiritual journey?

How are you feeling about where you are on your journey?

Desires

There's no doubt that feelings can be variable, ever changing and unpredictable. But they are an important part of our human operating system and deserve to be noticed, not least because they tell you something about what's going on at a bedrock level within. When I was able with a bit of hindsight to look back at my experience on Pillar, I could see that my feelings of frustration came from a desire to be in control of the situation, to get the outcome I wanted. And that desire for control was rooted in a need to achieve the hard thing, and to be seen to do so. My emotions were flagging up my deeper desires if only I'd had eyes to see them then.

And as we've seen, James tells us that our desires strongly influence our actions. So, now let's take a closer look at desires. We carry desires deep in our souls, in the collective essence of who we are. Desires are like a gravitational pull, sometimes an urgent tug, towards something we sense is vital to our well-being.

We are all born with desires. Think of a baby as a bundle of needs and desires – to be fed and clothed and kept warm, for touch and attention and love. Babies don't have the capacity to consider whether or not their desires are legitimate or not; they just expect someone to meet their always urgently felt needs. As we grow from babies to children to teenagers to adults, that urge to satisfy our desires remains and strongly influences our feelings, thoughts and actions.[26]

God takes the fact that we have desires seriously because, like feelings, God himself also has desires – desires that emerge from his infinite love. He desired to be with the first people he created, and even came looking for them after they decided to hide in shame (Genesis 3:8–9). He desired to restore people to himself by sending Jesus. And try counting how many times Jesus asked people what they wanted or desired for him to do for them in the gospels. Look again at the story of the rich young ruler to see how Jesus was able to see through his seemingly legitimate spiritual request to challenge the real desires which lay beneath it (Luke 18:18–30).

Desires play a critical part in who we are and how we respond to life and to God.[27] And when our desires are not being met, our emotions let us know about it. The next time you feel angry, ask yourself why. What is the desire within you that is not being met? Perhaps you planned out your day and your boss has just dumped a whole bunch of high-priority work on your desk. You've lost control of your day. You can't do what you wanted to do and it's frustrating. Or perhaps you have a desire for harmony in all your relationships because you can't bear the disconnection that comes from arguing or falling out. You may walk around a particularly prickly person taking great care not to upset them. What emotions give that away? Perhaps fear, or a feeling of unease. Emotions tend to flag up underlying desires.

And because human beings are complex, working with our desires can get challenging. If only we felt one kind of desire, we might be able to cope more easily. But we also have to navigate conflicting desires, that is, desires which seem to be pulling in different directions. For instance, if I'm asked to take on a piece of work, part of me might feel that it's a great chance to show people what I can do and would love to do it, but another part of me might be afraid that I don't have the capacity to do the work well at the moment. My desire to 'shine' is conflicting with my desire to protect my time. Both are felt desires but are competing with each other for my attention. And then there are the desires we have which compete with the desires God has for us – to carry his image authentically in the world! So, I may desire to hear God and do what he says, but I also wish to protect my own sense of how to use my time or seek an easy, comfortable life.[28]

Of course, we don't experience those desires with their accompanying emotions in a vacuum; they affect how we think and how our body reacts as well.

The heart connection to our mind and body

An amazing feature about our contemporary age is the rate at which we are learning about how our minds work in harmony (or otherwise) with the rest of our selves. When Paul asked the Roman church to renew their thinking (Romans 12:2), I can't imagine he had such a detailed understanding of the multitude of roles the mind plays, engaging rational, imaginative and creative functions. It's our thinking mind that pulls together all sorts of signals from our senses and creates a comprehensible picture of what's going on around us. In close collaboration with our 'heart', our mind helps us to develop a view of what's right and what's not.

This plays into our theology and our image of God. We build an understanding of how best to interpret what we read in the Bible, we listen to those who teach us from the pulpit or mentor us as Christian leaders, we try to get a sense of what God's Spirit might be saying to us in prayer and we form an opinion on how we should live as Christians. Overlaid on (and sometimes at odds with) the cultural assumptions of right and wrong within our society, we grow a living 'moral compass' that helps us to make choices as we attempt to navigate the journey we are on as we try to follow Jesus through life.

Let's widen our scope beyond our heart and mind to include our whole human body. Taken as a whole, our body is an incredible miracle of creation, but as Christians some of us live life as if our bodies have no connection to how we are transformed spiritually. I try to eat well and exercise, but I never really considered how my body was integral to my relationship with God. What a spectacular example of a worldview that's the result of unconscious 'selection and emphasis', dividing the sacred from the secular or material!

Clearly, we are embodied people. But we are not just our bodies, though models and athletes may prioritise their physicality. We are spiritual beings learning to be human in the context of our physical bodies.

Herewith the 'science' bit. Our minds are housed within physical brains that contain some 100 billion neurons, each with up to 10,000 synapse connections with its neighbours. The incredibly complex networks that those connections make support both lower and higher functions: from keeping us breathing to learning languages or creating a beautiful painting. And as we learn, those networks develop through changes in the almost infinite permutations of connections between the neurons in different regions of our brain, each with its own particular specialism. Truly we are fearfully and wonderfully made, but perhaps we don't always grasp the half of it!

Quite apart from the fact that our brains that process thoughts and emotions are housed and sustained within our physical bodies, our bodies themselves react to emotion. Because, of course, our body's organs are interconnected with our brain through our nervous systems. An obvious example is the fight-flight-freeze reaction you might have when you hear footsteps behind you as you're walking down a dark street late at night. In response to the fear you feel, your autonomic nervous system increases your heart rate, reduces digestion, tenses muscles and does a number of other things to prepare you for what you suspect might be to come. Less obvious, but no less important, everyday examples of the connection between body, heart and mind are the ways in which we can feel emotion in our bodies: fear in the pit of our stomach, anger in our chest, stress in our neck and shoulders.

So, when Jesus told people not to fear, it looks like he was actually addressing their whole human operating system!

Perhaps an example of how what we might call our 'reactive spiral' works would help. Alongside healthy and helpful reactions that are designed to keep us safe from danger, for example, this is also a description of how our defended-self reacts to a situation that threatens to cause us pain, because it leaves one or other of our core desires unfulfilled (see the diagram opposite). Perhaps sadly we've been hurt by someone within our church community. Nothing serious... maybe they said something insulting about how we were fulfilling a role like teaching Sunday school or serving the coffee. It's a small slight, but unconsciously we feel shame. This is pain that we want to avoid at all costs, and so we look for someone to hold responsible (other than ourselves of course!) and pin the blame on the person who organised the coffee or Sunday school rota that week. Our defended-self takes offence and prompts a defensive reaction to the situation.

Here's a way of looking at the process that I've found helpful. Our desire was to have our emotional needs met by our community, to be appreciated and validated in our service. But that didn't happen, and we feel hurt as a result. Every time we think about it, we get a tight feeling in the pit of our stomach and unconsciously clench our jaw or our fists. It makes us both sad and angry. And every time we start to think about it, we can't stop thinking about it. We rehearse what happened over and over again, our thinking mind concocting a storyline internally to justify our desire for recognition and how others fell short. The key thing to note is that we are often oblivious that our minds are caught in this relentless cycle, even though it may end up changing our attitudes or behaviour: *Well, I'm never going to put myself on that rota again!* and *I'll make sure to steer clear of that insulting person from now on*. What a self-reinforcing spiral of misery!

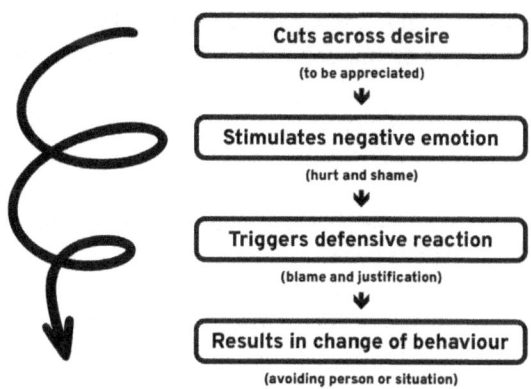

Our subconscious reactive spiral

Somehow through that experience of life, we have learnt to respond to a situation and a person in a negative way. After enough time, we may even forget why we're mad at said offending person, but physically, our neural networks have already laid down some connections, or pathways, that create a defensive habit that will hold us captive. Unless, that is, we recognise what's going on and do something to make a change. Because the good news is that our well-worn neural pathways can be refreshed and reoriented with God's help. But it won't happen unless we consciously switch off our 'autopilot' and start asking ourselves some penetrating questions.

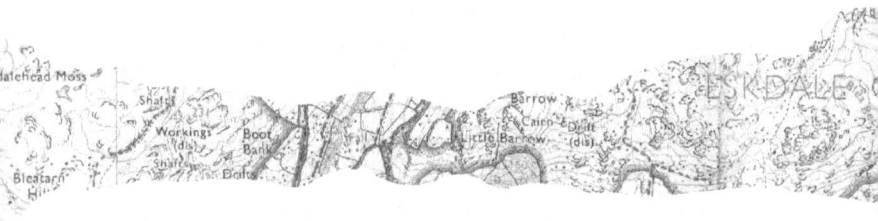

How getting to know what's going on inside us can help to save us

In the agony of the cross, Jesus prayed, 'Father, forgive them, for they do not know what they are doing' (Luke 23:34). I wonder how often he has prayed that on our behalf since then. Without some level of self-understanding, we'll struggle to be truly cognizant of why we're doing some of the things we do. But with God's help and our active engagement that can change.

I'm quite sure the religious leaders felt they were preserving Judaism for future generations by exposing Jesus as a blasphemer and liar. But what do you think was really going on in them at a deeper level? I wonder if they were aware that, perhaps, their underlying motivations might be to hold on to their position of power as the 'oracle' within their community and that their disgust and anger hung essentially on shame, that is, the strong possibility that they might turn out to be 'not enough'? Well, it seems not.

But before we indulge in any further finger-pointing, what about us? Do we really understand why we do what we do? For example, why we're intent on showing up our colleague at work to be seen for the lazy slacker we believe them to be, or why we consistently avoid interacting with people we find threatening or shy away from situations that might contain conflict? Or why we suddenly fall into a pit of incandescent road rage or why we wouldn't dream of learning a new skill (because we might possibly fail)? If we could only see below the water line and connect our conscious decisions and actions to our feelings and subconscious desires, we might discover the person behind the mask that God already knows and wants to liberate.

Let's break this down even further: most of us don't tend to notice the underlying desires that drive our core emotions. For the sake of simplicity, we will choose three common emotions: anger, fear and shame.[29] We're usually much more aware of what we are feeling than of the unmet desire underneath that emotion. These unmet desires produce a strong internal reaction, and we look for some way to fulfil them or someone to blame if we can't, in order to fend off or quench the pain.

For instance, we can feel *angry* or frustrated when something or someone stops us doing what or going where we want to (hence the road rage that rises when another driver cuts across our path). When we feel that we've been wronged or treated unjustly by someone else, that feeling can stay with us and linger. We mull it over and nurture the discontent within. But that can mean that we miss the opportunity to grow. Instead of gently seething, how might we see God's formative purposes for us and look beyond the immediate or obvious, even surrendering our need to be right, justified or always free to fulfil our own goals?

In the same way, *fear* is triggered when we think we lack security and feel unsafe. Quite often this happens when we try to anticipate 'the unknown'. We become anxious when we think about future events, like being intimidated by people who threaten our sense of well-being (hence the wish to avoid conflict). Many of us imagine future scenarios where we or our loved ones might face difficulty, pain or even death. These uncomfortable images play in our heads, threatening our desire to be equipped to meet every eventuality in life. How might we accept that some pain and loss is beyond our ability to avoid? How might we grow in surrendering those fears to God, deriving a sense of ultimate security based on his faithful character, allowing him to work out his plans, for others or ourselves – whatever comes?

And *shame*? As we've seen, that's often driven by the desire to appear well in front of others, to protect our reputation, competency or self-worth (hence the drive to make the work colleague appear worse than us). We are told that God values us highly, but how can we let that head knowledge seep more deeply into our hearts?

We must also bring some balance here. Alongside a negative influence on our freedom to be who we are, each of these desires can also have a healthy protective function. For example, a healthy level of anger at a clear injustice can fuel a courageous response when handled with maturity. So, how do we discern what's driving us?

A first step is to notice what's happening in everyday life through the lens of our unmet core desires. If you take another look at my experience on Pillar as an illustration, you'll see that each of those desires (for physical and emotional security, validation of my self-worth and a measure of control over what happens to me) came into play in both unhealthy and healthy ways: wanting to have my own way (control) that split the group; being seen to lead courageously across a difficult traverse (validation) that led others into risk; and eventually admitting to a healthy fear of falling off it (security) that helped to keep us safe!

You might like to try that for yourself. Notice what's happening in your day and ask yourself how you are feeling about it. Can you spot any unmet desires beneath those feelings?

The lens of personality

The combination of heart, mind, soul and body that we've explored so far come together to form our personality – the characteristic ways in which we process and interact with life. Our personality can give us a clue as to which of those core desires we feel most strongly.

There are all sorts of tools to help us look at personality. Two of the most popular ones are the Myers-Briggs Type Indicator (MBTI) and the Enneagram. MBTI looks at our 'thinking preferences', while the Enneagram focuses more on our core motivations and the mix of rational, relational and instinctual 'intelligence' that we use most naturally.[30] No tool or scheme can fully describe the miracle of God's creation in human beings. Only God sees the whole: including our deepest self that is 'hidden with Christ in God' (Colossians 3:3). But an awareness of the different ways in which we and others might be reacting to life as it happens through our defended-self can be helpful as we seek to understand what our natural impulses might be and how they might detract or hold us back from becoming more like Christ.

Take my friend Jenny, for instance. Jenny is an exceptionally relational person, often guided by her feelings of fulfilment when she's able to help other people. As a nurse this makes her an excellent carer, and she's lauded in her Christian community for that willingness to serve. But if left unexamined, her strong underlying need to be needed can drive her to expend herself in the service of others at the cost of her own well-being. She can also get really upset if people don't recognise her service to them! Jenny leans towards what Enneagram theory would describe as 'heart intelligence', greatly valuing relational connection and desiring approval or validation from others.

Then there's Kevin. A natural leader, Kevin is highly motivated to rescue those he sees struggling with powerlessness and poverty in society. It makes him cross to witness what's going on around him. That strong sense of justice has given him the energy to create an effective charity working with oppressed peoples. And yet that same desire to change what's wrong with the world can also make him a difficult and exhausting person to follow in his relentless mission, especially in how he judges other people and the quality of their contributions. Kevin leans towards 'gut intelligence', being quite instinctual in his responses to life.

As for me, I have a tendency towards the rational, putting my trust in reasoning and logic, which can make me seem a bit aloof or distant. What I have noticed in myself is a fear of not 'having enough resources' and this leads to a strong desire to make sure I keep plenty in reserve for every situation. I can struggle with the 'what ifs' of life and find myself creating all sorts of disaster scenarios and escape plans for things that hardly ever happen!

You may know people like Jenny, Kevin and me. You might resonate with one of us yourself. You can see that our deepest desires have potential to be fruitful, but if left unexamined, those desires can also become dominant and unhelpful. How can that be? I know that I tend to overprepare, because I'm afraid I'll fail otherwise; Jenny's moral compass would tell her to look after herself as well as others, but she doesn't want to risk their disappointment; and Kevin… well Kevin may just not be aware how he steamrolls over his staff in his urgency to fix the world!

Discovering more about your personality can help you to discern your 'default settings' – what your go-to motivations are likely to be – accompanied by underlying emotional states including the three common ones we've been exploring: anger, shame or fear. In this way we learn to work with God, to integrate our motivations together with love for God and love for neighbour.[31] We learn that we can't authentically be anyone but who God made us to be, so comparison, although universally practised in either negative or overly positive ways, is self-defeating in the end.

Understanding more about yourself will also help you to discern how others might perceive you (for more on this, take a look at the Johari

Window, as explained in chapter 6). In fact, increased self-knowledge, far from making us overly self-occupied, actually frees us to notice what's going on in others, understand more about how humans actually work and to be equipped to look beyond the immediate and obvious as Jesus often did with those he met, like the rich young ruler and Zacchaeus the tax collector (Luke 19:1–10).

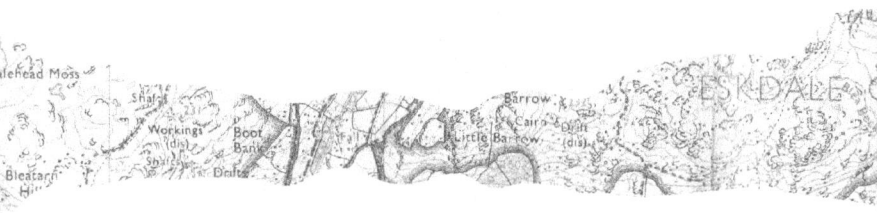

Where do we go from here?

This first part of the book has helped us to explore what's shaped the faith map we are carrying and how we see it through our human eyes. We've looked at the ways in which the map we've received has been formed by assumptions within the culture around us and the traditions in which we find community and fellowship. And we've seen some of the ways in which we look at that map through 'who we are'. We start to recognise how the way we're made can affect how we interpret the map we've been given.

So, when you are next listening to someone preaching or reading a passage of scripture, you might ask yourself: *How am I hearing what's being said?*, *What's the emotion it's stirring within me?* and *What does that tell me about myself?* And as you live as a Christian day to day, ask yourself the same questions. And then take what you sense about yourself to God in prayer, because it's in that place where our faith map intersects our 'self' within the experiences of real life (as shown in the diagram on the next page) that God seeks to shape us and help us to grow.

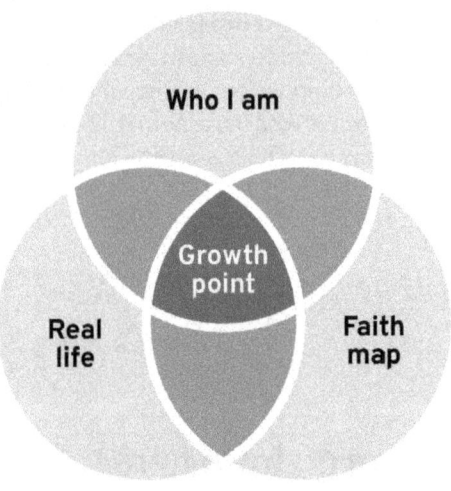

Our opportunity to grow

And it's through that landscape that we'd like to travel in part II.

Part II
Enlarging your map

4
Where are you on your journey?

Charles

Spiritual maturity is marked by being comfortable with the unpredictability of God.

ERWIN W. LUTZER

When attempting to navigate through the Lakeland Fells or the peat bogs of Dartmoor the determined traveller needs the most detailed Ordnance Survey maps available, known as the Explorer Series. At a scale of 4 cm to 1 km, it takes 403 Explorer maps to cover Great Britain, and that means you'll probably need several maps for a walking holiday in a big national park. Typically, as I unpacked my rucksack to tackle one of these kinds of treks, I would discover that I'd brought three of the four I needed for that trip but had left the crucial one at home!

On our spiritual journey, it's natural for us to stick to the first map we are given. But relying on that one map to see us through our entire Christian journey has its limitations. We learn lots of helpful things about our faith and the God we worship. We learn to pray in certain ways, and it shows us how to serve our church community and perhaps the wider community as well. But after a while many disciples, me included, may recognise that nothing much substantial has changed inside us. I do sense and enjoy God's presence with me, but I'm still the same old me. Even though I may have recognised my 'spiritual gifts' (Romans 12), the same temptations trip me up (Romans 7) and consistently manifesting fruits of the Spirit that truly reflect godly character

(Galatians 5) is sadly lacking. It's like I've changed my function and appearance on the outside, but not the reality of myself on the inside.

But that twinge of discontent we feel when we recognise how far we have still to go is not a bad thing. It's like God is touching our hearts with his love and encouraging us to draw closer, go deeper, unquestionably become more like Christ as well as doing our best to act like him. So, what is it that can hinder that deeper transformation we are promised as new creations in Christ (2 Corinthians 5:17)?

Perhaps that initial map we hold just doesn't cover enough ground to get us there. And as we explored in chapter 2, we'd benefit from examining it again and updating it. Drawn as it is with selection and emphasis influenced by certain cultural and Christian assumptions our map may be incomplete or missing some critical dimensions or regions. And we can expand our horizons, allowing ourselves to be enriched by the writings of other Christians who have walked this way before us – including perhaps some whose perspective is beyond our own tradition.

However, wherever we are on our map, once we feel that call onward it is imperative that we don't just 'stay there', assuming that whatever we are perceiving or experiencing today represents all there is or will be on the path of discipleship!

Every time explorers set out to discover new territories and extended the boundaries of their cultural spheres, cartographical evidence had to be drawn quickly to lay claim to those discoveries. In the early years of exploring the Americas, for example, Sebastian Münster published a map in 1540 that showed the Spanish flag over the West Indies.[32] The problem was, his focus on this valuable region left the rest of North America somewhat underrepresented! This must have been very confusing for subsequent explorers, who expected to see a thin strip of land only to find out as they pushed further west how vast the New World actually was.

I wonder if we're a bit like that. How much do we know or want to know about ourselves? Are we curious enough to keep pushing beyond the territory that we've already discovered and lies within our current consciousness?

To this end, I've noticed something odd about our stories of faith. Where we begin that story makes a big difference! If our story begins in Genesis 3 rather than Genesis 1, then faith tends to be grounded in the fall of humanity and the shame of our sin rather than in the glory of our humanity being made to carry the very image of God. The first perspective offers us an image focused on worthlessness and corruption and draws us to the work of Jesus on the cross in restoring our relationship with God – for which we are so grateful. But going back to include the creation stories in Genesis 1—2 also recognises that, while we are deeply flawed and need that restored relationship with God, the seed of God's original intent remains in our soul at the centre of our being, albeit covered by layers of self-inflicted shame.

It's not that one story cancels out the other; it's more a question of selection and emphasis. And that emphasis is crucial in determining our expectation for growing in the likeness of Christ.

As we saw in chapter 3, when we came to Christ, we brought with us the mask we had constructed with which to face the world, with all of its robust defences and protective layers born out of the nature, nurture and trauma we had experienced up to that point. A lot of our perception of and relationship with God and those around us can be determined by that defended-self, together with the shame it carries. And yet it doesn't represent the fullness of who God created us to be, the nature of our soul and the image of God we carry, if you like. In order to grow to the place from which we have the freedom to operate out of that God-given fullness, we first need to become aware of the role our defended-self plays in day-to-day life.

We may have been persuaded that it's only the visible fruit from loving and serving God that matters on our pilgrim's journey. But it turns out that, despite a certain Christian reluctance to pay attention to what's going on inside us, the path from spiritual childhood to spiritual maturity is marked by milestones of increasing understanding of ourselves. (For more on this, read David Benner, *Spirituality and the Awakening Self*.[33]) The depth and breadth of our self-understanding will always inform how we perceive and experience both God and others, which in turn impacts the quality of our ultimate fruitfulness.

Just as a young child possesses insufficient self-awareness to understand why they feel certain things or behave in a particular manner, so Christians who are growing in maturity must learn to equip themselves with wisdom by connecting the dots between their inner desires, feelings and thoughts and their outward actions. And here we become intentional about gaining a fresh perspective, learning to question ourselves and practising critical self-evaluation.

And so, in this second part of the book, we will build on the earlier chapters to address questions like:

- What's the process through which we journey towards maturity in Christ?
- How can we avoid getting stuck?
- How do we learn to grow through times of challenge?
- What can we do to cooperate with God in this process?
- How does a fresh perspective affect how we travel onwards?

Reaching the milestone of spiritual maturity appears to be taken for granted by the apostle Paul in his letters. Indeed he seems to feel that one of the goals of salvation *is* maturity! And he offers frequent encouragements for disciples to grow up into Christ (Ephesians 4:15) and to allow Christ to be formed within them (Galatians 4:19).

However, we can be quite competitive within our Christian communities, and few of us would willingly label ourselves as spiritually immature, especially if we've been walking with God for some time. Most of us probably assume that the older we get, the more wisdom we automatically acquire to apply to life's situations. But it's a bit like the slogan on those whimsical birthday cards featuring little old ladies madly tearing around on tricycles: 'Getting older is inevitable. Maturing is optional!'

In fact, maturing is never automatic as the years go by, and getting stuck at a certain stage or age of life, for all sorts of reasons, is common. So, it may not surprise you to learn that the same tendency applies to our faith journeys. But before we go there, it will help us to explore what spiritual maturity and immaturity look like. And what better place to start than the Bible.

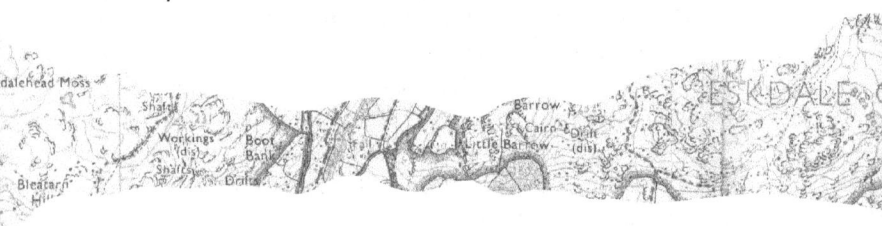

What does the Bible say about growing towards maturity?

The biblical portrait of how we grow in spiritual maturity parallels the basic picture of human development we have been outlining in the previous chapter. The apostle John uses the paradigm of graduated formation when he addresses the spiritual progress of sons, young men and fathers in 1 John 2:12–14. And this sort of biblical picture can help us to reflect on where we've got to and to look forward to the next milestone as we travel towards our destination. New Testament authors employ this picture of our faith developing in maturity many times in their writings to the early church (e.g. 1 Corinthians 2:14—3:4; Ephesians 4:12–16; Hebrews 5:12—6:3).

In common with raising small children, the first nation of God-followers profiled in the Old Testament were issued laws and guidance to provide a moral framework and a moral compass. These helped them to know who was in charge (God) and why obedience was a correct response to entering a unique covenant as a nation with God. It's interesting to note the progression in the Bible from an emphasis on 'obedience and repentance', which mostly concerns itself with external behaviours and practices, to the day when God would 'write his laws on their hearts' (Jeremiah 31:33; Hebrews 8:10).

Although children are taught to obey, and then to say sorry when they get it wrong, it's reasonable to assume that they rarely understand why they choose to disobey in the first place. And yet God intends that as spiritual adults we understand the impulses and desires behind our choices: 'Do not be like the horse or the mule, which have no understanding but must be controlled by bit and bridle' (Psalm 32:9). In other words, God doesn't want a 'transactional' relationship with us, informed only by obedience, but rather desires a response which emerges from a loving motivation to please and honour him. God's intent is for us to become 'living letters', as Paul describes to the Corinthian Christians: 'You show that you are a letter from Christ, the result of our ministry, written not with ink but with the Spirit of the living God, not on tablets of stone but on tablets of human hearts' (2 Corinthians 3:3).

To help us transition from mere obedience to the same kind of familial relationship that Jesus enjoyed within the Trinity, he introduced a new kind of 'living map' in the gospels, one which went beyond observing the law to one that required wisdom and discernment to interpret the situations we face in life, to be able to represent God's heart. This approach called for the transformative action of the Holy Spirit, together with an in-depth understanding of the reality of the human inner life. And you can see this in Jesus' teaching in the sermon on the mount, which has a laser-like focus on our underlying thoughts and heart attitudes (Matthew 6—8).

The point here is that rules and commands do provide a moral compass of sorts; they show us the right thing to do. But they don't necessarily transform the inner person such that we are then empowered to change our responses. Surely this was Paul's whole argument in Romans about the limits of the law. And yet, every belief we operate and every choice we make is 'forming' us spiritually in one way or the other.

Imagine for a moment the impact that regularly practising humble forgiveness might have in the face of being wronged. Such a decision changes the neural pathways within us that our defended-self has trained us towards in always having to be right (or to be seen to be right). A forgiving impulse can also soften our heart and open within us a wider acknowledgement and empathy towards the common failings of all humanity.

By contrast, rigidity, dogmatism and judgemental responses shrivel this generosity of spirit, reinforcing old neural pathways, thus shrinking our hearts and minds towards something much 'smaller' and less Christ-like. Could this be why Jesus was constantly challenging the religious leaders of his day? Their strict adherence to the rules generated an outwardly acceptable religiosity (something which isn't unknown to us as Christians today) instead of the much harder and complex work of noticing and retraining what's happening in the mind and heart. And if we're honest, we also know that we are regularly deceived by our own hearts regarding our true motives, even if we are seen to be acting rightly (Jeremiah 17:9).

To connect inner change to growing maturity, there is an expectation in 1 Corinthians 13:11 that we will gradually become aware of our childish ways (childish thoughts, speech, behaviours and dependencies). 1 Corinthians 13:4–7 seems to indicate that even the nature of how and who we love must alter as we mature, moving from the default impulse of only considering 'what's best for me', to being able to think about and embrace how this will serve 'the other'. These strategic steps move us towards a more adult faith in which we are not only fully known by Christ but know Christ more fully for ourselves.

Despite a consistent emphasis on 'growing up' in scripture, I wonder how often you have heard a talk on the subject of how we grow in spiritual maturity or the dangers of getting stuck in immaturity? And why do you suppose New Testament writers felt the need to focus on it as a constant theme? Could it be because those in the fledgling early church were doubling down on what they felt they had already grasped and Paul was afraid they would stop too soon, would fail to 'go the distance' and finish the race (2 Timothy 4:7)?

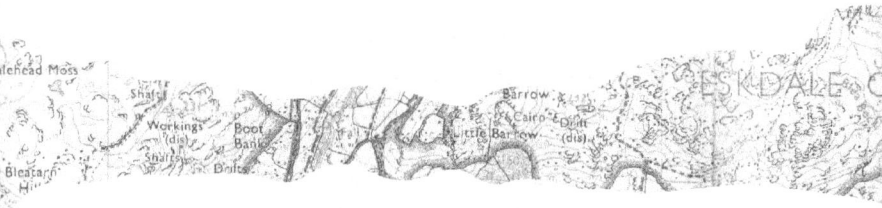

How can we recognise immaturity and maturity in everyday life?

As we go on now to consider what immaturity and maturity look like in the Christian life, might it be reasonable to suggest that the Bible appeals to both natural and spiritual sensibilities at the same time? It is hard to conceive of a naturally immature person (psychologically, emotionally and intellectually) exhibiting true spiritual maturity. In his book *Emotionally Healthy Spirituality*, Peter Scazzero links these qualities of emotional and spiritual development, underlining how important it is for Christians to cultivate self-awareness and understanding in order to grow in both.[34]

Largely unnoticed by us, we can show our *emotional* immaturity in many subtle ways. Turn back for a moment to the stories of the people we met in chapter 3, Jenny, Kevin and me.

Despite Jenny operating a good degree of emotional intelligence or literacy with regards to other people, she is not so in touch with her own feelings or the desires which lie underneath them. This stops her from seeing how God could help her with her need to be needed and to free her from measuring her self-worth by how she is received or appreciated.

Kevin's leadership qualities unravel quickly when faced with the disappointment of noticing that his team aren't trying to solve the world's problems with the same urgency he has. And he tends to withdraw or even manipulate them when not getting his own way, which can seem like bullying. Kevin is in danger of thinking that he is 'God'.

As for me, intellectually I realised how I am threatened by personal criticism, especially if I feel I have researched and prepared an informative presentation which is just not going down well. I can take disagreement personally, often becoming defensive. But I'm beginning to realise that I'll only be able to offer a mature emotional response if I can discover a reliable place of security, indeed be able to situate my very identity in my relationship with God.

Spiritual immaturity also has many faces. Within a Christian community it may present itself as perfectionism, or legalism, operating strict boundaries and a tendency to stigmatise anyone deemed to be different.[35] As we noted in chapter 2, a faith stance which tends to not tolerate challenge to its assumptive frameworks or viewpoints may indicate unexamined foundations, and it may focus more on visible, outward signs of conformity or achievement than transformed inner motivations or heart attitudes.

Many of us will naturally look to those who are exercising a relatively high level of function in our community as role models for maturity. Having served in leadership circles within a number of Christian contexts, I am familiar with the fact that those with the highest profile, the people who seem most committed to serving God, are often perceived by their flock as possessing the highest degree of maturity and wisdom. Unfortunately, the emphasis on function, particularly in the earlier stages of faith, can also mean that those of us in leadership can be the least self-aware, if we are too busy to investigate how our own defended-selves operate.

Sadly, this observation is confirmed by Christian scholars Janet Hagberg and Robert Guelich.[36] Even if that Christian leader you most respect looks to be mature because of their proficiency at preaching or pastoring, unresolved issues may continue to lay hidden behind all the activity and focus on outward appearances. It can be very hard for leaders to 'let their guard down' and be vulnerable.

It is entirely possible to arrive at a high level of responsibility and still be self-serving, legalistic, immature and inwardly fragmented. Christians are all too aware that some leaders are drawing significant public attention these days when they are found to be failing or falling from grace. The influence of their defended-self may never have been identified, let alone dealt with.

The giveaway for all of us, including leaders, will be seen for instance in our responses to situations of great pressure, as we find ourselves either giving into or bullying those around us, often without even being aware why we are reacting that way or how to stop. When we feel attacked by others, the defended part of ourselves may, in contrast, wish to crawl into a closet licking our wounds but never really knowing what we are trying to protect. Scazzero highlights this sort of issue quite freely, and some might say bravely, in his own admissions about Christian leadership from an immature level of spiritual and emotional development.[37]

According to the Christian psychologists F. LeRon Shults and Steven Sandage, the portrait of a genuinely mature person therefore includes being able to recognise, manage and take responsibility for their own thoughts and feelings.[38] Ideally, they will carry a healthy self-narrative, which seeks to come to terms with past experiences and wounds and demonstrates an awareness of the assumptive frameworks represented by their personal cultural and family backgrounds. Common religious or spiritual characteristics of maturity include a tolerant, generous attitude and respectful curiosity towards those different from themselves in religious, cultural or gender-related terms. And this is often expressed as a greater ability to show selfless and genuine concern for others, even with those outside their tribe.

Of course, those who lead are not alone in this. All of us are called by God to grow in Christian maturity. Be on the lookout in your own life, therefore, for habit patterns that you wish to conceal, but still impact how you interact with others.

Jesus' emotional and spiritual maturity

The scriptures tell us that the source of our identity and well-being is to be found in reference to Christ (Colossians 3), and yet many Christians look to their professional or familial roles, or even their church, community or leadership, to define and fulfil this for them. We know that God has given us friends and family to fulfil a certain degree of our emotional needs for love, acceptance and validation. But this can tip into unhealthy dependence when we find ourselves demanding that others meet our emotional needs (with or without their knowledge) or if we expect them to make our life and what's happening to us their top priority. We might then hold them responsible for sorting out our issues so that we can feel good about ourselves. How would you react if others failed to do this? Would it nurture unforgiveness or resentment within you? These are clear indicators of undeveloped character within the hidden defended-self, no matter how passionate our declarations about following Christ may be.

Let's take a look at our role model, Jesus, through this lens. We know that Jesus represents an example of someone who had to acquire wisdom as he developed, ultimately learning obedience 'from what he suffered' (Hebrews 5:8). In other words, he hadn't already arrived by age 8 or 18 or even by 33! Isn't this what the concept of discipleship evokes for us – a lifetime of learning? And we know that Jesus was the opposite of a self-oriented defensive person, instead radiating self-giving, self-emptying love (Philippians 2). But what else can we infer about his maturity from what we read in the gospels?

Sometimes the gospel stories are so familiar that we miss small points along the way. Obvious but perhaps seldom acknowledged qualities point to someone who wasn't swayed by others' agendas nor demanded that his most fundamental needs be met by his friends and family. That is not to say that he was some sort of superhuman who didn't have the same needs as us – to belong, to be loved and accepted, to feel secure, etc. Although he valued friendship and delighted in the way people like Mary, Martha and Lazarus opened their homes and ministered to him, the time he spent with his Father cultivated a sense of his true self and purpose. This enabled him to reflect the authentic image of God that he carried – 'The Son can do… only what he sees his Father doing' (John 5:19) – keeping him on course even when what others wanted of him cut across that (Matthew 16:21–28).

And Jesus didn't stop too soon in his growth and development, as he might have done if he had remained within the boundary lines of the life of a Jewish carpenter's son. He kept going, kept learning and kept allowing his own map to be extended. Somehow, he was able to see far beyond the obvious or immediate, even from an early age when he spent time acquiring crucial wisdom in the temple (Luke 2:46–50). I doubt his aim was to dishonour or frighten his parents by staying behind in Jerusalem – it's just that the map that was developing for him represented a far bigger landscape that he had to explore!

Perhaps Jesus used this same long-range perspective to see beyond the sin in people like Zacchaeus (Luke 19:1–10) or the woman caught in adultery (John 8:1–11) – sin that so offended religious leaders but to him called for the restoration of God's original design for them. He could see beyond the cultural map he had been raised in and could reach out to people utterly unlike himself because he perceived who God had made them to be and could still become. It was this same vision that enabled him to tell parables that both confronted and consoled people because he knew what was needed, even when it wasn't what they were expecting or desiring. He also regularly signposted the future realities of coming judgement (e.g. Matthew 12:36) and encouraged his hearers to strike out for their ultimate destiny instead of settling for short-term pleasure. Perhaps offering this wider lens helped them to distinguish between true and false treasure (Matthew 6:19–24).

Ultimately, taking the long view gave Jesus the motivation to suffer being misunderstood and publicly shamed without losing his sense of self in relation to the Father (Hebrews 12:2).

Of course, there is a risk in citing Jesus as an example of anything, let alone maturity, because we assume he had supernatural abilities that we can never match. But the emotional and spiritual maturity that God invites us to grow into (as human beings like Jesus) is not unattainable in this life. By way of addressing that issue, allow me to share a passage of scripture which has been very significant to me over the years. It's a well-known passage, often included in the liturgy of nine lessons and carols at Christmas time. This is because it's assumed to be a prophetic declaration of wisdom personified, signposting the coming Messiah, Jesus himself. I am referring to Isaiah 11:1–5:

> A shoot will come up from the stump of Jesse;
>   from his roots a Branch will bear fruit.
> The Spirit of the Lord will rest on him –
>   the Spirit of wisdom and of understanding,
>   the Spirit of counsel and of might,
>   the Spirit of the knowledge and fear of the Lord –
> and he will delight in the fear of the Lord.
>
> He will not judge by what he sees with his eyes,
>   or decide by what he hears with his ears;
> but with righteousness he will judge the needy,
>   with justice he will give decisions for the poor of the earth.
> He will strike the earth with the rod of his mouth;
>   with the breath of his lips he will slay the wicked.
> Righteousness will be his belt
>   and faithfulness the sash round his waist.

Taken in its historical context (2 Kings 16—18), we can see that, like many passages of biblical prophecy, this one has both a near-term and longer-term application. Isaiah was writing at the time when God's people were divided into two nations: Israel in the north and Judah in the south. Ahaz was king of Judah but very much ruled out of his own ego or persona, despising God's ways and instead embracing pagan practices. When Judah was threatened by the northern kingdom of Israel and the Arameans, Ahaz invited Assyria to defend Judah. This turned out to be disastrous for Israel, which was conquered by Assyria and its people exiled.

In expressing his desire for a wise leader, Isaiah was looking forward, praying for a king who would rule wisely and out of a sense of God's heart for the people. He probably had the son of Ahaz, Hezekiah, in mind, who did indeed turn out to be a God-fearing and wise king. But the passage also presages the coming of the ultimate wise leader of God's people, Jesus, which is why we use it in Advent.

The key for us in understanding what it takes to become emotionally and spiritually mature is to look at Isaiah's description of the wise ruler. He is given the 'Spirit of the Lord' accompanied by wisdom, understanding, counsel, might, knowledge and the fear of the Lord – all elements of godly character. But, crucially, his use of these gifts to make just and righteous decisions is attributed to how his humanity works in coordination with the Holy Spirit. We're told in verse 3 that he intentionally looks beyond a naturally human self-oriented capacity (what he 'sees with his eyes' and 'hears with his ears') and draws on the Spirit of God that rests on him. And for us in a post-resurrection era, we might interpret that as living out of the image of God we carry, enlivened by the Holy Spirit who has been given to dwell within us – within our soul or our 'deepest God-designed self' you could say.

Let's pause and take this in for a moment.

That's what I call seeing far beyond oneself, one's own perceptions or assumptions, one's previous experiences or cultural and religious maps. That's the kind of far-reaching sight that lies at the end of a long slog up Helvellyn as you take in the stunning 360-degree vista at the top.

This same Spirit has been promised to each of us as we turn to God in Christ and enables us to enter into the relational joy of the Trinity, as Jesus did. Such wise living is not beyond us, reserved only for Jesus. But if this is the case, why don't most of us experience this kind of God-grounded wisdom? Why do even experienced, high-profile leaders find themselves compromised, like David with Bathsheba (2 Samuel 11:1—12:20)? Why are we so often locked into fairly limited, incomplete, short-sighted worldviews or behaviours instead?

The purpose and process of emotional and spiritual growth

We have looked at pictures of emotional and spiritual immaturity and maturity, and hopefully can see the benefit of our journey from one towards the other. But what is actually happening as we cross that bridge? What's the process of putting off our old defended-self to put on the new? And what can get in the way?

What's happening as we mature?

Imagine an artist painting an exquisite portrait of their child, choosing the most vibrant colours and fitting composition to demonstrate their great love for that child. As the child grows older and learns to conceal who they really are, the portrait acquires layer after layer of varnish, creating a thick veneer until the child can't even remember what their original portrait looked like. But the artist hasn't forgotten and in order to reveal and restore that lovingly crafted image, begins a campaign to painstakingly scrape away all the layers that obscure it until the original portrait begins to emerge bit by bit.

You may never have heard the gospel story told in this way, but it's an apt metaphor to encapsulate the heart of God from the time you were first conceived until now. Before we first consciously encounter the person of God, we are tainted by our Genesis 3 fallen nature, an image or persona that is incomplete and, as we've seen, oriented towards keeping ourselves safe and significant. Only God knows what the true version of you was designed to look like; only he knows how to facilitate that restoration project.

But this project cannot happen without our active cooperation, because it is we who make the decisions about how to live our lives. Casting off our old self to put on the new involves understanding what needs to be surrendered, what needs to 'fall to the ground and die' (John 12:24), leading to a gradual but fundamental transformation of our inner being.

In short, we have a choice. We can actively resist this painful process of being stripped back, preferring self-orientation which feels comfortable or recognisable, because we foolishly believe it will continue to achieve our own agendas and meet our needs. To remain in that original undeveloped, immature state, however, means we will more than likely be limited to what we see with our own untransformed eyes and hear with our original ears. And so, God in his love invites us onward, to learn to surrender the person we think we are, the portrait we have unwittingly composed, and discover instead how to live authentically from the image of God we carry in our soul, to learn how to offer to the world that which we were gloriously made to be.

What's the process?

Many Christian thinkers (alongside Hagberg and Guelich) have helpfully mapped some of the most common features of the journey of faith over the centuries. And there is a remarkable consistency between the progression they describe, across both time and tradition, from mystics like Teresa of Ávila in the 1500s[39] to more modern theologians like the Protestant scholar Walter Brueggemann and the Franciscan writer Richard Rohr.

Most of these schemes observe the same sort of pattern, and it's one that is laced throughout the biblical story as well. In studying the Psalms, Brueggemann noticed a progression of faith – orientation (when the world seems ordered and God appears to be in control);

disorientation (when chaos ensues bringing confusion and faith-disruption); and new orientation (when the storm is weathered leading to an expanded, more mature understanding of faith).[40] These encapsulated the stages Israel cycled through in how they experienced their relationship with God over the years, especially moving from their unique status as a nation in covenant with God to the shock of eventually being exiled to Babylon, losing their monarchy, land and temple. Perhaps you can also spot echoes of this in how King David penned his psalms to express how he was feeling in different phases of his life, both good and bad.

For every new disciple, our journey begins as spiritual children (whatever physical age we may be) with an 'oriented faith', learning about this new and amazing God, often through the eyes of a Christian community with the perspective of whatever tradition we find ourselves in. We discover forgiveness and perhaps learn about our self-worth in God's eyes. In this early stage, we are normally dependent on trusted leaders to teach and guide us. And like a sponge, we soak up the information we need to form our initial faith map. After a while we begin to contribute to the functioning of our community, learning to use our gifts to serve those, perhaps through our church into the wider community as well.

This is a wonderful introduction to the Christian faith. But we are not intended to remain there indefinitely. In fact, it is hard, if not impossible, to mature fully without experiencing some level of disorientation and emerge into new orientation. It's a pattern that can repeat itself in our lifetime, helping us to grow stronger like trees who must survive high winds and drought, visibly evident like a code within the rings which form inside the trunk. Or we may only experience it with any great significance once. We will visit disorientation and new orientation in later chapters, but for now, let's take a closer look at what happens in this early oriented phase, and particularly why we might get stuck here.

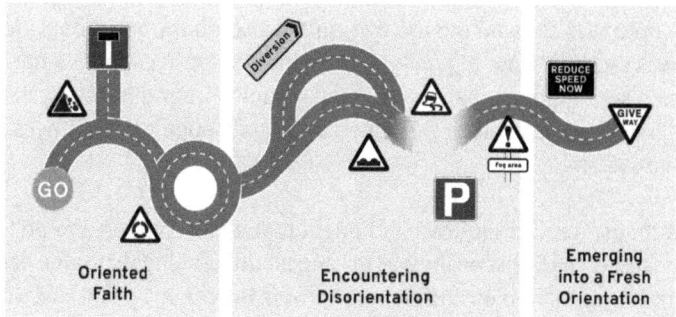

Different stages of the faith journey

What can get in the way of us moving on?

First and foremost, it may be that we are just not aware of the fact that there are subsequent stages of faith to travel through as we get to grips with the need for change.

This first phase of our walk can be a great joy. We know what's right, we know where we are ultimately going, and we have some sort of relationship with God. What's not to like? And yet, as we have seen, we enter this phase still reliant on a persona that is at best a partial representation of our true self and at worst an extensive fabrication. Something has to change for us to progress from that state.

When I first became a Christian, my experience closely followed what we've described as oriented faith. I felt that I so needed the forgiveness of the God who made me and was truly glad to receive it. I began my journey in a childlike way with an innocence, a freshness, that seemed vivid and vital. Comparable to the way we might feel during the first stage of a romance or new friendship, I tended not to notice many of the negative or more challenging aspects and was probably not using much evaluative or critical thinking at this early stage.

In that first flush of faith, I also experienced a strong sense of belonging in a community of fellow Christians and felt safe and secure with people who showed me the way and answered my questions. I felt I was tackling those big questions we introduced in chapter 2, deriving a sense of personal identity and meaning from this new system of beliefs, which in turn generated a certainty about the rightness of that system.

At that stage in my journey, I thought that all I would need to do for the rest of my Christian life was to keep plodding along that same path until I eventually died and went to heaven. How wrong could I be! God has a much greater and richer intent for this life than that. My hope was that death would release me from all the encumbrances of my finite human self, and my deep longing for God and desire to be like him would finally be fulfilled. But it seems that the strength of God's love for us, and indeed of the deep desire that is instilled in our hearts for God, invites us on a journey of change and transformation towards deeper communion with him in the here and now.

If we listen carefully to Paul as he writes to the Corinthian Christians, we can see that although we will always in this life perceive God imperfectly (1 Corinthians 13:12), it seems that God wants us to experience something of the unity with himself that Jesus speaks of in John 17:21 and enjoy that unity before we get to heaven. This unity can only happen once our fiercely defended-self becomes porous and surrendered to the indwelling Holy Spirit and we learn how to become more like Christ, more like the people God intended us to be in the first place – from the inside out.

However, we may not be aware that there is more to come if our faith map (and that of our Christian community) doesn't extend beyond an initial, well-oriented stage. Let's face it, this part of our walk is familiar territory to us; it makes us feel good about our Christian faith, and many of the landmarks are consistently recognised and validated by our own Christian communities. By default, if not actively stated, our faith map at this point may be presented or perceived as being complete, leaving us to conclude that this is all there is and is all that there needs to be!

How to tell when you're stuck

You might be wondering at this point how you can tell if you are in that place. Maybe you're thinking, *I feel okay with where I am, but what might I look out for going forwards?* Or perhaps you feel a sense of discontent but can't quite put your finger on why that might be. To help with this task, here are a number of indicators of what can happen when we outstay our time at this earlier stage. As you read them, think about how they might (like Ahaz) reflect the ways we can habitually default to our human perception rather than (like Hezekiah) recognise that true wisdom is to be found in God.

Our image of God

Sometimes our ideas about God can calcify. We still have the picture of God or Jesus we formed when we first became a Christian. Jesus himself experienced this sort of issue when he visited his hometown. You may remember the story told in Mark 6:1–6. It seems that those with whom Jesus grew up either hadn't heard about the person Jesus had become, the ministry and reputation he had acquired since they last saw him, or simply didn't want to acknowledge it. In the age of social media, where we can easily track what's become of people we grew up with, this is not an uncommon reaction. To us, that person who has made a name for themselves and has exceeded all expectations we held for them is difficult to accept because in some ways we desire to see them as the spotty youth or ordinary soul they used to be. We cling to the original story we knew because we may feel inferior by comparison, or simply find it hard to imagine them growing beyond that original version.

This reluctance on the part of people in Jesus' hometown to keep updating or enlarging their perception of who he was appears to have seriously affected Jesus' ability to demonstrate his divine nature and be the same kind of conduit for God's grace and power that he had shown in other contexts throughout his adult ministry. And it's very likely that Jesus' hometown friends and family would have struggled even more to imagine how his story would ultimately play out. Is this what Jesus may have been referring to by mentioning the folly of trying to pour new wine into old wineskins (Luke 5:37–39)?

Consider your own view of God, and whether it is still the same as it was earlier in your Christian journey. If it has changed, can you identify how?

Our modes of learning

Whether through insecurity or just my ignorance of other points of view, at early stages of faith, I found I was very attached to what I considered to be the accepted 'right way' of believing or doing things and less curious about unfamiliar territory, either theological or spiritual. Interestingly, I found out that this curtailing of curiosity is a hallmark of adult learning in any subject. This is because the way truth is presented and perceived at the point of entry can easily become the touchstone for how truth is measured for the rest of our lives. Unfortunately, this also reduces the chances of our perspective changing as we grow older. Why is our natural impulse sometimes to seek to preserve and protect what we think we've got hold of already? Why do we fail to be open to new ideas or consider an enlarged vision of what God may be leading us into?

In his book *What Prevents Christian Adults from Learning?*, John Hull suggests ideological hardening might be at play here, defining this phenomenon as a state of mind where members of a group perceive their truth to be the truest truth because their traditions, leaders, discourses or literature confirm this for them.[41] Although the Bible is purported to be the only source of truth by many Christians, what is often being exercised here is a strong faith in or attachment to a particular idea or interpretation of the Bible as espoused by a particular tradition, context or religious leader. This brand of certainty can lead to what is known as 'premature closure', which is the belief that the truth a person holds in their hand at any given time is all the truth that exists. Such a strong assumption, whether conscious or unconscious, precludes the idea that growing up in Christ may involve a fundamental dismantling of one's present body of ideas to facilitate a different onward journey.

In addition, Dallas Willard observes that the need to 'be right' is strong in Christians generally because they have consistently been told that they *are* right in holding Christian truth.[42] Sadly, this can easily become an attitude which pins the person to their original framework and is a common feature within close-knit ideological communities, either religious or political, often resulting in tribal mentalities, which sadly create us-and-them categories.

How open are you to learning new things or leaving behind things that no longer work for you?

Our ways of discerning

As I began to move past my earliest stages of faith, I also noticed what I can only describe as a kind of super-spiritual lens that I myself had operated and that many others I knew had used to interpret their lives and discern the meaning of challenging circumstances. Let me explain.

I firmly believe in a supernatural realm and a God of power and miracles. I also believe that there is an enemy of God and of all humankind, Satan, who seeks to disrupt God's purposes by suggesting alternative truth to disciples, as is evident from Genesis 3. But judging by the frequency with which he is referenced in some traditions, being blamed for pretty much every kind of difficulty Christians might face, I have started to question whether this same enemy was being credited with far more power and influence than his pay-grade possibly allowed for!

Whether it was related to having a bad day or the need to visit the hospital for a tricky procedure, it seemed that every undesirable or difficult experience I expressed to Christian friends was met with the same response – that it was 'enemy activity'. While it is impossible for us to establish the true boundaries or sphere of power in which Satan operates, I began to wonder if the real travesty of this assumption was that God's intentions for our spiritual growth within demanding situations might be missed.

If we simply attribute every cause of our distress to the 'enemy of our souls', we risk missing an opportunity for growth. It may be that sometimes we ourselves are at least in part responsible for our situation (e.g. finding ourselves at odds with a colleague or friend) or that God is asking us to exercise trust despite not understanding why some life-event has happened to us (e.g. an accident or bereavement).

Let's not bypass the hard and less glamourous work of developing much-needed self-knowledge and surrendering to God's process of inner transformation by over-spiritualising situations which happen not to be our preference.

Can you identify any responses you have made to unwelcome events that fit this description?

Updating and enlarging our faith maps

If we are noticing any of these indicators of being stuck on our journey, this has implications for how we handle our faith map. If we perceive one stage of the journey, one section of the wider map, as being sufficient to guide us through the whole of life, we might get confused when God begins to challenge us to grow beyond that paradigm. If we don't anticipate that there are further stages of faith to come, we won't be prepared to travel beyond the borders of the initial map we're holding.

It's all a matter of not stopping too soon. Of resolving to keep up with our evolving faith-story. To keep enlarging our sense of who God has called us to be and the path we must travel to get there.

So, here's a hypothesis worth considering: what if faith was never intended to stay the same? What if the reasons why you believe, the motivation you have for following Jesus, and the way you perceive and treat yourself (let alone others) were all meant to evolve well beyond what you might have originally imagined? If you knew the route God had prepared for you tomorrow involved changing your mind, habits, attitudes, viewpoints and character (all of which seem written in stone today), how would you feel? Are you prepared to add some additional 'Explorer' maps to help you keep going on your journey?

But surely God is the same yesterday and forever, you might say. Yes, God is, but we (hopefully) are not! We may resist our image of God changing because we associate it with the unchanging truth we've received or that our church preaches, without realising that often these represent a particular understanding or interpretation of the gospel and wider scriptures, arrived at and adhered to at a particular stage of faith to which we are 'being faithful'.

Ask yourself: what were your first impressions or expectations of Christ when you came to know him? Have they changed or developed, or, like the people in Jesus' hometown, are you holding fast to what you first knew of him? As a young convert, I was presented with a Jesus who was there to be my best friend, meet all my needs and generally make my life better and easier. With such an introduction, not surprisingly, this understanding has had to change quite significantly. I probably assumed that God would never let me suffer or let anything bad happen to me, and I certainly didn't recognise how difficult and painful experiences might help me to grow.

A friend of Mary's once said to her, 'I wish I could return to the deep and singularly focused faith I had when I was eight years old – it was so pure and so rich.' Mary suggested to her that her faith may have seemed deep and singular because she was eight, without much awareness of the complexity of God or the world. Of course, Mary was not dismissing the faith of a child; indeed, as Jesus says, 'the kingdom of God belongs to such as these' (Mark 10:14), but it is child*like* faith that is commended (Matthew 18:3) not child*ish* faith. As Dick Van Dyke once said: 'Scripture says you should put aside childish things when you grow up. I take that to mean wilfulness, self-centeredness, and things like that – not imagination, creativity, and joyful curiosity.'[43] Now that Mary's friend was in her 30s, her 'faith' should naturally have moved on. The reference point for her wasn't meant to be backwards in her journey, but forwards.

And so it is for us. We 'press on towards the goal to win the prize for which God has called [us] heavenwards in Christ Jesus' (Philippians 3:14). It may be helpful to remember that we're all children of God, but God wants us to come to know him as grown-up children who can relate to him in adult ways, not as infants or toddlers, always wanting to have their needs met straight away.

As we discussed in chapter 3, when we realise that we are ourselves the lens through which we perceive God and others, we understand how much that might affect how we relate to both God and the world around us. Especially as we've now started to appreciate the barrage of filters that our defended-self has erected!

From time to time, I'm asked to help others in the tricky business of discerning God's will. Some approach this task with a transactional, almost sterile tone: 'If I say yes to God for this, I expect him to make it come together for me really easily', or, 'I expect God will send me to *[insert undesirable location]* because it's the last place on earth I'd want to go'! Others seeking guidance feel fearful of 'getting it wrong' and somehow missing God's best for them. Seen through this transactional lens, God seems distant, demanding, ready to jump on us in judgement. I wonder if Jesus was trying to address this perception by suggesting that he no longer called his disciples servants (who aren't necessarily parley to their master's heart or intent), but now considered them friends to whom God could open his heart and share his wider purposes (John 15:15)?

I saw this play out first hand in a conversation with a young woman called Emily. She was looking for a new job and as she weighed up how God might be leading her, she showed an unusually high degree of self-understanding (her core desires and weaknesses) and a real openness to God. Despite her relative youth, Emily's very developed relationship with God helped her to notice how he seemed to be opening some doors in this process. But at the same time, she was also able to look beyond those potentially 'encouraging signs' to some equally important aspects. What, in all humility, might she learn from her prospective colleagues and what 'loaves and fishes' could she offer to that workplace?

Emily told me that her interviewers had been impressed by the fact that she stated her weaknesses and limitations alongside her perceived strengths quite openly and told her how unusual this was. For me, it spoke of genuine evidence of having a 'sober judgement' of herself, as is encouraged in Romans 12:3. Privately and before God, Emily took careful note of how she was speaking to herself about her own hopes and fears and how she differentiated between those and hearing God's still small voice within. Most of all, she wisely weighed up the uncertainty and possible challenges that God might ask her to face in this new position against their potential transformative value in her spiritual life.

You might ask where all this wisdom and maturity had come from? How was it formed? If only we could go to church, read our Bibles and pray to receive it by osmosis. But alas, it's usually cultivated through a much more demanding process. This level of wisdom is formed specifically through facing trials, difficulties which require us to consistently surrender our own life agendas (James 1:2–5). In Emily's case, it was the by-product of costly choices and an attitude of surrender she had deliberately chosen through many years of chronic illness.

Reviewing your map

Pause for a moment to reflect. I wonder how you are viewing your faith map as you read this book. Do you sense that your faith map covers the whole journey? If not, where do you feel that you are in relation to its boundaries? Is it perhaps time to unfold the next page of the map you might need to help you move forward?

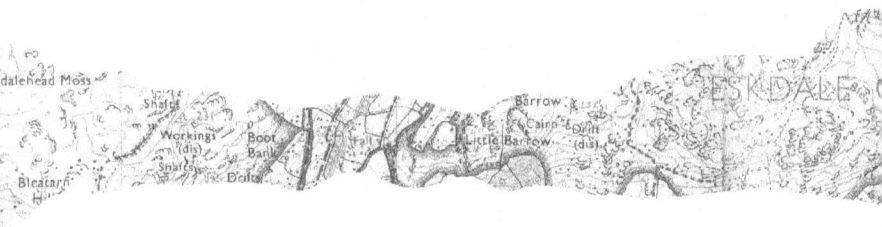

Where do you find yourself on the journey of faith?

Perhaps you've sensed for a while that it's time to grow beyond the current boundaries. We can respond to this feeling in a range of ways: some might wonder who can help them grow and begin to explore new sources and resources which they hope will supplement their lack; some might wonder what it means that they are experiencing 'sameness' in their week-by-week experience or the dryness of their prayer times provoking them to seek something more; some may respond by praying for God to do something and wonder why he hasn't yet; some sink towards despair as their relationship with their church community and even with God himself seems to crumble away and become less relevant.

It may be that you are alert to your need to grow in maturity and are ready to cooperate with God in doing the necessary work. You just want to know how. We'll be exploring some very practical pathways in chapter 7.

Or… you might be reading this book in pain and confusion, having been hit by one of life's tsunamis, and are asking yourself, *How could God let this happen?* And that can be so hard to swallow. There are no simple answers, but exploring the significance of walking in the dark or through wilderness as part of the way Jesus calls us forwards may help.

5
What happens when your map runs out?

Mary

We become lost in a trackless desert but if we persevere despite our disorientation, we begin to realise that it is only in losing ourselves that we are found.

THOMAS GREEN[44]

One year Charles joined a team of experienced walkers who undertook the challenge of navigating the Ten Tors in Dartmoor. Thankfully, I was in the nice warm support van! Part of the challenge was to complete the course using only a map and compass. This was fine when the next tor happened to be in sight and they could head straight for it. But in between those times they had to use the well-tried method of working out where you are from three significant landmarks – triangulation.

Triangulation has been an invaluable tool for map-wielding travellers for many years, and today it's the underlying principle that allows GPS to tell us both our geographical location and our elevation. First, you orient your map to north using a compass and then with that same compass take bearings on each of three distinct landmarks. Then you draw a line on your map from each landmark on the bearing you've taken. Where these three lines intersect is where you stand. Simple! Well, maybe not so much in the freezing cold and pouring rain with your map being blown about, but it worked for them, and they were able to plot a course for the next leg of their journey.

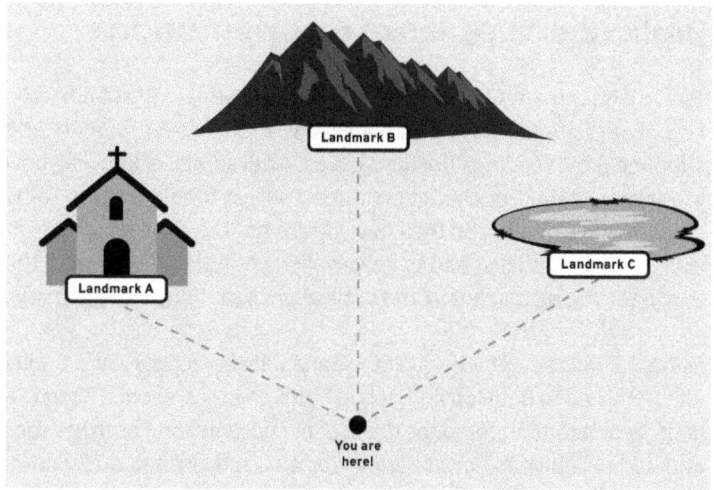

How to triangulate your position

But they hit a snag on the second morning when, already bleary-eyed from lack of sleep, a heavy impenetrable mist had descended on the moors, and they could no longer make out any landmarks from which to triangulate. All they had was a rough idea of which direction the next tor should lie in and their compass. Conscious of time, they set off with the trusty instrument in hand.

So what happens on your journey of faith when you hit unfamiliar territory or the mist comes down and you start to feel disoriented? Perhaps life deals you a crushing blow or you're struggling to connect with God like you used to. Perhaps you find yourself at the edge of your faith map, facing changes seemingly without the familiar landmarks to guide you forward. The fact is, whatever we assume will happen or hope will happen, not all journeys are straightforward. It is surprisingly easy to become disoriented, find yourself in a dead end or just have no clue where you are, how you got there or how to get to where you want to be.

Biblical examples of disorientation

And so it is for many Christian pilgrims at some point in their faith walk. Few of our faith journeys turn out exactly as we expect them to. And although Bible-reading Christians have the advantage of knowing how the stories of biblical characters turned out, at the time those same people were caught up in their own life drama. They had no idea what was up ahead and just had to keep walking out their 'route' until the end, often facing unwanted and unpleasant situations along the way.

Esther found herself facing a plot to annihilate her fellow Jews. Daniel was trafficked to Babylon and, set up by his enemies, spent a night in a lions' den. Naomi suffered the death of her husband and both her sons and had to return to her hometown as an impoverished and vulnerable widow. Both David and Elijah experienced times of persecution, violent aggression and acute depression. In those times, when there was no immediate rescue by God, they may have been tempted to wonder about his presence and purposes for them.

For Christians in some spiritual traditions, like the contemplative authors St John of the Cross, Thomas Merton and Dietrich Bonhoeffer, disruption or disorientation is integral, indeed necessary for growing on the path of faith. For others, such as those in some Pentecostal and charismatic movements, I've noticed that the emphasis in their received faith map with regards to navigating turbulent waters or bouts of disorientation tends to be on prayers for rescue, overcoming obstacles and rapid restoration, enabling these disciples to return to more certain territories and more victorious living.

This latter tendency may or may not typify the wider Christian community, but popular author Philip Yancey counters it with a striking reality check: 'I have to face the honest fact that Christians live in poverty, get sick, lose their hair and teeth and wear eyeglasses at approximately the same rate as everyone else. Christians die at exactly the same rate: 100 percent.'[45]

For the psalmist, and perhaps all of us, our question in times of distress or uncertainty might be: *Why would the God of the miraculous not intervene on my behalf, and do that quickly?* But perhaps we could reflect again on that most well-known of psalms, Psalm 23, which provides glimpses of the very varied nature of the landscape through which God may lead us: not just green pastures but also dark valleys; not only the context of still waters but also in the presence of our enemies.

It was through reflecting on the book of Psalms as a whole that Walter Brueggemann recognised the pattern of spiritual growth we described in the last chapter: orientation, disorientation and new orientation. Psalms of orientation tell of certainty and security that can commonly be felt to be the only true expression of a strong Christian faith (e.g. Psalm 16 or 19). But the problem is this doesn't always match up with real life, which can be marked by incoherence, suffering and injustice. Oriented faith rarely lasts through the whole of one's faith journey.

Psalms of disorientation were often written in highly stressful situations amid both individual and national crises. 'How long, Lord? Will you forget me forever? How long will you hide your face from me?', cries David at the beginning of Psalm 13. Plenty of other psalms also display extreme emotions of fear, confusion and turmoil (e.g. Psalm 63; 88).

Counterintuitively, it is in times of disorientation that we tend to grow most. Despite that, we rarely ask ourselves in such demanding circumstances, 'What can I learn from this unexpected turn in my life?' Or 'What response could I make to help me keep growing and maturing?'

What forms of faith disruption might we see today?

We all know that life in general is not necessarily easy and is rarely devoid of all difficulty and stress, but the particular experience of faith disorientation for Christians extends beyond the normal struggles of life towards a perception, on some level, of a 'breakdown' of one's map of the Christian journey – that is, that the anticipated Christian life might not be all that was assumed or promised.

In his books *Journeying in Faith* and *Chrysalis*, evangelical author Alan Jamieson has researched and identified obstacles and responses that Christians frequently experience as their faith map begins to be challenged.[46] They may, for example, become bored or disenchanted with the form of Christianity being expressed in their church or tradition. Commonly, this looks like rejecting the pedagogical norm of having the pastor or church leader do all their thinking for them, perhaps feeling that traditionally didactic forms of preaching don't allow for genuine discussion or opportunities to disagree. They may feel that there is little room for open-handed questioning or even low-grade objections.

As people develop their intellectual capacity, they may also begin to question or temporarily doubt their beliefs more strongly. For some people, the perennial existential questions (chapter 2) start to assume more than merely background interest. And other questions, which those in every generation seem to ask and plague even the staunchest believer, get more urgent as time goes by. Questions such as: why does a God of love permit evil or suffering or why does God give people freewill to choose if they always seem to choose badly?[47]

I don't suppose many of us actively seek out uncertainty or disillusionment, especially in relation to religious beliefs we used to hold without question, but which may now feel lifeless or untrue. But I've found in walking alongside people in this state that even discovering new and equally plausible sources of truth can be disruptive because it upsets their unexamined assumption that only one type of source or person could be considered a legitimate conveyer of truth. This is especially so for truths that don't originate within their faith tradition or even fall outside the traditional bounds of Christianity.

Faith disruption can also be the fruit of more personal and emotional circumstances. I don't know if you've ever lost your job or an important self-defining role. Many who have report feeling as if they are a failure, seemingly unproductive, and are caused to wonder what their purpose in life is. New parents or full-time carers, whether chosen or not, may suddenly feel they have lost their independence, freedom and identity. Some people might find themselves wrestling with other crucial parts of their identity, in confusion about their sexual orientation or gender specificity. These sorts of emotional struggles can also challenge the Christian's 'assumptive framework' about who they are as people and as Christians, and once significant threads like these come loose, the whole piece of fabric can begin to unravel quickly.

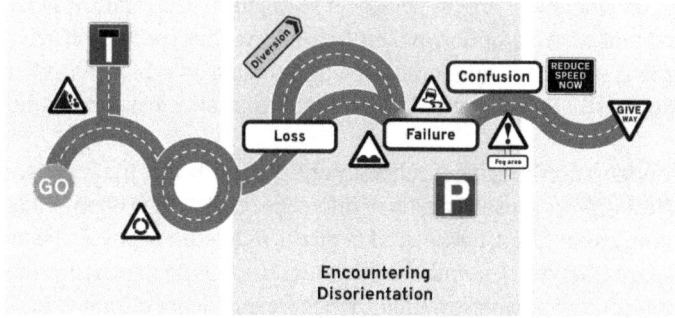

Some triggers of faith disruption and disorientation

Kathy Escobar runs a refuge in Colorado, not for battered wives, but for battered and weary faith 'wayfarers'. The pastiche of individual expressions of doubt and confusion contained in her book *Faith Shift* provides a picture of emotional and psychological distress which I would confirm to be very common in those encountering faith disorientation:

> My initial questions and doubts have only led to more questions and doubts; I've lost my connection to God and therefore the church; the Bible doesn't seem true or make sense any longer; I feel anger about what I was made to believe or how I was forced to behave; religious activities that used to bring peace or meaning now feel like fingers on a chalkboard; calling myself a Christian now feels dishonest, I don't know how to label myself any longer.[48]

Such descriptions of faith disruption are only examples. They can't be definitive because disruption doesn't necessarily follow any pattern. One observation I would make, however, is that often disruption experiences have as much to do with how Christianity is practised, presented or perceived by the individual disciple as perhaps a fundamental problem they may have with God himself.

You may or may not resonate with these heart-felt admissions, depending on where you are on your own faith journey. But for those who find that such disruption in their faith journey has sparked off a more serious sense of disorientation, it may be helpful to explore further the nature of that specific experience and its significance in our maturation.

Disorientation in its most generally understood form is the experience of losing one's sense of reality or reference points. It can happen if one becomes confused, bewildered or afraid, as a result of physical issues (such as dizziness), mental health issues (such as dementia) or simply losing one's way when travelling. When we experience disorientation in our faith journey, the gradual or sudden challenge to our faith-related worldview causes similar patterns of confusion, anguish and fear.

So this symbolic losing of one's way affects dimensions of our emotional, psychological and spiritual well-being. Despite the plentiful signposts in scripture we have already mentioned, this almost always feels like an unexpected turn to our spiritual story. For instance, even though Jesus repeatedly told his disciples that it was necessary for him to die and to rise again, they still were not expecting the events of

Good Friday. And when Mary arrived at Jesus' tomb on Easter Sunday, she expected to wrap his dead body with spices, not encounter his resurrection being in the garden.

The picture of disorientation we have painted so far can appear somewhat negative. For some it can be, leading to a breakdown in trust and a hiatus in their relationship with or journey towards God. And this can plunge them into what feels like a spiritual wilderness. For others, disorientation provides a necessary wake-up call to reassess what we assumed were our vital landmarks, inviting us to see through the clutter of our faith landscape more clearly and decide what may be past its sell-by date.

Whether we are distressed or clear-sighted, it's still a good idea to ask, *How could this experience be significant towards growing in Christian maturity?* Addressing this question means drawing on some of what we've covered in previous chapters: reviewing the assumptions or shape that our original faith map represents; referencing the way we come to or understand faith through who we are as human beings; and acknowledging our tendency to get stuck in the earlier stages of our spiritual journey.

What's going on in disorientation?

One of the reasons we become disoriented in our faith is that our original map may not cover the ground we find ourselves travelling through. We wonder why nobody told us that at some point the familiar landmarks of our faith might change or disappear altogether.

At present Charles and I are running a group in our church for those who are asking questions and struggling with their faith. Unlike some initiatives which seek to shore up previous belief frameworks, our aim is not to talk those who question back into recapturing their original form of faith or to get them to return to a path which possibly no longer makes sense to them. Rather, we are inviting them to articulate their stories, express their emotions and embrace tools with which to critically evaluate the map they are holding: to reimagine what faith might look like going forward. In other words, in looking beyond their present faith experience, no matter how distressing, there is potential to discover why and how their disorientation bears great potential for spiritual growth within God's grace-filled economy.

And despite many years of following Christ, what we sometimes do discover lurking in our inward parts is often quite a shock to our system! Unless intentional work has been done, many Christians remain self-determined, pursuing self-oriented plans.

This is why Paul speaks of the need to die to our old self (Romans 6:6) – easily said, but horrendously difficult to do! Requiring a sea change in our way of thinking and 'doing life', this points to the true meaning of the concept of *metanoia*, a repentance that transcends mere guilt or sorrow over one's choices or attitudes. A fundamental change in outlook is what the concept implies, a reordering of our orientation, a comprehensive change in the way in which we go about – well, everything!

For many of us this just doesn't happen without something big to stop us in our tracks. Our neural pathways are so rutted and worn that they simply won't change without significant disruption. And that's where disorientation comes in. For our defended-self to acknowledge that only God can truly manage our lives, it must encounter something big that it can't manage by itself. Listen to this summary from Richard Rohr:

> Until and unless there is a person, situation, event, idea, conflict, or relationship that we cannot 'manage', we will never find the True Manager (God). So, God or Life makes sure that

several things will come our way that we cannot manage on our own. Self-made people, and all heroic spiritualities, will try to manufacture an even stronger self by willpower and determination – to put them back in charge and seemingly in control. Usually, most people admire this, not realizing the unbending, sometimes proud, and eventually rigid personality that will be the long-term result.

It is the imperial ego that has to go and only powerlessness can do the job correctly. Otherwise, we try to engineer our own transformation by our own rules and with our own power – which is therefore, by definition, not transformation. It seems we can in no way engineer or steer our own conversion. If we try to change our ego with the help of our ego, we only have a better-disguised ego. To borrow a quote often associated with Albert Einstein: 'No problem can be solved from the same level of consciousness that created it.'[49]

In the midst of what may feel like some sort of 'spiritual tsunami', it's good to remember that disorientation is never meant to be an end in itself but is intended to lead us into a new orientation towards God, ourselves and others. And this new orientation, this freedom to recover and restore our original God-image within, is precisely what Christ died to achieve.

Saul's journey to new orientation

Let's look at a prime example of all three stages of orientation, disorientation and new orientation in the life and times of a man formerly known as Saul. Saul began with such certainty that his Jewish worldview was right and absolute. This was a man solidly in the first phase of faith orientation. It took a major intervention on the road to Damascus to knock Saul from his firmly held position, and this resulted in a lengthy period of disorientation and a change of name (Acts 13:9).

Scholars believe that Paul spent several years in relative obscurity, using the time to gradually develop a very different perception of God, God's purposes and his own part in that 'new story' (Galatians 1:15–19). But of course, this was only the beginning of his new orientation, in territory he could never have anticipated he might have to navigate. Both Luke and Paul himself document the spectrum of early new oriented life, from those exciting if dangerous missionary journeys planting new churches (e.g. Acts 12) to the letters Paul wrote in prison as he awaited a death sentence (e.g. Galatians 1—2).

It's reasonable to assume that this was not how Paul initially thought his life might pan out. We see him later writing with confidence the material that has since become foundational to Christianity, providing landmarks of faith through theology, ethics and vision. However, we cannot underestimate the long and drawn-out process Paul underwent to transition from a largely Judaist worldview to a newly formed Christian one.

As I study how Paul's experiences may have informed what he wrote about, this process also seems to have rearranged crucial aspects within Paul's character and sense of self: reorienting him away from a self-determination (Acts 8:3) and probable pride as seen through his self-referential tendencies (Acts 9:1) to a humility that enabled him to grow a contentment no longer linked to pursuing his own agenda or having his perceived needs met in his way (Philippians 1:21). All of the above makes sense when we notice that Paul's internal reorientation appears to have been accomplished through acute suffering and undoubted times of fear and uncertainty (2 Corinthians 11:21–33).

Those are my observations about Paul, and you may draw different conclusions. But before we rush past the demands of disorientation towards finding a new orientation, it's good to consider what God may want to accomplish through seasons of faith disruption. And if we turn to observations that others have made about stages of faith through the centuries (chapter 4), it can help us to discern what may really be happening.

Disorientation often challenges us to let go of our early images of God and expectations of the Christian life, in order that we might develop a bigger, more expanded, yet nuanced picture.[50] But more than that, disorientation also causes us to face some of the truth about ourselves.

However, this threatens the status quo and rattles the cage of our defended-self. Faced with exposing the wounds we bear inside – our fears and insecurities and years of shame – our defended-self doesn't usually willingly cooperate with this kind of campaign, so something has to challenge its controlling position and inner narrative. And this is the point at which we face that 'unmanageable thing' to which Richard Rohr refers in our previous quote. We 'hit the wall' in the form of something that we just can't handle by ourselves.

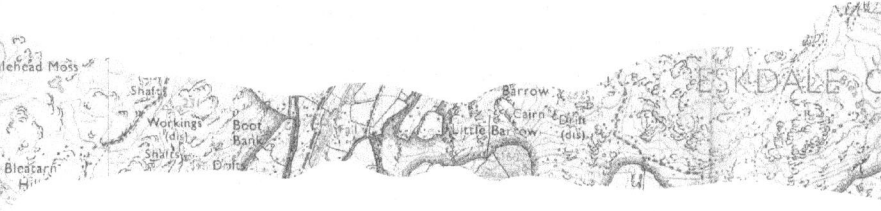

How can I tell if I've hit the wall?

If at this point you are wondering whether you or someone you know has hit the wall, here are some characteristics that might help you assess:[51]

- Our previous spiritual habits and rituals lose their effectiveness. We may find that our worship style or prayer life doesn't seem to work or nurture our relationship with God any longer.

- Our relationship with God shifts in some way. We may also struggle to perceive God in the same way as we used to or are confused by the fact that God no longer appears to be behaving as 'normal' (as if there were ever a 'normal' for God).
- It may feel harder to access God. We might feel less connected to God or that he is speaking less clearly than he used to or is no longer manifesting his presence in the same way.

We may also find that when we share how we are feeling with those who haven't passed this way before, it may look to them like we're backsliding, encountering a 'dry phase' or that God is simply 'testing our faith'. That may well be so, but possibly not in the way it's being suggested. Hitting the wall usually feels much more serious in spiritual terms because the combination of all these factors can sometimes make us feel like we are losing our faith altogether. And indeed, in some senses we are, because the shape of our faith walk is veering away from its early or original form. And this appears to be a necessary precursor to developing a more mature, complete one.

This wall is difficult for all who encounter it, and it is encountered in different ways. Some experience this stage while retaining their sense of God's presence with them and love for them, even though their defended-self may be doggedly resisting surrendering to God. Others, however, find that their sense of God changes so drastically that he feels distant, strangely remote. It's like their inner compass has become shielded from the magnetic field, their sense of God's love, that in the past has always drawn their compass needle towards him.

This is the path I found myself on a few years back, and although God takes each of us on a unique path, it may help those struggling with a more severe state of disorientation for me to share how it felt at the time.

Walking in darkness

One day, I completely lost my way. And it all began with a furious stand-up argument. With God.

I had known for many years that my relationship with God had begun to deteriorate, my prayer life not consisting of much more than whining about how I felt God had let me down. But one day, it all got too much, and I decided that I'd had enough. I began to shriek out my frustration to God and – in common with all heated arguments – gripes and grievances that had been building for years came tumbling out like a stream of hot lava. It was actually a relief to be able to express things I never thought I'd say out loud, least of all to God.

The shouting finally culminated in a metaphorical, but no less dramatic, slamming of the door. 'We're done!' I declared to the Almighty defiantly. 'Don't bother to speak to me any longer.' And like the prodigal son, I envisaged myself marching off down the road to make my own way in the world. Like the prodigal son, I felt my Father was not delivering what I assumed I needed or desired. At least, not in the way I wanted.

I've always wondered whether I would have taken that decisive action had I known what lay in store in the days and months that followed. For starters, the silence was absolutely deafening. I had walked with God for the better part of 60 years and had never experienced life without sensing his presence, always chatting and consulting God throughout the day in a most natural fashion.

But now... now, there seemed to be no God to chat to.

I felt utterly on my own.

At first it was something of a relief to let the noise in my head die down and just be still. I knew perfectly well that as a frail human being, I was not capable of taking a single breath without God's help. But I had to remind myself that there were many people out in the world happy to ignore the Almighty for their entire lives. For me, even though I knew I had metaphorically walked away from him, what it really felt like was that God had moved away from me, perhaps to Australia – which was the furthest geographical point I could think of. And worse, was ignoring my spiritual equivalent of emails or letters.

Yet strangely, deep within my inner being, I knew this situation was not one borne of God's anger or a desire to punish me. Somehow there was this deep inner sense that I hadn't irretrievably sinned or broken some higher spiritual law. I knew that God doesn't mind us ranting and getting our feelings out (otherwise the psalmists would have been in deep trouble). So I concluded that God had perhaps withdrawn his felt presence from my life for purpose. But it was purpose I couldn't yet possibly fathom.

I was plunged into a steep learning curve. I found out, like many others caught up in disoriented faith patterns, that church is quite a dull place when God is no longer really in the picture. Singing songs about him or praying to him seemed unproductive and meaningless. I began to attend Christian gatherings less and less and withdrew from the list of those available to speak on a Sunday morning in the realisation that it would be hypocritical to talk about God's love or purposes when you weren't sure of either.

Having been a part of Christian contexts and communities for much of my life, this new experience felt very odd. I was beginning to lose my bearings and significant landmarks on my spiritual map, and I started to worry that I might never regain them in this strange new existence. It couldn't have felt more unfamiliar than if I had been Alice, having fallen down the rabbit hole into Wonderland. The upshot? Without a Christian role to play or specific group to belong or contribute to, my sense of personhood and purpose in life began to lose all direction and meaning.

Any experience of disrupted faith always affects our sense of shared faith within our Christian communities. Up until then, I thought I had a perfectly fruitful relationship with God but didn't realise the extent to which that had been shaped, reinforced and enabled by the mutual faith I shared with like-minded Christians. Now that I was walking a path which others, like Job's friends, didn't seem to understand, my usual sources of wisdom and fellowship couldn't really help. They seemed as clueless as I was about how I had got lost or how to rectify the situation. And so, I fell out of 'fellowship' and lost friends – like the psalmist expresses in Psalm 88:5-8.

I'm sure it was offered in good faith, but friends who declared that God would never withdraw a sense of himself based on verses like 'Never will I leave you; never will I forsake you' (Hebrews 13:5), clearly hadn't also read Psalm 69, Lamentations 3 or Job 16 – passages that encapsulate the raw and confused emotions that abandonment experiences evoke. Our by now familiar principle of unconscious 'selection and emphasis' seemed to be at play again.

Something worth noting at the time for me was that all the reference points suggested by Christian voices to help verify the reality of my faith seemed to point backwards – to what my faith had looked like in the past. While there was some merit in this, there was also a universally expressed disbelief that my troubled situation could hold any spiritual value whatsoever, on the basis that it just wasn't 'possible' to be disoriented after becoming a Christian – only beforehand when God was unknown to someone. On one level of course this is perfectly reasonable. Making the decision to follow Christ means that old beliefs will be exchanged for new ones, but the problem comes in framing this initial transition as complete, entering a new state of belief which precludes any further transitions or disruption. As one Christian commentator notes:

> One of the problems with the usual model of spiritual or religious development we've inherited is that it too often places the 'spiritual crisis' only in the past – 'I was lost, now I'm found'. So, we're allowed the single pre-Christian spiritual crisis which catapulted us to conversion, but this is now safely

behind us (hallelujah!). And we're taught to view any post-conversion spiritual crises as dangerous, to be feared and avoided. We're afraid they will lead us out of the security of faith into heresy and apostasy; will pluck us off the straight and narrow way where we're safe and saved and throw us into perdition.[52]

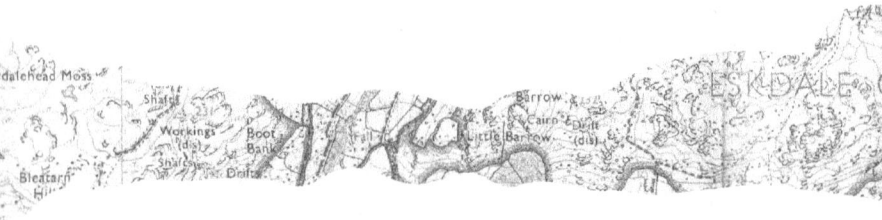

Navigating with new landmarks

Although I had little sense of the way forward, slowly, almost imperceptibly, new landmarks began to appear on the horizon – landmarks that I found I could use to triangulate and help me navigate this strange new landscape. These included a strong inclination to pay closer attention to my personal experience, to consult the wisdom of Christian traditions outside my own, and to study a wider variety of scriptures and biblical characters which, until now, had not seemed particularly relevant. Let me explain how these new landmarks became so important to me.

The validity of personal experience

Fortunately, I was in the habit of keeping a journal to reflect on my life with God and what it meant. I also already had a spiritual director who, from the vantage point of being a Carmelite, listened deeply and validated my experience. From her tradition, wandering in a spiritual wilderness or pitch-black darkness seemed perfectly normal, even desirable for spiritual growth. She advised me to read books by St John of the Cross, Teresa of Ávila and the Desert Fathers to discover why.[53] Although those authors were less familiar to me, unexpectedly I found that they were the only ones accurately describing my current faith experience. By acknowledging that the loss of landmarks was quite common and by situating my experience within a positive paradigm of spiritual formation, you could say they extended my faith map and supplied new cartographic skills with which to discern my new landscape.

My spiritual director also took my emotions seriously. As we observed in chapter 3, we are created in God's image, and just as he is an emotional being, so are we. No doubt biblical characters in extremis experienced a range of emotions, including some rather violently negative ones as the prophetic books and certain psalms witness. Yet we Christians often struggle to accept that we experience the same sorts of feelings, and sometimes we are even advised to ignore them or pray them away. I had someone say this very thing to me the other day. Very humbly he had confessed that he was struggling to maintain his faith of earlier years and was told to dismiss his feelings by what he described as more mature mentors, because they would only lead him astray. But feelings arising from experience are often the first red flags that help us notice what's going on underneath if we pay them attention.

Sadly, many testimonies from those whose faith has been disrupted witness to what is and isn't deemed appropriate to express (or feel) in their Christian communities – forcing some who are caught up in faith maelstroms to hide their feelings:

> The pressure to keep a brave face on is very real, and yet it feels fake and deceptive to do so. It would be self-indulgent to let it all hang out because we are there to focus on God, not ourselves. Even so, the tension exists and makes it hard to want to attend.[54]

And yet, Jesus paid close attention to the way his disciples were feeling after his death and resurrection: Mary's anguish in the garden; Thomas' doubts; Peter's sense of shame when Jesus spoke with him over breakfast on the lake shore. And we find that God often sought out his people who were suffering emotionally, showing no sense of rebuke that they might be doubting him or didn't understand what he was doing as they railed against him (e.g. Hagar and Elijah) – although that didn't stop God from asking a typical spiritual direction question, like: 'What are you doing here, Elijah?' (1 Kings 19:9).

Perhaps the fear for some disciples is that citing or even feeling negative personal experience will diminish the veracity of objective truth as presented by the scriptures or cast a negative light on God's character. Gordon Lynch brings balance to this debate when he suggests that while Christians do not have to base their lives or theology exclusively on their feelings, uncritical thinking can be just as damaging to the development of a mature faith as an uncritical evaluation of feelings.[55]

Although most Christians are encouraged to 'listen to the voice of God', we're rarely encouraged to listen to our own lives, listen to what we are saying to ourselves. This includes noticing our many emotions and accepting them as authentically ours. Otherwise, there is dissonance between what we as Christians believe we are meant to feel or think and what we do feel or think. As Dan Allender and Tremper Longman write:

> Ignoring our emotions is turning our back on reality. Listening to our emotions ushers us into reality. And reality is where we meet God. Emotions are the language of the soul. They are the cry that gives the heart a voice. However, we often turn a deaf ear – through emotional denial, distortion, or disengagement. We strain out anything disturbing in order to gain tenuous control of our inner world. We are frightened and ashamed of what leaks into our consciousness. In neglecting our intense emotions, we are false to ourselves and lose a wonderful opportunity to know God. We forget that change comes through brutal honesty and vulnerability before God.[56]

During this period, I often felt as if I was the only one navigating such ferocious and unwanted feelings. But as I studied the contemplative tradition, I realised that I was far from being alone, saints of old having freely documented and provided commentary on such experiences for centuries. Although many these days refer to a dark night of the soul in generic terms to cover various difficult or distressing circumstances, it was St John of the Cross living in the 16th century, who first used this particular label to denote a specific spiritual experience. He described the dark night as 'a period when God interrupts the normal flow of the Christian journey by withdrawing his presence and the enjoyment pilgrims once took in spiritual practices or sources'. John underlines the feeling of having entered a darkness: 'A darkness and absence that turns a formerly flourishing spirituality into a sense of loss and grief at what is no longer experienced.'[57]

To many Christians, sentiments like these appear to be some sort of detour away from God's true path, or worse, be leading towards a fruitless dead end. But in my own experience, and having now counselled others, what is apparent is that stumbling through darkness can in fact lead to a luminous portal – rich with opportunity to encounter greater mysteries about God. Felt absence may simply represent a loss of the God we *think* we know.

While some navigate this 'wall' still feeling God's presence and ultimate love, it's fair to say that most of our early faith maps don't include a route along which we might face these struggles without a felt sense of those vital features. I never doubted the theological truth that God was alive and well and even that God loved me, but for the first time in my life I simply couldn't *feel* the reality. And it made me realise that although there are many ways that help us conclude that God is present (e.g. the testimony of scripture, the wonder of creation or witnessing the supernatural in signs and wonders), what most strongly convinces us on an emotional level is the way we sense him from within the depths of our soul.

So if as young disciples we are introduced to God in this relational way, there will be the expectation of some sort of reliable felt-sense of his 'presence' and even 'intimacy'. One commentator acknowledges this, saying:

> The faith of Christians is built on Presence. Whether in the pillar of fire, the still small voice, or the Incarnate Son, God has been Emmanuel, 'with us.' He has promised never to leave nor forsake us. In thousands of hymns, we have sung of an experienced intimacy with God in Christ.[58]

For a committed Christian, then, there is nothing more devastating than a sense of Divine Absence or spiritual loneliness. But at least reading about St John's dark night confirmed that my experience of God's withdrawal, though painful, was entirely real and had significance. For instance, as James Finley, commenting on St John of the Cross' teachings, explains, God may have to withdraw a sense of himself or 'wean' us off our original ways of engaging with him:

> We may be accustomed to experiencing God in certain ways through prayer... and so we go for a rendezvous with God, but God doesn't show up in the normal way because he is weaning us off our dependency on finite ways of experiencing the infinite presence of God. This is just to clear the way for the infinite way of experiencing the infinite presence of God... when we pass through the veil of death to eternal glory.[59]

Sources of wider wisdom

Few Christian writers within my own tradition at the time seemed to acknowledge or be able to accompany me through what was for them an unimaginable path, so historical writers such as St John of the Cross and contemporary writers from other Christian traditions like Thomas Merton, Thomas Green and Christopher Chapman became my truest friends and Sherpas. These fellow trekkers and guides, who had also navigated through terrains which seemed pretty sketchy, often summed up my own feelings with immaculate precision, such as this from Thomas Merton:

> For now, oh, my God, it is to you alone that I can talk because nobody else will understand. I do not know anything about it myself, and all I know is that I wished it were over. You have left me in no man's land.[60]

So it was as I tuned into the frequency of this newly discovered sphere of Christian tradition that I began to understand that God was perhaps purposely working in my life in some overarching way. But I wondered whether I was ever going to hear from God or feel him in my life again, since baffling radio silence from the heavens continued, becoming the sound track of empty static to my spiritual life.

I didn't know then what I have since discovered, that silence is a liminal threshold, a doorway through which Christians can discover God in a completely different way. The notion that the God who dwells within the vast 'unexplored country of the soul'[61] was utterly different to what I had been used to (e.g. connecting with God more through energetic songs of praise or vociferous prayers of intercession). Often overshadowed by the more visible religious rituals, I gradually found that the soul is waiting to be discovered, like the proverbial door at the back of the Narnian wardrobe that becomes the entry way into all manner of unnerving new understandings or experiences of God. Largely untried and untested by many in today's fast-paced societies, stillness, solitude and silence seemed to be crucial tools for many ancient writers and traditions, allowing a stilling of stormy waters to offer clearer vision down into the depths of the soul and beyond towards the infinite love of God.

In these ways, noticing and regularly sharing my experience with wise and trusted advisors who had knowledge of dark nights and their purpose, and taking on board new insights and paradigms from other Christian traditions, I was helped to re-triangulate my position on my now somewhat enlarged map of faith as many landmarks began to be reimagined, reframed and reinterpreted.

Deeper reading of scripture

Despite this, and still not feeling any active sense of God, I continued to read the Bible every day, though sometimes it was agony to do so, especially when someone within those pages was having the kind of meaningful encounters I lacked. But that resolve became a third and final triangulation landmark. As I began to perceive familiar scriptures through a new lens, while desperately trying to find God, frequent biblical references to navigating the desert, wilderness or darkness started to jump off the page.

Abraham, Moses and the fledgling nation of Israel were all tested in the heat of the wilderness or desert, as were Elijah, John the Baptist and Jesus himself. Even today, desert environments test the human spirit like few other places, teaching wanderers how to survive in harsh circumstances, underlining human vulnerability and powerlessness. Similarly, in spiritual terms, being plunged into such bewildering landscapes strips back the Christian pilgrim's expectations about their own self-sufficiency and challenges the props and assumptions that underlie the proclamation or practice of their faith. The desert is a place where the reality underneath our self-curated portraits begins to emerge, as old varnish is slowly stripped away and the true undefended-self can begin to be restored.

I found that biblical figures such as Jacob, Joseph, Jonah and Job turned out to be great examples of seeking a sense of God's presence or purposes while in 'dark places' (Genesis 33; 37; Jonah 1—2; Job 19). How many of us realise that some of the most significant aspects of Jesus' life occurred in the darkness of the womb, the tomb and most acutely through the crisis of experiencing God's seeming desertion during his crucifixion (Matthew 27:46)? The very heart of the Christian gospel after all is a moment of dereliction, loss, tragedy, emptiness and seeming meaninglessness. Christ went into the void, which makes it all the more surprising that his disciples today don't expect to share in his sufferings, even if only symbolically through learning to surrender our self-oriented perspectives and choices.

The very fact that these sorts of accounts are included in the canon of scripture confirms for me that true spiritual maturation must include some aspect or phase of walking in darkness, confusion, loss or death. 'For whoever wants to save their life will lose it, but whoever loses their life for me will find it' (Matthew 16:25).

All this time I had been asking: *What possible purpose could God have with regards to my spiritual formation in such a time of disorientation?* Slowly I was catching on to the fact that this painful and drawn-out phase of my faith walk might turn out to be a highly significant turning point. An opportunity – no, an invitation – to change my perception of both God and myself.

But how?

What can change our perspective in hard times?

One of the emphases that individualist, consumerist western culture has brought to our Christian faith map is an expectation that God will answer all our prayers the way we want them to be answered. We are encouraged to trust God for our core desires, but we want to retain the right to define exactly how and when they should be met. For example, when we describe or declare God to be faithful, often what we are unconsciously assuming is that this faithful quality will be to our liking or specifications. It is this atmosphere in our Christian culture that unwittingly helps to keep the illusion of 'self-in-control' firmly in place.

Despite not sensing God nearby for a long time by then, even I never doubted that God was faithful. But I was coming to understand that he is faithful to his own plans, not ours. Our natural desire is to return to easy, pain-free normality (if that indeed is normal) and get past the 'bad' or 'painful' stuff as soon as possible. This is often what we naturally pray for, but by God's grace that's not always what we get. It may not be what we need to help us become mature. Paul discovered this the hard way when he was given a 'thorn in the flesh' to stop him becoming conceited (2 Corinthians 12:7).

God knows that, while alleviating whatever the issue may be will reduce our physical or mental anguish, an instant answer to prayer rarely transforms us in any lasting way. We just go back to our 'normal' without becoming any more Christ-like than we were in the first place, albeit grateful for the relief! Sometimes we must embrace walking through the painful experience on the basis of trust, unable to see much prospect of relief. That's hard, but it's also where there's potential for change.

It seems that God tends to have a more comprehensive, longer-term plan to draw us further and deeper into who he really is and the freedom he really wants for us – freedom to perceive a much larger spiritual landscape. For instance, having been raised with a comfortable, cosy picture of my 'best friend' Jesus, as my original map was challenged, I began to engage more with a sense of the cosmic Christ, the co-creator and sustainer of all creation (Colossians 1), the God who was the ground of my being (Acts 17:28). I therefore became more aware and appreciative of the God who could be found beyond church, within nature and in secular contexts, as well as within my Christian community. I didn't seek this change, it just slowly evolved. And with it, tracks were laid for a far deeper experience of God in the future as well.

Since suffering is never our preference, it represents a form of 'not getting our own way'. And this often becomes a rich context for our transformation, as the letter to the Hebrews lays out:

> Endure hardship as discipline... God disciplines us for our
> good... No discipline seems pleasant at the time, but painful.
> HEBREWS 12:7, 10–11

What might the author mean by discipline? We perhaps first think of a parent disciplining their child for doing wrong. But the point of that kind of discipline is to provoke long-lasting, impactful change. In this case, it appears that out of a profound love, God disciplines us for our good, that 'we may share in his holiness' (Hebrews 12:10). The gap here may be that you and I have a very different understanding of the concept of 'good' in comparison to God. And we may understandably think to ourselves: *Nothing that feels this bad can possibly be considered good, can it?*

Perhaps a modern-day example can help us here.

The popular survivalist Bear Grylls personifies this kind of training in the TV programme *Running Wild with Bear Grylls*, in which he takes celebrities into the wild to test their inner resilience through a series of difficult challenges far removed from the comfort of their normal environment. Bear seems intent on thrusting his 'disciples' into situations which force them to confront head on their weakest points or worst fears. But it becomes apparent that he does so not out of some sadistic streak, but out of an intense belief that anyone can grow if they are committed to the process, however painful. It is this unique vision that Bear holds for his celebrities (more used to being feted by fawning crowds on the red carpet than scrabbling in the mud for live grubs to eat for dinner) that is truly inspirational. He appears to believe that they are capable of far more than they believe about themselves.

And this made me ask, in the midst of my own dark night, was this the 'good' that God was trying to cultivate? Was there something I could learn from Bear's approach about God's way of lovingly facilitating my spiritual growth? Instead of abandoning me as I assumed, was he there in the background, trying to grow some resilience and perseverance in me instead?

Slowly I began to perceive my struggles somewhat differently. Instead of God doing something unwelcome to me, could he be initiating a grace-filled process designed to get to the root of various problems within me instead? I am reminded of the double meaning of the word 'harrowing': working both as a description of extremely unpleasant circumstances we must navigate in life as well as an agricultural term meaning 'to dig a deep trench in a field for increased fruitfulness'.

You see, before that fateful day when I had my row with God, I had begun to pray that I would come to know him better. That might have been a little foolhardy in retrospect! But in desperately searching for God in what became a nightmarish landscape, the one person I didn't expect to meet was me. The real and unadulterated me. And this is what often happens in the extremis of difficult seasons: the me I don't really want to see begins to emerge in all of its terrifying dimensions. Perhaps my day of reckoning with God had arrived?

One of my friends described it like this: 'God doesn't seem as interested in investing in our false or defended-self as we are. He'd rather spend his time and effort in cultivating and revealing the God-intended person he originally made us to be.' Just like the loving portrait painter, God doesn't polish the layers of old varnish, but instead he patiently scrapes away those layers to reveal his true, original image beneath.

However, unlike inanimate paintings, we are called actively to participate in our own restoration. This is underlined by the significant condition that is attached to reaping the full harvest from testing times, as described in Hebrews 12:11: 'No discipline seems pleasant at the time, but painful. Later on, however, it produces a harvest of righteousness and peace for those who have been trained by it.'

I don't know about you, but I interpret this to mean that if we don't catch on to what God is doing and cooperate, it's entirely possible that much of the potential fruit of walking through hard or disoriented seasons might be lost. And what a sad waste that would be! We all know that it's too easy to lose perspective when drowning in any kind of struggle or long-term period of suffering or loss. This flags up to me how crucial it is to have access to mature wisdom in the form of mentors or spiritual Sherpas who will come alongside us and listen empathetically to our legitimate emotions of pain or protestations of injustice. People who will help us make sense of where we are and what God might be doing as we navigate really distressing circumstances, whether that be hitting a wall or a dark night.

Perhaps that is why James tells his readers to welcome their 'trials', 'because you know that the testing of your faith produces perseverance. Let perseverance finish its work so that you may be mature and complete, not lacking anything' (James 1:3–4). It seems that these challenges to our faith are to be recognised and interpreted as an important part of the way we grow in maturity, not giving in, not losing hope, but staggering on, however uncertainly.

To test James' theory, I began to consider what Jacob's night-long wrestling match with God was all about (Genesis 32:22–32). How was he meant to benefit or grow from this encounter? What strikes me is that Jacob walked away with a much bigger, more complete picture of God, and perhaps a sneaking respect he hadn't originally possessed for both God's power and his personhood. But Jacob also emerged into the dawn with a new sense of his own personhood, being given a new name and future role. And it's not a surprise therefore that those with eyes to see and hearts to embrace God's process have consistently witnessed to these two kinds of revelations as common fruits of the 'harvest of righteousness'.

As for me, I certainly didn't walk away from this disorienting phase of my faith walk 'braver and stronger', as many 21st-century sages like to suggest are the inevitable outcome of surviving difficulty. But a different type of resilience was birthed, alongside a clearer vision of God's fierce and unrelenting mission to reorient my whole being towards himself. And just as Jacob declared after another 'night experience', 'Surely the Lord is in this place, and I was not aware of it' (Genesis 28:16), I also emerged from my night of God's seeming absence with a new idea of how God might be present to me. Perhaps God had never been so close to Jacob as he was when God appeared shrouded in dream-like mystery or in the midst of outright wrestling. Perhaps I too could learn to sense God in shadow, in struggle, in silence and in surrender.

And like Jacob, I also crawled into the dawn of my own next stage of faith sporting a kind of limp, no doubt a symbol representing a self which could now embrace a more apt kind of weakness and humility. One designed to help me see through and beyond the illusion of self-sufficiency or self-constructed certainty. A continual reminder perhaps that there is a much-needed process of identifying what we are most attached to within our defended or self-serving illusions or idols so we can wholeheartedly learn how to surrender them to God (Jonah 2:8–9).

To put this another way, having chosen to follow Jesus, our 'conversion' as disciples extends far beyond that first decision, to a daily practice of dying to our old self and being born again, not just perceived as a once-for-all event, but part of a pattern that probably continues for the rest of our lives.

Let's pause to ponder that for a moment.

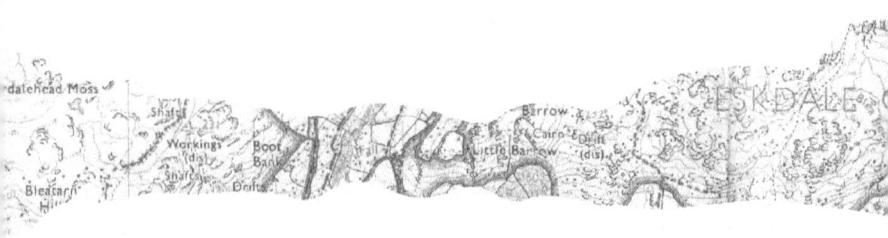

> ## Engaging with disorientation
>
> Take some time to reflect on this series of questions. If you are starting to sense some challenges to your faith map:
>
> - Have you noticed any ways in which you have begun to question your early assumptions about God and your faith?
> - When have you struggled to understand God's purposes in demanding or distressing circumstances?
> - How did you resolve your questions? Did anything cause you to struggle with your image of God or his plan for you?
>
> Or, if you have been wrestling for a while:
>
> - Reflecting on your experience of the wall, how does seeing faith disruption as 'Instruments shaped to the contours of the hand of God' (Ignatius) strike you?
> - How do you feel about submitting to the 'crucible' of transformation by following Jesus through dark and bewildering terrain?
> - If you feel resistance, what might be standing in the way of the change of heart or mind needed to enable you to reimagine your landscape of faith, to rethink your faith map?
> - What landmarks do you continue to cling to as you look towards your onward faith journey and are they serving God's call towards of spiritual growth?

A huge takeaway from my own experience of this crucible has been the conviction that God is far more serious than we could ever imagine about restoring and reorienting our inward parts. And that this serious intent is born out of his infinite love for us.

But why? Why is this so crucial to God? And how do we practically recognise and cooperate with his 'transformation campaign'?

6
Where is your centre of gravity?

Mary

*When the scientists finally discover
the centre of the universe, a lot of people
are going to be disappointed that they're not it!*

BERNARD BAILEY

Around the turn of this century, the world of basic navigation and wider cartography changed forever. The first global satellite navigation system became available to the public in 1995. At first it wasn't very accurate, but by the early 2000s GPS had started to catch on. And currently there are four different global systems operational. The result has been that instead of unfolding a cumbersome paper map which demanded that you locate your starting point before you could begin your journey, now when you switch on a satnav what pops up in the middle of that map is always… you! Your location. And the offer of bespoke routes that suit you.

It's not surprising that this was such a game changer in map-reading, because that's what we've always been most interested in – knowing where we are and recommendations for routes that will take us where want to go in the most efficient way. What's more, using a satnav, especially on a mobile phone, enables us to participate in a 'living map', which, unlike traditional generic paper maps, constantly updates us about changing circumstances or conditions, all the while keeping us in touch with our own orientation.

We can use this most popular device as a metaphor for how we perceive our lives as well. Our tendency to look at everything and everyone from the perspective of how they relate to or impact us is not only doable, but completely acceptable in most of western society, with little thought for the implications of such an orientation. So let's think about what it feels like to live at the very centre of our life map and find out how this affects our life trajectory.

The reality of our self-orientation

A good first question might be: what does it feel like to be you? Never mind where you are on your faith map, what does it feel like to look out at and interact with the rest of world from within yourself, using your own perspective, your own past history and your sense of current story? That may seem an odd question and you may never have been asked it before, but most of us live within the reality of our own 'state of being' every day, consciously or not.

When we begin to follow Christ, even as part of a loving church community perhaps, it can still feel like the way we live our life is very much down to us. The difficult choices we must make, the burden of unpleasant memories we harbour, the weight of weaknesses and sinful habits we cannot seem to shift – all erect unseen barriers to others knowing us as we would like to be known.

Because, however close we are to other people, there is no one else who can completely know or share our precise emotional, psychological and physical makeup or fully key into our hopes and dreams. Family, spouses, friends and Christian community can lessen or dilute the sense of aloneness, terror of failure, fear of weakness, shame and death, but who can cure it or chase it away completely?

We are stuck with ourselves and the version of self we are most familiar with and carry around is all we think we've got, so we tend to hang on to and protect that 'self' for dear life!

This sense of separation is something we carry from the moment we first recognised ourselves as an individual in our youth. Without a sense of connection with the infinite love of God, we build our own castle from which to face the world (chapter 3). Consequently, when faced with the core existential questions we rehearsed in chapter 2, we look to ourselves for answers, and this habitual reflex stays with us even when we come to know that our questions can only be addressed by the God who made us. It seems to be baked into our neural pathways!

That same self-referential mindset triggers the many ways in which we defend our central position, reacting instinctively to cope with shame and pain. And it's that strongly defended position that means we may need experiences like the wall or a dark night of the soul to help break us of the habit.

We are painting a bleak but realistic portrait here! And for Christians it can be hard to admit how deeply and intricately we continue to be self-oriented after coming to Christ. But without inner transformation, our innate, finely tuned sense of self remains firmly in charge, however we justify or try to conceal it.

We've mentioned the idea of the defended-self throughout these pages, the self who is trying to control, for example, what happens to us or how others think of us, and this idea of self is often associated with the concept of ego. While the word 'ego' does not appear in the Bible, principles that call out the dangers of becoming egocentric certainly do, cropping up in verses and stories which illustrate the fruit of pride and self-righteousness (e.g. Proverbs 8:13; Isaiah 14:12–14; Matthew 23:12; Luke 18:9–14).

Psychologically, the basic concept of ego is related to a healthy sense of self. But in popular usage 'ego', or more specifically 'egocentric', has generally come to be associated with an exaggerated sense of self-importance, resulting in an excessive preoccupation with self. Clearly, this sort of self-orientation is not in keeping with the Christian call for humility, particularly as it relates to Jesus' actions detailed in Philippians 2:5–11. The preceding verses (Philippians 2:3–4) encourage us to 'do nothing out of selfish ambition or vain conceit. Rather, in humility value others above yourselves.' And they seem to point towards the journey Christ-followers are expected to make as we become more like Christ; that is, that we should not simply look to our own interests, but also to the interests of others.

It's worth considering at this point that there may be a subtle distinction between being selfish (prioritising or pursuing one's own goals and desires at the expense of others) and self-orientation, which connotes being so preoccupied with one's own thoughts and feelings that those of others may go entirely unnoticed or unconsciously ignored.

Either way, many parents try to help their children to make this transition away from self-orientation as they grow into adulthood. Their hope is to expand their child's sphere of awareness away from a focus on self towards a sensitivity and responsiveness to others. Ironically of course actually becoming parents naturally trains us away from our innate self-oriented impulses, because we're suddenly called upon to prioritise another human being's needs. No wonder some are reluctant to take that plunge as people weigh up what appears on the outside to be an unattractive sacrifice!

However this comes about, it seems that tackling the self-oriented impulse we carry from an early age is a key part of the way God desires to change and mature us. And, correspondingly, as maturing Christians, I would assume that God desires that we too become more knowledgeable, more acutely sensitive to his ways, his character, his purposes for the world, and how they contrast to our own instinctively human ones, trapped as they are in more self-determined tendencies.

Evidence for self-orientation

What we've seen in the last couple of chapters is that a degree of self-orientation does serve some necessary functions, such as motivating us to recognise abuse or toxic forms of dominance, practise healthy self-care and take responsibility for ourselves and our actions. However, growing beyond this natural human state of self-orientation in spiritual terms, so that we can increasingly embrace the fullness of the image of God planted deep within, means that the life of discipleship is one of relearning and reorienting ourselves to a whole new way of thinking and being. Unfortunately, it's not as easy as simply believing or declaring that 'God and God's ways are at the centre of my life now'!

Let's take a look at the subtle ways that self-orientation might play out in the life of an average adult. And to do that, we're going to become micro-specific.

For instance, what are you like when you get on an airplane for a long flight? Do you look at the seat next to you hoping no one turns up to occupy that seat, especially if it's a night flight? Do you retreat into your little bubble, colonise the space by arranging your belongings, hunker down under your headphones, trying your best to ignore everyone around you? Do you roll your eyes or feel hard done by when you spy the baby a few rows away, who you suspect will intrude into your world when they start crying at 2.00 am? I know what I'm like in these situations. In fact, I detest flying in anticipation of having to navigate those very scenarios.

And how about the airport check-in queue – maybe it was long and tedious, so how annoyed were you when someone didn't quite understand how queuing works, blithely rolling their suitcase in front of you? Most of us head for the shortest queue in any context to avoid having to share our time, energy or attention with anyone outside our little world. Where does that strong preference come from? Why do we feel so angry when our goals for ease and comfort are blocked?

I have a feeling I know where it comes from within me.

It's because I prefer to occupy the centre of my universe. And despite singing songs inviting Jesus to 'be the centre' of my life, unless I pay conscious attention to my actual undeniable desires and aims, my long-ingrained habitual preferences will continue to direct much of my thinking and behaviour.

This may not be obvious. What about the times we do a favour for a friend in the hope of receiving gratitude or take on extra work in the office in the hope of recognition, validation or even a promotion? A seemingly altruistic gesture may conceal a hidden but very real self-orientation. The same goes for volunteering at the food bank or indeed playing any role that many others deem selfless or worthy. Are we motivated because we care or because we hope to earn 'brownie points' or to get recognition for our service? Perhaps a bit of both if we're honest. You can often tell what your true motivation was if you don't receive the validation or reward that you were really chasing (Matthew 6:2). Just check on how you feel.

Every time we feel superior to someone with whom we disagree – or worse, feel contempt for them in what we judge to be their vastly inferior state of education, knowledge or life choices – the standard against which we are making this judgement is ourselves, our view, the conclusion we've come to, based on our history and accumulated understanding (which might change one day, but for now leads us to judge the other person).

Sadly, we often fail to recognise these kinds of scenarios as 'sinful', because we may not have outwardly behaved in a way that necessarily displayed our inward feelings of pride or annoyance. But they are examples of just how caught up in ourselves we can be, particularly when we feel no one is looking or judging how Christ-like we are in that context.

Biblically there is a different perspective.

> Not that we dare to classify or compare ourselves with some of those who are commending themselves. But when they measure themselves by one another and compare themselves with one another, they are without understanding.
> 2 CORINTHIANS 10:12 (ESV)

> Do you see a person wise in their own eyes? There is more hope for a fool than for them.
> PROVERBS 26:12

We may have grasped that Christ is meant to occupy the central position in our lives, but we continue to suffer instances of everyday self-orientation that are harder to spot than we might imagine. Being transformed into the image of Christ is certainly not for the faint-hearted.

Walking alongside others in spiritual direction, I've found that this process often begins with intentionally stepping back to view ourselves with some critical objectivity. This is because we tend to run on autopilot and need a wake-up call to do the necessary self-reflection, much as Charles Dickens depicted Ebenezer Scrooge in *A Christmas Carol*, published in 1843. Scrooge was unable to see himself and perceive what he was really like until the various ghosts dropped him into scenes from his life – past, present and future – in which his hardness of heart and condescending attitude were made plain, along with the impact it was having on others. What Dickens doesn't tell us explicitly are the reasons why Scrooge had become like that. And that, of course, is the crucial thing that demands forensic investigation by us – about ourselves.

Let's look at a case study to put flesh on the bone as it were.

Kate desires to follow Christ but has an ill-defined sense of self, stemming from a childhood in which she didn't often feel validated. Even though she is vaguely aware of this, she has developed an unwanted habit of always comparing herself to the people she knows. And she finds herself judging each one in terms of how they contribute to or detract from her need for recognition. Jealousy and envy are her constant companions and, despite being creative with many artistic gifts, this unconscious craving to be perceived as an equal (if not superior) to her peers feeds a cycle of bitterness, resentment and anger when the desired praise is not forthcoming. Being around Kate can be quite difficult, because she exhibits a typical victim's mentality, interpreting every response she receives as a comment on her self-worth. So even close friends and family find themselves tiptoeing around her on eggshells, soothing and appeasing her sense that 'life just isn't fair'.

I wonder how you might respond to Kate if you knew her? Does anything in her profile resonate with your own inner dialogue?

Don't feel bad if you're thinking, *Oh dear, I'm sometimes a bit like Kate!* It turns out that comparing ourselves to others is a common (if not a subconsciously continuous) pastime. And many people also experience the uncomfortable feelings of inadequacy and shame that prompt an envious response in us. Distressingly, certain kinds of media, such as celebrity magazines, detail the elevated lives of the rich and famous specifically to provoke these kinds of feelings. And social media takes this to a whole new level, providing a 24/7 hotbed of stimulus for this soul-destroying syndrome, as multitudes vie to curate their self-image for the benefit of the world at large.

Envy and jealousy underlie much contemporary anxiety and sense of isolation. They also frequently ignite or fuel the fires of warfare (both interpersonal and international). One of the most devastating things about being caught in this entangling web is how hopeless it can make us feel, driving us to assume that our life will never be as we feel it is meant to be. Another sad byproduct is the way it can render us oblivious to how we are impacting those around us.

Kate's story demonstrates how miserable self-orientation can genuinely make us – how claustrophobic it can feel to be locked into our own self-constructed world of overwhelming negative thoughts and feelings. Without a radical change of perspective and motivation, we simply haven't got the resources or vision to free ourselves from such a downward spiral of emotional, psychological and spiritual morbidity.

I've chosen to highlight just one form of self-sabotage, but the above portrait and its impact on our inner and outer lives could equally apply to fear and anxiety, anger and malice, pride and arrogance.

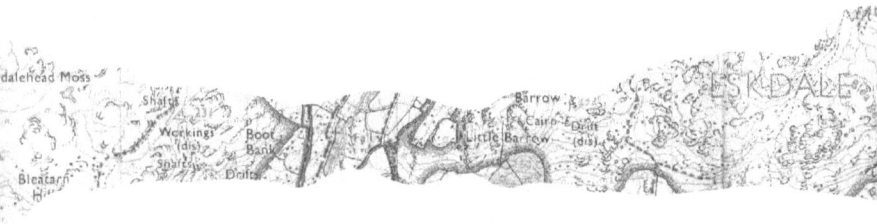

God's counter-initiative: a Copernican Revolution

The good news is that there is someone whose sole desire is to change those unnoticed default patterns. Someone who does know what it's like to be human and also knows the full extent of what it's like to be you. Someone capable of changing you from the inside out. And part of his cunning plan to achieve that is to help us to discover what it's like to be like him, to be transformed into his way of thinking, perceiving and loving.

That person is Jesus, but even though we may pray to be changed or pray for relief from the unwelcome fruits of our self-orientation, he doesn't just snap his fingers to reverse this trend or take away the feelings instantaneously. Our default perception has been laid down over so many years of neural activity, convincing us of the truth of the worldview and behaviours we have unconsciously curated, that it must undergo a long and detailed process of gradual reorientation.

But first, something fundamental needs to happen to wake us up to the true state of affairs within and God's potential purposes in that. Most Christians discover that spiritual transformation requires a sort of personal Copernican Revolution at the very heart of their thinking and core beliefs.

But the Copernican Revolution didn't happen easily.

As a stargazer, Charles has always been very conscious of the motion of the 'heavens' relative to him and his telescope planted firmly here on earth. It seems to him that the stars (including our own sun) apparently move across the sky, and his telescope needs some quite sophisticated equipment to keep it tracking 'their movement' so that he can take good astrophotographs.

These days, of course, every school kid learns that our map of the solar system is heliocentric. It clearly has our star, the sun, at its centre, anchoring all the planets that orbit around it, including ours, with its immense gravitational pull. But a heliocentric solar system has only been our belief for the past four or five centuries. Before that, it was the geocentric map of second-century astronomer and cartographer Ptolemy that reigned supreme in Arabic, Byzantine and Western thought, placing our home planet firmly at the centre of not only our solar system but everything else in the universe as well.

The Copernican Revolution, as it has come to be known, comprehensively challenged the prevailing map of cosmology. And at the time, the church was fully behind the earlier geocentric view, citing biblical support in verses like 1 Chronicles 16:30 ('The world is firmly established; it cannot be moved'). So, when Galileo's observations (building on the theoretical work of Nicolaus Copernicus) threatened to shake this foundational belief, they were strongly resisted.

In our own small way, the revolution we face in our spiritual formation is just as challenging. In dethroning our defended-self and surrendering to the reality of God at the core of our being, we too can become strongly defensive. After all, we are being asked to let go of a lifetime's perspective that places ourselves firmly at the centre, albeit a perspective of which we are often unaware, especially as we might think we've already ticked that theological box by deciding to follow Christ in the first place.

And there's the rub. If I asked you if the earth went round the sun instead of the other way round, you'd probably say something like, 'Of course, don't be silly.' But if then I had said, 'Did you see that glorious sunset last night', you probably wouldn't have noticed the inconsistency. This is because our *operative* belief can be different to our *professed* belief. We profess that the earth goes round the sun because that's what we've been taught. But we live quite happily with an internal model in which the sun rises and sets around us. And in the same way, despite our declarations that 'Jesus is Lord', until quite substantial work has been done to reorient our desires, emotions, thoughts and will, we unconsciously continue to be the centre of our world.[62]

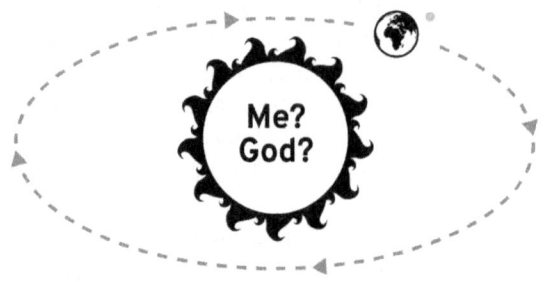

Where are we really?

What is Jesus offering to transform?

So how do we factor in this new reality? It was some 350 years later that the then Pope (John Paul II) acknowledged Galileo's brilliant insight.[63] We don't have that long! And so, in these next two chapters we'll explore what's required and some of the most effective ways that Christians over the ages have found to partner with God towards effecting their own transformation.

Accurate self-knowledge

If the first step involves seeing ourselves in a more objective manner, a good second step is to catch on to the fact that the self we believe ourselves to be isn't necessarily all there is to know, and it possibly isn't even what we think it is. In truth, only God has the ultimate capability to introduce us to ourselves, because the self we carry around without much thought is largely a construct of our own making, an accumulation of past stories, memories, thoughts and feelings as well as future plans and desires. This unexamined self, hidden from view and largely unattended to, is what continues to drive our unconscious self-orientation. But I've discovered that we can't really tackle this if we continue to insist that it's 'un-Christian' to pay attention to oneself, because without due care and attention, our ignorance precludes any significant change.

A critical way to cooperate with God, therefore, is to become curious about that which lies beyond the scope of our usual means of sensing, understanding or perception. That means admitting not just that we are sinful, but that our self-centricity is so embedded into our complex human makeup we have no hope of recognising or dealing with it. Not unless we begin to intentionally shine a light on those hidden parts, the parts we're most embarrassed about acknowledging.

It might be helpful at this point to note the vital difference between being self-centric and being self-aware or exercising healthy self-understanding. And to this end two psychologists called Joseph Luft and Harrington Ingham created the Johari Window as a framework for distinguishing between four distinct types of self-knowledge.[64]

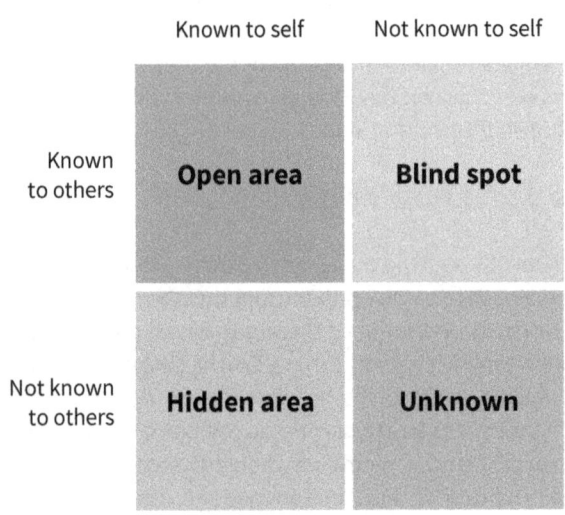

The Johari Window

These are categorised as:

- *open* – things known by you and everyone else who knows you (e.g. you are a certain height or are alive in the 21st century)
- *hidden* – things known by you but unknown to others, unless you disclose that information (e.g. negative childhood experiences)
- *blind spot* – things you are unaware of but others know about you (e.g. habits, strengths or weaknesses that are unconsciously communicated)
- *unknown* – things unknown both to you and others, but surely known by God (e.g. the way that your life will end).

Fully embracing the realities represented by the Johari Window is often difficult for us, especially the idea that there are things others know about ourselves that we don't know. Don't we lean towards wanting to be in charge of how others perceive us? Don't we spend a lot of time carefully curating both our image and behaviour to project the person we desire to be known and accepted? But, of course, many things, like a perceptive job appraisal or stingingly accurate gossip, can challenge this illusion – a truth which we could use to our advantage if we were willing to humbly seek honest feedback from trusted friends or advisors.

Let's return to Kate to see how this might work in her favour. Kate feels trapped in a cycle of comparison, which leads to envy, which in turn leads to self-loathing, although she is not necessarily conscious of this relentless chain playing out in her heart or head. Something she might consider is to bring all this to someone with known qualities of wisdom and spiritual insight – not to whine or complain (to be validated or soothed), but rather to be equipped to gain the self-knowledge that she lacks, to take the brave step to be helped to notice what is going on in her inner dialogue, express the emotions she feels and gain insight into why she has developed the particular inner narrative she rehearses so often.

Hopefully, this intervention might help Kate to understand how and where it all started and what triggers the unhappy chain into motion. In other words, instead of just continuing to accept the pattern of thought and behaviour, Kate could choose to take ownership of her own tendencies and failings, see them for what they are (self-oriented desires that her defended-self deploys to protect her fragile sense of self-worth), and receive counsel about options for breaking the cycle. These options may include spiritual prayer practices, which when consistently employed can help to interrupt the narratives she has unconsciously constructed and reorient her inner dialogue towards God's original intentions for her (more of which in the next chapter).

Reorienting our inner life by awakening to the fact that God has always been at the centre of our lives, 'for in him we live and move and have our being' (Acts 17:28), enables us to tackle the *roots* of our inner problems so that we are free to take new *routes* towards being transformed into the likeness of his son. 'It is for freedom that Christ has set us free' (Galatians 5:1).

All this becomes possible when we reimagine how we would look if we were transformed, instead of disqualifying ourselves or feeling hopeless because of our own ingrained sin and frailty. And a crucial part of this comes from exercising enough self-knowledge to acknowledge that we often can't break the chains ourselves. So, we reach out for help, both human and divine. We embrace skilled help, such as counselling, mentoring and spiritual direction, and engage in prayerful dialogue with our creator, all as part of God's provision for us. Such a choice also fulfils a God-given desire for authentic connection with others – helping us to not feel so alone and isolated in our entanglements.

Deeper connection to others

It's undeniable that as humans we crave profound connection to others, prizing harmonious relationships and authentic interaction that helps us to feel known and accepted. Celebrations, family gatherings at Christmas and birthday parties, and communal activities all feed our deep-seated impulse to engage meaningfully with others. But true connection, declares the sociologist Brené Brown, 'doesn't require us to change who we are; it requires us to be who we are… Trying to fit in and hustling for approval [are] hollow substitutes for belonging… and are the greatest barriers to belonging.'[65]

Not surprisingly, therefore, this may be where we find the theology and the spirituality of the Trinity coming together again. Because God never created us to stand alone or use ourselves as the sole point of reference, the Godhead becomes the ultimate family into which we are freely invited. And this represents the definitive community in which each member, though different in function, doesn't need to compete to be at the centre but is always other-oriented. I am often struck by this invitation, rejoicing that a unique form of unity in both purpose and in essence of being generates such profound and utterly unconditional love, one that stretches far beyond what we could ever imagine was possible.

At the heart of coming *to* Christ is to be welcomed into that inexpressible community in the here and now (Hebrews 2:11), and by gradually becoming *like* Christ it can change so much of our earthly experience. The way I look at it, heaven may not so much be a utopia as a dimension in which to discover and enjoy all that humans were originally designed for in a loving unity with God. These are qualities that have potential to cascade through all of our relationships even now and save us from the sense of aloneness and unacceptability we carry from birth.

This leads us to another aspect of our connection with others. You may never have given it much thought, but your physical being occupies precious space on the planet, an inimitable place within a family line. You were born to particular parents within a distinct culture, at a specific time. And if you have children, even when you die the memory of you will be retained within your family line, which may go on long after you and the immediate generations surrounding you.

Why is this important? Some have asked the same question about biblical genealogies, that is, why they so regularly appear in scripture. Perhaps they are there to underline the fact that we all came from somewhere, that we belong in a family chain, even if it's largely invisible to us, lost in the fog of history. This means that your existence, by definition, isn't autonomous and could never be entirely self-oriented, because you exist against a much larger canvas in the history of humanity. It may explain why such TV programmes as *Who Do You Think You Are?* have become so popular, because knowing who we are involves knowing where we come from and to whom we belong. Family trees thus represent an important form of cartography socially, culturally and anthropologically.

Despite what the serpent promised Adam and Eve (that they could 'be like God' – Genesis 3:5), living within the reality of this connective thread suggests that our ultimate happiness was never designed to be understood or fully realised in a self-centric manner. In fact, the whole Bible story from creation to consummation presents a faith map for navigating a journey towards a reality that is far beyond us as autonomous individuals, a reality that addresses our deepest existential need to find meaning and purpose in our lives within the wider story of and connection to all humanity (Revelation 22).

Belonging to the human race means we are intrinsically entwined with all sorts of people who aren't like us, born as they were at different times and in different cultures, and this is even more so when we become a Christian. One clear emphasis that Paul makes in his letters (1 Corinthians 12:12–26; Galatians 3:26–29; Ephesians 2:12–16) is that our spiritual family tree is now an extended one, connecting us to the lives and stories of all those who are part of God's family, past, present and future. Most of them we are unlikely ever to know first-hand, and some sadly we might actively choose not to know.

Yet becoming like Christ brokers the freedom to leave self-centric points of reference, prejudice and bias behind to embrace a new and profound sense of identification with others. In Zulu culture this is like the concept of *ubuntu*, which roughly translates as 'I am because we are.' Coming to know Christ kickstarts this process, showing us what's possible, but becoming like Christ frees us from the tyranny of self-only impulses, facilitating a love that is able to transcend our natural assumptions, boundaries and barriers towards every person under the sun. This offers us a shared sense of humanity, because we now understand that all carry the image of God within (Revelation 7:9).

Christ-orientation in the world

Becoming like Christ involves a gradual inner transformation that allows the image of God in which we were made to take centre stage. But what does that look like?

By planting a garden in Eden (Genesis 2:8), God created a context for people to flourish, thriving on beauty, purposefulness and fruitful relationships (Genesis 1:28; 2:22–25). And in Jesus we see someone on a mission to restore that intent to a broken and fallen world, engaging with the world around him with a heart to address individual pain and desire. Just look at how the gospels record him consistently questioning those around him to discover what they carried in their hearts, what they struggled with and what they were chasing to fulfil their deepest needs (Matthew 20:32; Mark 10:51; Luke 18:41; John 1:38). Perhaps the more God-oriented we become, the more these qualities will be cultivated in us and shine forth from us as well.

So how do we become more Christ-like in the way we relate to those around us – both closer friends and family and the stranger? What might change our perspective, especially when things get tricky – that is, embarrassing, confrontational or upsetting in some way?

Let's consider that neighbour, work colleague or family member you can't begin to fathom or get on with. Have you considered the reasons why they are as they are? If you were presented with their comprehensive backstory, like we often have the advantage of seeing in films or books, might you have more empathy for them, motivating you to react better?

Perhaps we can think of this as a chain reaction. Understanding something of how I work internally offers me insight into others and compassion borne of solidarity and a shared humility over what it means to be a struggling human.

No more 'us and them' or even 'me versus others'.

Let me give this theory a pointed edge. When someone comes to see me for counsel about their faith walk, they usually relate a story from their life, either positive or negative, and I accept it at face value, because it represents their lived experience. But I always know there will be more to the story than what they are expressing. For example, if their story concerns an interaction with another, I will want to ask probing questions to widen out the angle of their lens, to help them discover other dimensions: greater self-understanding, 'other-understanding' and God-understanding. So, I might ask: 'What was going on inside you during that situation?' Or: 'How do you imagine the other person was feeling during your relational conflict?' Or: 'Why do you think you responded as you did, and why do you think they responded as they did?' And finally: 'How are you speaking to God about your actions or your thoughts?' Or even: 'How are you praying for the other person?'

Simple interventions like this help to expand an inner narrative beyond well-worn neural pathways firing away as usual to protect our defended-self from feeling pain. Unconscious selection and emphasis can also be playing out, if we find ourselves rehearsing the same story over and over, using the same points of reference, which trap us in the same limiting conclusions. By questioning aspects of their story, I provide an opportunity for those I accompany to step back, reflect and become more aware of their own potential drivers. In widening out their version of the story, there is an opportunity to reimagine the interaction from various angles – different dynamics going on underneath or a different outcome, perhaps. I believe this is a core part of exercising faith, that is, reimagining what seems unchangeable, irretrievable, undesirable or downright impossible.

After a few years of this kind of counsel I find that people instinctively start to learn to question or interrogate themselves – making it a regular part of their own prayer life. It is not a bad practice to embrace.

You could try this kind of intervention for yourself in the course of everyday life...

Opening ourselves to a fresh perspective

After situations where you feel hurt or confused, instead of going home, grinding your teeth or allowing your resentment to build up, you might try asking:

- *How complete do I think my understanding of the situation was?* (Bear in mind that we often think that we know more than we actually do if we only rely on assumptions and past interpretations.)

And to help you evaluate your relationship to the person who has hurt or frustrated you today:

- *What might I have missed or was simply outside my 'view finder' due to my limited or incomplete knowledge?*
- *How might my recall of the situation now be influenced by my own emotional wounds or unresolved issues, or even my personality type?*
- *What response might facilitate greater spiritual maturity within me?*

These sorts of questions help to reorient us away from our default self-oriented position based on our own sense of hurt, rejection or fear. But the greatest favour we can do for ourselves is to resist the assumption that the way I interpret the situation, the other person or even God's involvement (or seeming lack of it) represents the final, definitive truth for all time. The fruit of such a choice? A softer, more open-handed heart alongside a humble willingness to keep the enquiry open.

And how might such a response impact our relationship with God? Instead of asking him to save us from the person at church we find irritating, the boss we can't stand at work or someone in our family who causes us stabs of pain every time we interact with them, we learn to view such situations as opportunities for cultivating Christ-like qualities, qualities that God is patiently trying to grow within us like compassion or forgiveness. As Morgan Freeman (playing the role of God) suggested in the film *Bruce Almighty*: 'If someone prays for patience, do you think God just makes them patient or do you think he gives them opportunities which require them to learn to become patient?'[66]

Peter's story of reorientation

Someone whose journey of reorientation is well documented (often somewhat painfully) is none other than the apostle Peter. Although he was one of the earliest disciples and leaders of the fledgling church, when he began Peter didn't appear to be a person you would describe as patient, forgiving or particularly reflective. Not endowed with much self-awareness, perhaps!

Peter adamantly wanted to follow Jesus, but his own self-oriented impulses highjacked that aim again and again. For this to change, Peter had to experience a period of faith disruption (rather like Paul, as described in the previous chapter), which for him came in the form of Jesus' arrest, death and resurrection. Peter signed up to follow the man he thought would lead them all in a rebellion against the occupying Roman powers, only to find his dreams in tatters as Jesus was led away to be crucified. All Peter had left was his shame at denying this man in whom he had placed all his hopes. Then three days later Jesus is back, but different somehow. Peter's faith map must have been completely scrambled by this point. I wouldn't be surprised if there had been many times during this bewildering period when Peter asked

Where is your centre of gravity? 171

himself the same question we have posed throughout this book – 'How did I get here, and is this all there is?'

But Jesus was vitally interested in the real Peter, who lay trapped within his personality, motivations, gifting and history, seeking to free him from his self-referential tendencies and erroneous expectations. And Peter's short but acute period of disorientation was a significant part of that process. For Peter to change, he needed to know much more about the reality of his defended-self and discover more of who God had really made him to be.

So, in his compassion the risen Jesus meets Peter on the beach for breakfast, helping him to realise the source of his shame (which we might remember would have been fuelled by feeling that he was 'not enough'), and calling up the deep love that he knew Peter held for him (John 21). Notice that Peter didn't argue with Jesus, but his pride was hurt as a result of Jesus asking him the same question, 'Peter, do you love me?', three times.

Why do this? Why poke the wound of Peter's shame and humiliation? It's clear that he was already in pain but didn't seem to know what to do about it. My own interpretation is that Jesus considered it to be a day of reckoning for Peter and also a day of introductions. I think Jesus had always perceived the disparity between Peter's external words or actions and the state of his inner life. Forgive me for projecting my own sense of possible motivation into this story, but I feel Jesus could be saying:

> Peter, I've known who you really are all these years, and have loved you passionately anyway. Today I'm introducing you to you. You need to come face to face with yourself. Today your old untransformed self is now capable of meeting the God-image within you. Becoming more aware of how my image burns within you will enable you to enter into all that I died for you to possess – freedom from your attachment to yourself, your plans, your preferences, your pain and shame. And the

outcome will be that people will see something of me whenever they meet you. Something of the light shining within bearing witness to the fact that transformation and reorientation *is possible*, making better connection, curiosity and clarity a reality. And this will represent the founding principles of my newly shaped God-oriented community.

What a bracing and unexpected Copernican Revolution! Before, Peter's own plans for himself and the nation of Israel were driving his every assumption, action and declaration, which meant that up until his death, Jesus was a good fit for Peter's faith map. But being plunged into a dark night wilderness through experiencing the crucible of his failure, humiliation and shame, Peter's hitherto unrecognised, self-oriented stance was exposed to the light, illuminating the underlying desires that drove his actions. And that, through Jesus' intervention, facilitated the change.

I don't believe that Peter's desires were evil or wrong, they were simply enmeshed in outdated or incomplete understandings, the kind we have associated with an unexamined map in this book. But Jesus wasn't just trying to rearrange Peter's map so that he would go the right way; he was also rearranging Peter the map-reader from the inside out. Unlike anyone else in the universe, Jesus thoroughly understood what it was like to be Peter. He was able to look out on the world through Peter's eyes and understand why he was chasing the hopes and dreams he did. No one else could offer this depth or breadth of understanding and empathy. Jesus was issuing an invitation for Peter (and all his subsequent disciples) to join him in recognising and embracing the God who lives within us. What we simply don't understand is how much better it will be for us (and others) when we become reoriented.

In short, Peter's wasn't a painless, simple or instant exchange, trading in one outdated map for another updated one, because it involved an excruciating but memorable day of reckoning with himself, about himself and about his future. And even after that, it took years for

Peter to fully 'walk out' that reoriented faith in his actions as leader of the early church – see Galatians 2:11–13 for an example of Peter's continuing struggle with his desire for validation by others.

I wonder if the key change in Peter's character, which altered the direction of his future ministry, was not just understanding God's new plan or even being empowered by the Holy Spirit (Acts 2). Perhaps it also included perceiving and surrendering his strongly self-oriented heart to Jesus' infinitely greater invitation to join him in his campaign and to enter into his Trinitarian community.

So it looks like it's not just me and Jacob who wound up with a limp, but it would seem Peter didn't escape unscathed either.

Developing a working strategy

Where does this leave us? Being willing to embrace the work of disorientation to achieve a completely new orientation seems like it will always be an ongoing feature of the life of faith. But a fair question might be how do we get started, or how do we carry on what has been started in a more fruitful manner? And what might get in the way? There are some common assumptions which act as obstacles to our good intent.

The first is the assumption that becoming like Christ is exclusively a work of God's grace, only the result of a touch of the Holy Spirit, or something we receive automatically by studying theology, claiming the truth of transformation, attending church, receiving the sacraments or discovering our spiritual gift or ministry. As Curt Thompson writes:

> It is not uncommon for those who live in the West to expect transformation to happen if they simply recite the verses that assure us of such an outcome… We are familiar with the language God is faithful, God will provide, Jesus loves and forgives you… These words are both true and helpful, since theological facts have great worth, but they are not helpful on their own in getting us to live the way we want to live. They do not reflect our total experience and may not provide enough practical guidance.[67]

That may feel shocking to you, but bear with me. Ask yourself this: if our transformation was solely down to the work and grace of God, why are most of us not much further down the road of being like Christ, such as carrying his mind and heart as Paul recommends (Ephesians 4:13)? God's grace is self-evident, but we also have a vital role to play in 'working out our own salvation' (Philippians 2:12).

Despite the many other Pauline imperatives which clearly put the onus on us to be intentional (Romans 12:9–13), somehow the Christian life can still be perceived in fairly passive terms: accept Jesus into your life, listen to sermons, take in information, attend homegroup and pray for God's power to transform you. We may also pray the confessional prayer on a Sunday morning and feel forgiven for that person we know we hurt last week, but still fail to realise or deal with the root cause of what drove us to hurt them in the first place. Paul's encouragement in Philippians 1:6 – 'Being confident of this, that he who began a good work in you will carry it on to completion until the day of Christ Jesus' – doesn't mean that we can just sit back and wait for that to happen.

You may also have heard Christians express a sentiment along the lines of: 'I'm just an empty vessel through which God accomplishes what he intends to do. I just need to get out of the way so that Christ can work unhindered through me.' I believe this represents an inaccurate reading of verses which speak of 'losing your life' or 'denying yourself' (e.g. Luke 9:23). Denying or dying to yourself doesn't represent obliterating the person that God has lovingly created and is in the process of restoring. Rather, as we've just seen in our review of Peter's story, it is more concerned with laying down our 'old self', our self-oriented default mode, the self-construct which stands in the way of that God-image being revealed in and through us.

For the activists among us, the hard work of our faith can become reserved for outward acts of compassion, kindness and justice. All of these are such vital parts of loving our neighbour, and yet prone to being derailed in one way or another unless they are built on the foundation of internal transformation. Outward right living and the inward journey of transformation – that is, heart, mind, body and soul – are like two sides of the same coin. It's hard to behave like Christ on the outside in a consistent or sustainable way without fundamentally becoming like Christ on the inside.

Paul addresses so many practical issues in his epistles that it's clear he intends we should work out our salvation (1 Corinthians 5—8 are good examples of Paul's urgent admonitions in these areas), retaining both personal agency and responsibility. God doesn't do this for us. Indeed, we are all too capable of resisting God in this process. One or two honest people I have worked with have admitted to me over the years that they didn't want to be a Christian any longer because they weren't up for the hard work of true transformation into Christlikeness, which is truly sad. But at least they acknowledged that it *is* hard work.

So a great question with which to end this chapter is: what is *my* work in this endeavour to implement my own Copernican Revolution, and what is *God's* work? In other words, what do you think *you* must initiate and take responsibility for, and what is the work that only God can achieve by his loving grace?

Martin Laird writes: 'What we alone can do, we cannot do alone. What God has started without us, God does not complete without us.'[68] We are called to a working partnership with God.

Earlier we spoke of Paul's frustration expressed in Romans 7 when we find ourselves 'in the dark', unable to comprehend why we fail to do the good works we want to do as those trying to follow Christ but instead do that which we don't want to do. In Romans 8 we find him rejoicing in the forgiveness and freedom that Christ has won for us and the Holy Spirit signposts for us.

But to move between those two states, we also have a responsibility to set our minds 'on what the Spirit desires' and avoid setting our minds 'on what the flesh desires' (Romans 8:5). The flesh here is Paul's euphemism for our old self, our untransformed defended-self. What Paul doesn't give us is an everyday strategy for changing our mindset, dying to our old self and putting on the new.

In the next chapter, therefore, we will offer a few suggestions for how we can go about this based on the lives and practices of seasoned saints over the centuries.

7
How do you navigate from a new perspective?

Charles

Spiritual transformation is not a matter of trying harder, but of training wisely.

JOHN ORTBERG

There's no shortage of advice on what it looks like to behave like Jesus externally. But what helps us to become like Jesus internally? How do we move from striving for outward conformity to thoughts and actions born out of an inner transformation? Most of us would probably welcome a practical working strategy that guides us on our quest to gain a fresh perspective: a way of bringing our old defended-self into alignment with God's Spirit. Like the earliest Christians we imagined as pilgrims ('people of the Way') in chapter 1, we too are on a lifelong journey. We too are pilgrims who are asking questions, seeking to grow, enlarging their vision and expanding their horizons. What most pilgrims have in common though is as sense of intentionality. Pilgrimage is not a random amble through the countryside, but a purposeful trek, aimed at learning and growing along the way towards the hoped-for destination.

Two of Mary's friends had this in mind as they set off for a day's 'pilgrimage' in the Lake District, not up a mountain in this instance, but around one of the most beautiful lakeside settings, Derwent Water. As a married couple, Jane and Steve had gone through a lot of change in recent months and wanted to anchor themselves again in God's purposes. So they set off with a clear intention to encounter Jesus together as they walked, through what they noticed along the way. In particular the story of Jesus calling his disciples (Mark 1:16–20) was uppermost in mind. This turned out to be a very fruitful strategy. Here's an extract from their own description of that day:

> As we sat down at our first stop, a question that emerged for both of us was Jesus asking us 'Do you see me?' So, using that as our first question, we asked God to give us revelation of who he is, through what we noticed on the walk. Imagine our delight when a few moments later, we came across a large upright stone with this engraved on it:
>
> *The Spirit of God is around you. In the air you breathe. His glory is the light that you see. And in the fruitfulness of the earth. And the joy of its creatures. He has written for you day by day his revelation as he has granted you every day your daily bread.*
>
> The walk continued and the more we became aware of our surroundings, the more it was as if God was directly interacting with us. We noticed a giant stone table and chairs carved from rock, which seemed to be a symbol of God dwelling with us, inviting us to eat and joining us around the table. That gave us a real sense of joy and encouragement. And later, when we had to add extra miles to the walk because of flooding, we were reminded of the reality that the journey is not always straightforward, but the more time we spend walking with God, the more rewarding it is.
>
> I felt such a deep sense of peace at the end of the walk, and I believe that even in one day I was able to grow spiritually in a way that made me more resilient to the storms of life. I am so glad that we put time aside intentionally to seek God and it has made me aware of the need to do this more often. 'Blessed are those whose strength is in you, whose hearts are set on pilgrimage' (Psalm 84:5).

Jane and Steve were intentional about their walk that day. They had a strategy. And in the same way, we also need a strategy for our journey to be fruitful. Looking beyond the obstacles we identified in the previous chapter, what can help us to become more intentional about how we grow on our walk of faith?

To make a start, let's imagine where we are on our journey relative to some of the landmarks we've covered so far. Do we understand what influences our map and where it has come from? Are we beginning to grasp who we are as map-readers and what fundamentally drives us in this life? Are we fruitfully growing through the early stages of our faith journey or perhaps finding ourselves confused and at the edge of our known faith map, our familiar landmarks lost in faith disruption? And have we taken the brave step of doing a comprehensive self-audit to work out what's really going on in our inner world and how we can begin to respond in less self-centric ways?

That last question demands some closer review.

We are currently living with what Ronald Cole-Turner suggests is 'a double identity, old and new. We are being transformed, but for now the juxtaposition of old and new is often bewildering, making us incomprehensible to ourselves.'[69] So how can we make sense of this jumble of perceptions and devise a strategy to address it with some consistency or order?

What will help us to change perspective?

Let's go back to where we left off at the end of chapter 3. If you remember, when our core desires are not met, they stir in us negative emotions. If our perspective is self-oriented, then to avoid feeling the pain of these emotions, instead of leaning into God we react defensively. This impulse can become compulsive, like a hamster wheel that goes round and round in our thoughts and emotions, forming well-worn grooves in our neural networks that cause us to react to people and situations in certain ways – most of which we are unaware of. And those pathways are normally driven by self-interest, not the selfless love that we as Christians espouse.

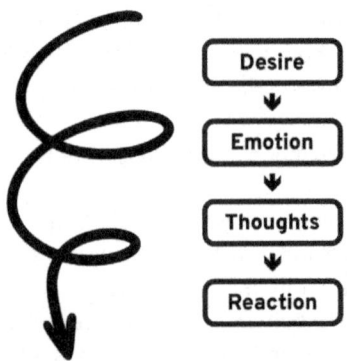

Our subconscious reactive spiral

Thinking back to the case study in chapter 6, for example, Kate's longing for validation meant that she treated her relationships largely as a means to get the recognition she craved and that meant she was not free to offer a healthy, 'other-oriented' sort of love.

A meaningful strategy for change at any stage of our journey will involve addressing each of our defended-self characteristics in turn, while learning how to put ourselves in a place where God can work with us to accomplish change.

At this point, it's helpful to pause, ask some questions and exercise your imagination a little:

- What could you do to interrupt the hamster wheel?
- How could you become more aware of what's going on?
- How might you own your thoughts and emotions?
- Why do you react like you do?
- How might you embrace a God-oriented perspective?
- How could you respond out of this fresh perspective?

Just addressing one of these questions won't necessarily find you in a greater place of freedom or help you to become more Christ-like. It's like using the London Underground – you often have to use more than one line and in the right sequence. If you want to travel from, say, Harrow to Kennington, you take the Metropolitan Line, then change at Baker Street to the Bakerloo Line, followed by another change at Charing Cross to the Northern Line to Kennington. To get where we want to go spiritually, we need to walk through and explore each of these six questions together, like planning our route on the Underground.

Along the way, we'll refer you to some spiritual disciplines that are particularly relevant to a specific question. These are explained in more detail in the Appendix. Some spiritual disciplines may be familiar, some will be new, but either way it's important to approach them with the right posture. In other words, please treat these suggestions as an invitation to get serious with God about effecting change in your inner life, and don't expect the disciplines to have some sort of 'power' in themselves. It is not spiritual disciplines per se that transform us into the likeness of Christ. Without the work of God's Spirit within, practices guarantee nothing. Adele Calhoun offers sound counsel in this regard: '[Spiritual disciplines] simply put us in a place where we can begin to notice God and respond to his word to us… Spiritual disciplines give the Holy Spirit space to brood over our souls.'[70]

Remember, spiritual formation is always a work of partnership between us and God.

What could you do to interrupt the hamster wheel?

This is where our earlier reflections on neural pathways come into play. As a reminder, the connections within our brain, once formed and used repeatedly, become preferred pathways for signals to travel. And they are persistent. It's like walking familiar routes in our houses, from our bedroom to the bathroom, or taking a shortcut through the park on the way to work. The more we walk these paths, the more they make marks or ruts in the carpet or in the ground and become like a footpath. These ruts underlie some of our unconscious selection and emphasis and this everyday habit of thought and response is a way that the brain stores our experience as knowledge.

We may feel our thinking systems are set in stone, unchangeable and even burdensome. Our deeply rutted reactions are so familiar, so much a part of the fabric of our consciousness that they can really make us feel prisoner to these habits. In our case study, Kate began to become aware of how she was behaving, which was a start, but that awareness alone didn't change her.

Here's the good news: our neural pathways can continue to change and develop throughout our lifetimes.[71] Now for the less good news: unlike when we were children, absorbing new information and ideas easily, as adults laying down new neural pathways often takes a lot more intentionality and plain hard work. As you'll know if you've tried to master any new skill set like a foreign language recently, it takes training and discipline to be able to switch from your native language to a new one with anything approaching fluency.

This is especially so if we are consciously trying to walk away from thought patterns that are connected to strong emotions, like fear, anxiety, disappointment or anger. Strong emotions are able to fuel the formation and operation of our defended-self. The thinking mind and feeling mind work together and mutually reinforce patterns, especially those laid down through trauma or in crisis.[72] For example, it has taken

How do you navigate from a new perspective? 183

me most of my life to recognise and start to deal with the patterns of thought and emotion laid down by years of attending the kind of school where the only thing that counted was how you performed – academically, artistically or on the sports field. In that environment, my worth as a person was seldom valued in terms of character attributes such as compassion or integrity.

Once we wake up to the need to become more self-aware, there are ways in which we can help ourselves in this process. Our two pilgrim friends, Jane and Steve, for example, chose to take a day out from their hamster wheel of routine and spend time with the clear intent of noticing what God might show them about their life and call together. It was a fruitful hiatus in their everyday life, and we might follow their lead. But we also need to learn how to do this each day to some extent.

Picture yourself on your giant hamster wheel, running hard, spinning the wheel but getting nowhere. This is what happens when we get stuck in old patterns of repeating thoughts and emotions. For the apostle Peter it might have been, 'I can't believe I denied knowing Jesus. What a traitor I am! How could he ever forgive me for abandoning him at a time like that?' Round and round as the levels of shame and feelings of worthlessness gradually build with every turn of the wheel.

Now imagine taking a stick and poking it into the hamster wheel. The wheel grinds to a halt and your cycle of thoughts goes flying. Take a moment to ask yourself:

- What kind of a stick do you need to interrupt the hamster wheel of your inner dialogue?
- How might you develop the habit of deliberately 'surfacing' from that inner dialogue at regular intervals in your day and taking an evaluative look around?

Sometimes God intervenes through other people to help us to stop and notice what's going on. Think of the apostle Paul, who had to confront Peter about his reluctance to eat with Gentile Christians for fear of offending those Jewish Christians who continued to uphold their original circumcision laws. The 'stick' that Paul inserted into Peter's 'wheel' was to remind him of the new truths that the gospel of Christ represented (Galatians 2:11–14). But it's much better if we can learn to do this sort of noticing for ourselves before things go too far.

On a broader level, Jesus often threw a stick in the spokes to interrupt commonly accepted religious assumptions and point to that which lay beyond dogmatic thinking; for example, telling the Pharisees who objected to his disciples gathering heads of grain on the sabbath: 'The Sabbath was made for man, not man for the Sabbath. So the Son of Man is Lord even of the Sabbath' (Mark 2:27–28). There's a danger that any form of religion, including our own experience or tradition of Christianity, however new and innovative initially, can eventually default to the 'same old, same old' pattern, rituals in worship, expectations of how God will act, endlessly spinning away without us noticing or continuing to ask some basic reflective questions every so often. A metaphorical stick is definitely needed to interrupt this sort of flow as well.

How could you become more aware of what's going on?

By interrupting the repetitive cycle of our inner narrative, we give ourselves space to take note of what's happening within us. We take the time to 'notice what we are noticing' and this helps us to keep adjusting our perspective. But we still need to be intentional about how we use that time fruitfully. For example, Jane and Steve made a point of stopping periodically to ask themselves what they had noticed along the way. And we can do the same as we travel through the moments and events of each day we are walking through life, even if it's more routine than a beautiful lakeside stroll.

To paraphrase Brian McLaren, what we pay attention to determines what we see; what we don't pay attention to determines what we miss seeing.[73]

This is self-evidently true, but why is that? Because what we pay attention to tends to be another powerful factor in forming those neural pathways that wire our brains in certain ways. So we repeatedly respond to certain people or situations in the same old defensive ways. Attention and intention are the two struts that support the operation of our wills, that is, what we notice that we feel needs to be done to protect ourselves or avoid pain, and then resolving to do it. For example, like many others I suspect, my performance-oriented upbringing predisposed me to thinking of God as someone who was primarily interested in how well I served him rather than loving me for who I was. So I strove to serve in my church community. This was not a bad thing on the surface, but it was driven by a distorted image of God, so it didn't do much to help the quality of my ongoing relationship with him or with others in that community. My attention was focused on achievements and failures, so I missed seeing so much else that is important to human existence.

What this means is that our neurophysiology, our psychology and our spirituality all actively partner with God as we grow in Christian maturity. The renewal of neural pathways is important as we seek to grow spiritually in a way that affects how we behave. Paul recognises this when he encourages the Ephesians 'to be made new in the attitude of your minds' (Ephesians 4:23). Even though we may read this encouragement in scripture, it all too often comes across as an imperative – offer your bodies, be transformed, do not conform (Romans 12:1–2) – and we might not be clear how to put these directives into practice. But the fact that Paul often uses the imperative form in his admonitions for the Christian life tells us that the will is involved in addressing our issues.

So, what can help us to notice these thoughts and emotions circling around on our inner hamster wheels? There is a centuries-old prayer practice that's particularly useful here, called the Examen, which has returned to popularity in recent years. You can find a step-by-step guide in the Appendix (see p. 240), but in outline this practice helps you to look back on your day and invite God to highlight and provide insight into significant moments. What were you thinking then? What were you feeling? How were you relating to God in that moment? How were you relating to others?

Taking note of the feelings that our inner narratives evoke is key here because as we've seen they are signposts that we can use to identify unmet desires that drive us. But before we get to that point, it's important first to treat those often-negative emotions carefully.

How might you own your thoughts and emotions?

Let's start with the thoughts we notice when we stop to give ourselves space to reflect. One of the most significant contributions to our growth in spiritual maturity is our ability to discern and differentiate between those parts of our story that have their roots in God's design for us and those we have invented, over-emphasised or sublimated to create the image we need to project to avoid or quench emotional pain. This is yet another example of selection and emphasis, appearing in many forms, such as choosing a particular part of an action or interaction we have with other people to major on. Sometimes the very thought that causes us pain looms far larger in our consciousness than its importance deserves. For example, many of us remember the one small criticism, however buried it might be, among a sea of praise in any feedback we're given.

Equally, as I begin to take more intentional notice of what's was going on inside, I increasingly recognise the sound of my inner voice chattering away every minute of the day. I spin stories to myself about what's happening, who I believe has mistreated or misunderstood me or failed me, almost like a soap opera playing on the screen of my mind.

One person complained to Mary that she felt Satan was taunting her as she lay awake at night and felt quite helpless to resist listening. They talked about whose voice this might actually be, how neural pathways worked and how constant reinforcement makes 'a groove', which she was able to change through creating new 'grooves'. And together they concluded that in this case, it was really her own voice she was listening to (albeit something that our enemy might well celebrate or leverage). With practice she has become much more able to discern the difference between her inner critic, God's loving guidance and Satan's accusation. Perhaps this is one reason why John encourages us to 'test the spirits' (1 John 4:1).

So, some questions you might like to ask yourself at this point:

- What kinds of inner narratives or storylines do you tend to use?
- What is the nature and tone of that voice with which you address yourself?
- What sort of tone of voice do you sense God might want to use in talking with you?
- How are these tones of voice similar and how do they differ?

You may not have noticed these tones of voice before, but it's amazing how astute our basic awareness becomes once we decide to pay attention to them. There can be a self-referential, self-elevating quality to some of our inner stories – ensuring that we always cast ourselves as either the hero or the victim, while others are cast as the villains. Alternatively, we may constantly be putting ourselves down or rehearsing shame-fuelled memories. Interestingly, both kinds of narratives are caught up in the 'eddy of self'.

Alongside our thoughts and inner stories, we feel emotions in response to people and situations in everyday life and the inner narratives that they stimulate. These emotions can also become associated with well-worn neural pathways that mean we tend to respond emotionally to the same situations and people in the same ways. Jane and Steve felt very positive about their day of pilgrimage, enjoying their freedom to sense and celebrate God throughout that day, whereas Kate found herself caught up and imprisoned in the negative feelings associated with never being able to get enough affirmation. For me, going back to my early school experiences, I grew to react with fear to those carrying authority and power over me. And I still have that tendency, which can really get in the way if left unidentified. Often, it's completely irrational, but annoyingly it happens nonetheless. Being aware of that doesn't necessarily mean I don't still feel fearful, but it does help me to engage with God to accept and work with that fear.

How do you treat your negative emotions?

I don't know about you, but when I feel something negative, I tend to push it away, lock it in a box and try to ignore it. I might employ a distraction to help me by indulging in something nice like that chocolate I'd been saving. How many adverts have you seen that involve chocolate as a way to deal with life's ups and downs?

You may be thinking, *Yes, the chocolate tastes good, but it never lasts long enough*, and you'd be right. A first step towards dealing with negative emotions is first to notice them, like our thoughts, and then to acknowledge them and give them some hospitality. Imagine instead of pushing away a negative feeling, you choose to entertain it. Really? Well, yes, actually. I don't mean the circumstances that gave rise to the negative emotion, but the emotion itself. After all, this is part of you responding naturally to something sad, bad or threatening (try Welcoming Prayer part 1 – see p. 242).

For instance, I might find myself pushing away feelings of dislike for another person, because I know I am supposed to love my neighbour – every neighbour! But if I do that, I miss understanding why I responded like that, which could give me a vital clue that helps me grow and become more loving. And whatever it is, that uncomfortable feeling will tend to resurface at some inconvenient point anyway so we might as well see it for what it is up front. This sets us up for some honest dialogue with God about how we really feel, and we will come back to that when we address a later question in this 'underground journey'.

Why do you react like you do?

Let's pause to reflect. Do we understand why we are compelled to speak as we do or feel as we are feeling? Are we connecting the dots between our emotions and the inner narratives relentlessly going on inside? How much do the stories we write on the pages of our inner thought life represent the outworking of those emotions?

We might be shocked if thought bubbles appeared over our heads like they do in comics, broadcasting our inner mess to others. How embarrassing! All our judgemental thoughts, our feelings of fear, shame, arrogance and ignorance alongside the meaningless trivia and petty, self-centred thinking displayed there for everyone to see. Perhaps we'd be really motivated to change our thought lives if that were the case, but would we know how? What would it mean for us to 'take captive every thought to make it obedient to Christ' (2 Corinthians 10:5)?

I am grateful those thought bubbles are not visible. But as we saw in chapter 3, noticing our thoughts and acknowledging our emotions are critically important because, properly interpreted, they can help us identify deep desires operating within us. And these desires are often the fuel that keep the engine of our habitual thoughts, actions and behaviour running to satisfy the needs of our defended-self.

Desires sit at the root of our reactive spiral and tend to stimulate certain emotions when left unfulfilled. We've touched on some of the most common of these in earlier chapters: our desire for validation from others; for security; and for some measure of control over what happens to us and others. Each of these desires or felt needs creates within us an emotion and a perspective that tends to vary depending on our personality, way of processing life or prevailing impulse.

Let's put these factors together now in exploring how we might understand our reactions. To keep things simple, we will stick with the three common types of personality we illustrated in chapter 3 through Jenny, Kevin and myself. If you remember, Jenny was more inclined towards a relational impulse, Kevin was more instinctual in his responses, while I lean towards a rational approach. Here is a summary of the common need (or desire) for each type, the emotion that's felt when that need goes unfulfilled and the perspective that develops:

- *Relational impulse, valuing connection with others*
    - The need for *validation* by others makes us worry that we did or said something to offend or fell short in some way. What should I have said? How could I have done that better? How can I make amends?
    - The emotion we feel is *shame*.
    - The perspective that this nurtures is: *I never seem to be enough, and it's crushing!*

- *Instinctual impulse, acting on 'gut feeling'*
    - The need for some measure of *control* over our environment makes us want to impose our will over situations or other people, or point out what's wrong, or resolve or withdraw from differences and disputes.

- The emotion we feel is *frustration* or *anger*.
- The perspective that this nurtures is: *Life doesn't seem to be good enough (and by the way neither am I), and it's so frustrating!*

* *Rational impulse, living in our heads*
  - The need for *security* makes us devise endless ways of keeping safe – imagining a range of potential disaster scenarios and worrying about questions like 'How will I cope?' or 'What will happen to me?' We desperately try to solve them in advance to make sure we are ready, that we have enough 'in the bank' for what might happen… maybe… sometime.
  - The emotion we feel is *fear* or *anxiety*.
  - The perspective that this nurtures is: *I never seem to be able to do enough to make myself feel safe, and it's overwhelming!*

To some extent we all carry a combination of these responses or impulses, but you may find that you lean more consistently towards one more than the others.

In a nutshell, if we stop to recognise and welcome the feelings that arise within us, they can help us to identify the desires that are fuelling them to meet the demands of our defended-self. Try using a Self-Lectio approach (see Appendix on p. 244). That sort of desire may lead to an action that may well be something we want to avoid, so what can we do to interrupt that part of the cycle?

How might you embrace a God-centred perspective?

So far, we've looked at the first four steps towards changing our self-centric viewpoint and the way we react to people and situations in life:

- Interrupting the hamster wheel of our thoughts and emotions.
- Noticing what those inner narratives are.
- Acknowledging what we are feeling about the situation.
- Understanding the unfulfilled desire that triggers our defensive reaction and can distort the way we carry God's image.

And we've identified some prayerful approaches that can help us at each step. Having diagnosed the issue, now it's time to make some changes with God's help.

The first thing to note is where we go to get our desires fulfilled. There is a tussle here between two different perspectives: I may desire passionately to love and follow God and become more like Christ. In so doing, I know in theory that I need to depend on God in all I do. But there are also competing desires in me and in you, that want to make sure we get our fundamental needs met by ourselves, in our way and on our timescale. This can be quite subtle, and on the face of it difficult to spot.

For instance, I may respond to a need to serve others by spending my spare time raising funds for a local charity. If I willingly do so because I genuinely feel that's what God has gifted and called me to do, that's great. But if there's a part of me that basks in the glory of being seen to be a 'good Christian', there's a problem and I may well react badly if something or someone gets in the way. In the first case I'm aligned with God's desire to take care of the needy, but in the second I'm serving my own desire to be validated by my community.

In Eden, God was fundamentally the go-to person to provide for our deepest human desires, as reflected by Jesus when he says, 'Your Father knows what you need before you ask him' (Matthew 6:8). Sometimes God provides for our legitimate needs through healthy relationships with family, friends or wider community – as is pictured in Genesis when God recognises that 'it is not good for the man to be alone' (2:18). Most of us would profess that we believe in a God who provides for us in various ways (Psalm 103). But operationally, day to day, most of us also look to ourselves or others to fulfil what we need.

This is tricky, because of course God has given us agency and responsibility to do what we can to provide materially for ourselves and others. We are not intended simply to do nothing and wait for God to come through with the goods. But while we are thankful to God for providing our material needs, often through the work of our hands, those unfulfilled desires can be very strong drivers.

It's at this fundamental level that we tend to ignore God and strive to redress the painful emotions that our unmet desires evoke through our own efforts. And for the most part we fail, or we damage others in our urgency to avoid that pain. The reason that Kate's friends and family feel they need to 'walk on eggshells' around her is due to her fundamentally deep desire to be validated in every response they make to her. If only she were able to find that sense of self-worth in her relationship with God, it might be a relief to all concerned!

The second thing to note is what to do about these well-worn self-referential habits. Two things must happen for there to be lasting change:

1 we *surrender* the attachment that our defended-self has to getting what it wants
2 we *look beyond* that perspective towards God as the source of what we truly need.

Sounds simple! But if our default reaction to unmet desires is solidly self-centric and has been for some time, then it's likely that we have grown attached to that way of doing things. Such attachments are not easy to shift and represent more of those deeply worn grooves in our patterns of thought and emotion. Instead of responding with surrender we may choose to resist letting go or deny that we are caught in a trap altogether. These in themselves are defensive reactions. It's in the title – this is our defended-self in full flow.

Shifting from attachment to surrender can be really hard, which is why some patterns of behaviour need external help. The twelve-step programme for addictions is one very powerful example.[74] But there is plenty of scope for us to engage with God in finding freedom well before deep-seated addictions set in. Try the second part of Welcoming Prayer in the Appendix for an example (see p. 243).

Let's go back to the defended-self perspective of each of the three impulses associated with our personality, and see what changing from a defended-self perspective to a God-centric perspective might look like.

- *Relational impulse*
    - *Defended perspective*: I am not enough (I fall short of God's and others' expectations of me).
    - *God-centric perspective*: God delights in you and has called you into human community to be a living illustration of his Trinitarian community of love (Zephaniah 3:17; John 15:9–17).
    - To change perspective means to dwell in God's embrace and from that place of acceptance lean into what you can offer to others; e.g. *I (God) love how I have made you and what you carry that can help others.*

- *Instinctual impulse*
    - *Defended perspective*: Life is not good enough (I want to change it/others/myself).
    - *God-centric perspective*: 'In him we live and move and have our being' (Acts 17:28); 'Therefore, as God's chosen people, holy and dearly loved, clothe yourselves with compassion, kindness, humility, gentleness and patience' (Colossians 3:12).

- To change perspective means to lean into God's design and saving action for the world and give yourself to others in that; e.g. *I (God) have got this! Join me in my work.*

- *Rational impulse*
  - *Defended perspective*: I just can't do enough (I don't know how to deal with the potential issues I might be facing).
  - *God-centric perspective*: I find God in the quietness of mind that allows me to let go of my anxiety and regain a realistic perspective, learning to recognise and draw on God's supportive presence and deep wisdom in the face of threat. 'He leads me beside quiet waters... He guides me along the right paths... You prepare a table for me in the presence of my enemies... Surely your goodness and love will follow me' (Psalm 23).
  - To change perspective means to trust in the wisdom of God that is available to you through his Spirit (Ephesians 1:17), and generously to offer this wisdom to others who may be in need of it; e.g. *I (God) am present with you, dwelling by my Spirit within you, and can supply wisdom beyond your own capacity. Rest in me.*

It's worth reflecting on those statements for a while to see which of them most resonates with you and allowing whatever God wants to say to you personally to sink in.

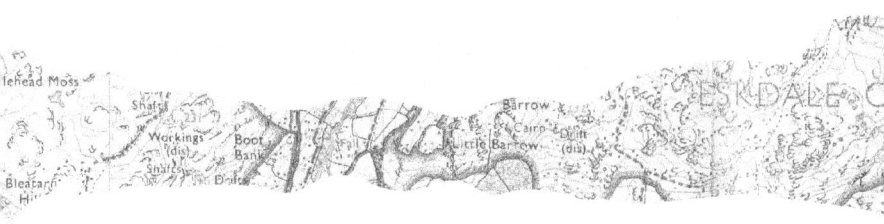

How do you respond out of this fresh perspective?

We began this chapter with a strategic framework for transformation. We are nearly there, but one final step is required to seal the deal. We need to follow through our inner work done in cooperation with God with an outward response to the people and situations that we encounter day by day. Remember the scenario we used earlier of ignoring others by putting myself in a highly self-protective bubble when, for example, travelling by public transport? Growing in emotional and spiritual maturity means that we have greater freedom from the attachments that trigger defensive or dismissive reactions to other people and situations and eyes to see how we can offer the image of God within us more authentically to those around us.

Recognising and prayerfully laying down our own efforts to fulfil unmet desires leaves us in a place of greater freedom. We are no longer subconsciously driven towards our own ends, and that allows us to let our focus turn from ourselves towards God and others. We might begin to ask: what is it of God deep within me that I would love to use in service of those who really need it? What aspect of godly character most resonates with me and could do someone else some good? How might I be generous with some of the nine fruits that the Spirit bears within me (Galatians 5:22–23)?

What could love look like as I give an appraisal to someone in my team at work? How could I bring joy to that person on the supermarket till today? Is there a way to offer a measure of peace to my troubled friend, or even the person I think of as my enemy? You get the picture. And there are six more fruits to choose from! The London Institute for Contemporary Christianity (LICC) has championed this sort of approach to fruitful living as a Christian in everyday life for many years.[75]

One of the reasons that this step is so important is that as we seek to offer the image of God that we carry to others, we are also in a sense 'calling up' that image. We are deliberately choosing to swap self-centredness with God-centredness, which naturally leans towards others. Whereas our subconscious was preoccupied with self-centred inner narratives, we now have the space to welcome the fruit of the Holy Spirit to occupy that space. You might even try praying 'Welcome love' or 'Welcome self-control' as a way to engage with God's fruitful intent for you. And then to live that out. This takes time and intentionality, but I have personally found it to be a very effective way of breaking out of my tendency to fear and instead embracing the 'self' God has made me to be. We have to train ourselves to be alert to those around us and sometimes to take a risk, if welcoming kindness and then being kind, for example, means putting ourselves out in some way.

A most poignant example of this sort of right action emerging from surrender to God is described in Matthew's gospel, as Jesus prays in the garden of Gethsemane (Matthew 26:36–46). Jesus becomes deeply disturbed in his prayer. 'My soul is overwhelmed with sorrow to the point of death', he tells those with him (v. 38). But somehow, he is, after a while, able to let go of those natural desires that are causing his deep distress, at least to some extent. He still asks his Father, 'May this cup be taken from me', but in the end surrenders himself to the way that God chooses for him, 'Yet not as I will, but as you will' (v. 39). Through this he is able to walk the way of the cross, trusting in God even when it feels like he has been abandoned.

Few of us are called to that level of self-sacrifice. And yet, as we learn to let go of our small but habitual preferences daily, we gradually become more able to respond out of our true self – the image of God that we carry that goes hand-in-hand with the 'unique God-given meaning in a person's life'.[76] As we use prayer practices to engage with God in this process, piece by piece our old neural pathways are being rewired so that patterns driven by our old dependence on self, with its habits of shame, are replaced by patterns formed by awareness of and a dependence on love.

You might be wondering what the prayer practice or spiritual discipline might be for this step. Responding to others out of freedom and love, out of the true person God made us to be, *is* the prayer practice or discipline. Could it be that our very action itself reinforces the internal work done with the help of the Spirit and helps to prevent us from losing ground? Maybe this is what James means when he writes:

> Anyone who listens to the word but does not do what it says is like someone who looks at his face in a mirror and, after looking at himself, goes away and immediately forgets what he looks like. But whoever looks intently into the perfect law that gives freedom and continues in it – not forgetting what they have heard, but doing it – they will be blessed in what they do.
> JAMES 1:23–25

Moving from internal change to external action is a vital step in completing the action of putting off our old self to put on the new.

What's really happening when we engage in this process?

We have focused in this chapter on a strategy that helps us to cooperate with God as he calls us up into the likeness of Christ. Many Christians assume that spending their lives seeking out the latest spiritual context like a certain kind of prayer, retreat or Christian conference will result in the most penetrating changes. And these can certainly act as God's vehicles to restore our vision and reset our orientation. But God's usual strategy seems to be a great deal more 'mundane'. 'God comes to us disguised as our life',[77] working through the situations and people we encounter to bring about change.

Take the prayer practices we've been exploring, for example. These are good to learn in the quiet of a private space, but not because they should be reserved for that context. Once we have learnt in solitude how to approach God in a particular way, we are equipped to let that approach infuse our everyday. For example, you might ask yourself some Examen questions in the middle of your day over a sandwich on your lunch break: when have I offered love today or withheld it? Where have I encountered God? Or we might surrender our desire to get validation from another by using a breath prayer that reinforces our confidence in being loved, such as: 'Nothing can separate me *[breathing in]*… from the love of Jesus *[breathing out]*' (based on Romans 8:39). And over time, as we cooperate with God's work in our lives from day to day, we find ourselves in a place of greater freedom to allow the image of God that we carry with us to emerge in what we say and do.

Well done if you have made it this far! We recognise that there are quite a lot of steps to remember in this strategy. We put together a simple acronym (PAUSE) for LICC's small-group resource *Growing on the Frontline*,[78] which you might find helpful. Try running through this sequence when you are out and about and life greets you with one of those challenging circumstances.

PAUSE

Pause: interrupt the hamster wheel of your inner narratives to notice your emotions and the thought patterns that accompany those feelings.

Acknowledge: take ownership of your emotions and welcome them as a part of you.

Understand: identify as far as you can the deep desire that is driving those emotions.

Surrender: let go of that desire and look to God as the cornerstone of a fresh viewpoint and the source of what you truly need.

Engage: embrace the image of God you carry and offer that authentically to those around you.

What might using PAUSE look like in practice? Here's a typical way we might use it when we're going about everyday life. Let's go back to where we began, with that Tube ride from Harrow to Kennington.

I'm meeting my boss this morning in Kennington, and as I rumble along on the Metropolitan Line I'm not in a good place. All sorts of possible scenarios are whirling round my head, most of them unpleasant! After a while, I take a deep breath and decide to stop myself spinning round in mental circles (*pause*).

What am I feeling? As I reflect, I sense that I'm stressed that my project is running over time; I'm a bit annoyed that I've been called away from working on it to this meeting; but mostly I'm anxious about telling her that I've missed the deadline. And so I take a moment to sit with those feelings and accept that, yes, that's where I am at this morning (*acknowledge*).

That feeling of anxiety seems to be the most significant, and I wonder what's behind it. Obviously, it's not great to disappoint your boss, nobody likes to have to admit that they have failed, and I know I have a particular issue with authority figures. I do enjoy their approval and tend to wilt under criticism. But I think that in this case, alongside that desire for validation, what's also behind my anxiety is that I don't feel I've got enough resources to deliver this project to the timescale agreed. And I realise that does fit with my tendency as someone who leans towards rationality to worry about whether I 'have enough' (*understand*).

At this point I quieten my own thoughts and turn to God in prayer. After a moment of silence, I imagine placing that anxiety about having enough resources and being thought well of on the altar of God's love and provision, and I entrust them to God's care (*surrender*).

By the time I get to the meeting in Kennington, I'm better prepared to offer an honest assessment of the situation, listen to whatever criticism there may be, but then to offer the best of who I am to get the job done as well as I can (*engage*). My perspective has moved from a self-centric sense of inadequacy to a God-centred sense of trust.

All this bears testament to something hugely significant that's happening within us. We are indeed engaged in our own personal Copernican Revolution in which the way we perceive ourselves relative to God is gradually transformed. As we develop those internal muscles of Godward surrender and trust, not only are we freed to act differently, but we are also freed to relate to God in a fresh and deeper way as well. We realise, perhaps somewhat embarrassed, that God really is God and not simply a benign and all-powerful figure ready to answer our prayers based on our agenda for ourselves. We discover something of what it means to be deeply flawed yet deeply loved. And, tentatively at first, we learn to put our full weight on the infinite yet unfathomable love that we realise gives us every breath that we take.

For some of us, this may be a monumental reimagining of the landscape of faith.

So, what about you? Where might your present perspective or life habits most need reimagining? And in which direction are you facing? In other words, where are you looking from and what are you looking towards?

8
How does 'looking beyond' change how you live?

Mary and Charles

Pilgrims are longing to take a journey of transformation. To do so, they leave behind the familiar and the known, and physically journey into a place and a future that only God can envision.

GEOFFREY TRISTRAM[79]

As I (Charles) uttered that *cri de cœur* on a Cambridge towpath so long ago – 'How did I get here and is this all there is?' – I didn't realise that God's reply would echo throughout the rest of my Christian journey. At the time I didn't really know why I was asking that question. But now I realise it was heavily influenced by both my perspective and perception at the time, two words which tend to be used interchangeably, but are not quite the same thing.

Perception is the way we understand or interpret something, an intuitive insight or assumption based on sensory input. The sensory input we tend to use as a default comes from our five physical senses. *Perspective*, on the other hand, represents our personal lens on the world, shaped by background, experience, beliefs and worldviews. Perspective concerns the place from which we are looking, and perception is how we interpret what we see when we are looking from that place.

This neatly summarises what this book has really been about. Because, as we've noted consistently, no cartographer truly starts with a blank piece of paper, which means that all map-making and map-reading, both literal and spiritual, demands that we become aware of the vantage point from which we are looking and the fact that our view will always be to some extent, inaccurate, distorted or limited.

Sometimes we forget that we are spiritual beings learning to be human more than human beings learning to be spiritual (attributed to Pierre Teilhard de Chardin). What we lack and need to cultivate is the habit of sensing and seeing from a spiritual perspective. This helps us to understand better how we perceive and evaluate what we believe to be true – about God, about the nature and purpose of the journey we go on with God, about ourselves and about pretty much everything else.

My question on the towpath provoked a long-term pilgrimage, one which invited me to look back, to look within and to look forward on many levels, some of which we've tried to share in these pages.

- Stopping at regular intervals to look back at the map I'd inherited and stages of faith through which I had travelled, so that I would continue to be aware how my background, my family experiences, my educational values, have and continue to inform my particular worldviews, spiritual paradigms and expectations.

- Looking within to understand the patterns of emotions, thoughts and desires that project images and stories on to the screen of my inner self. And wondering how my personality and learnt responses influence so strongly the ways in which I judge and react to other people and to God.

- Looking forwards, from where I am on my faith map, towards what I discern of my journey yet to come. And in seeking to grow in Christlikeness, the discerning practices that might offer pathways for spiritual growth.

Whatever form faith disruption takes in our lives, our personal Copernican Revolution helps to fundamentally change our perspective and allows us to moderate our thoughts, emotions and physical senses with the wisdom of our spiritual perception. As we first recognise and then embed that change using spiritual practices it becomes clear that our formation is no longer just about looking back, looking within and looking forward; it's also about looking beyond. God calls us up, out of our well-worn self-centric viewpoint to look at everyday life from a perspective that is centred with Christ in God. And that changes everything.

As human beings we are very much concerned with the business of living our human existence – until it runs out! As spiritual beings, our journey doesn't end with physical aging and death. We have a *telos*, an eternal destiny, that can have a profound influence on the way we live in the here and now if we are intentional about it. Either we tuck away our 'ticket to heaven' in a back pocket and get on with business of being human or we actively learn to live our human life in the present with an eye to what's beyond the horizon of our physical death.

If we're being honest, however, perhaps we need to admit that as humans caught up in this life, we often prefer the sort of faith map that is concrete, practical and well-defined, something we can understand and feel that we have a handle on. In a sense, it can be the sort of map we both perceive and actively, though unmindfully, shape to our own image. And so, we will tend to focus on the human face of God that is offered to us through Jesus in the gospels, select the 'nicer' psalms of praise and celebration, and the many encouragements that Paul offers in his letters. Of course, there is nothing wrong with any of these.

But just pause for a moment and consider the incarnation of Christ on which our faith rests. Jesus himself lived daily with a perspective that both included and looked beyond his humanity. Jesus was fully human, experiencing emotional and psychological needs and bodily functions as we do. He had to live within familial, social, political and religious spheres, all of which constituted the everyday, pedestrian, immediate, even perhaps boring, and visible realities of his life. But even as he fully entered those dimensions, Jesus was always mindful that they didn't represent all there was to life.

If we only dwell on Jesus' ordinary humanity, or veer to the other extreme and focus mostly on the supernatural realm of his miraculous signs and wonders, we miss how subtly and seamlessly Jesus knitted both together. He used the very ordinary and the seemingly mundane events and situations of life to signpost transcendent realities. In fact, he often asked people to see through or look beyond the seemingly self-evident, to consider those things with new eyes, from an entirely different and faith-oriented perspective; for example, lilies of the field, yeast, mustard seeds, lost sheep and lost coins (Matthew 6, 13; Luke 15).

Jesus introduced Nicodemus to the startling idea that there is both natural and spiritual birth, and in meeting the woman at the well he perceived someone whose questions needed answering from both an earthly and spiritual perspective (John 3—4). These meetings remind us how Jesus brought together the human and divine spheres, the finite and the infinite, in a unique way that no one before him had managed. And yet, he invites us to do the same, not to be limited to our human perspective but to intentionally look and live on two levels at the same time. He offers a form of preparation in this life for the life to come.

We want to spend this final chapter exploring what living with that sort of perspective might look like. It involves us learning how to look beyond our normal landmarks. On that towpath, stuck in my self-centric perspective, I just couldn't imagine what 'more than this' could possibly look like. But I sensed so strongly within myself that there had to be more. So alongside looking back, looking within and looking forward, we also need to be prepared to look beyond our finite horizons.

Looking beyond requires us to engage our imagination, guided by the Holy Spirit, because our rational or emotional selves will fall short of grasping what we haven't already experienced. Especially as we seek to engage with an eternal God using our finite faculties. So, buckle up as together we attempt to look beyond and reimagine our current ideas of God, ourselves, our relationships, our faith map, from a perspective that reaches far beyond our physical lifespan into the great unknown territory of that which lies beyond death.

Looking beyond my perception of God

Let's start with your relationship with God. How did you imagine your journey with him would go when you set off as a 'new Christian'? Perhaps that original expectation has been fulfilled, or maybe you found that it changed out of all recognition? What happens to the milestone we were heading for on the horizon when we are redirected by the unexpected, the difficult or the unfathomable? A typical refrain I hear as I walk with fellow pilgrims is: 'I didn't imagine my life would turn out like it has.' Or: 'I can't imagine what God is doing as I encounter severe knockbacks, disappointments, unfulfilled dreams or perhaps the reality of my own physical frailty.'

As we've seen in the last couple of chapters, we tend to perceive what happens to us, pleasant and unpleasant, from a self-centred perspective. And that's not surprising. But what would prompt us to enquire of God what else there may be to see within a given circumstance? What could help us to notice and then reimagine from God's perspective the assumptive framework we habitually use to evaluate our life?

A helpful angle might be to consider how you perceive or engage with God in the first place. Would it be as a loving Father, beckoning you with arms open wide? Or maybe, even unintentionally, you sense a stern headteacher with a clipboard who's continually evaluating your performance? Or do you envisage a friendly sibling, companion or guide, always available to advise and console you in time of need? These are just some of the contrasting ways that people use to describe how they relate to God. But what these pictures often have in common is that they haven't been subjected to much conscious examination or development. Not surprisingly, they are based on some aspect of previous human relational experiences, both positive and negative. This is natural, but perhaps a bit limiting.

So, as an experiment, let's use our imaginations to think beyond our normal anthropomorphic metaphors and try out a different picture of God and us in relation to God – a picture that might expand our perspective and point us towards the omnipresent and omniscient qualities of his infinite love. Try thinking of God as a vast ocean and yourself as a sponge immersed in that ocean. Instead of desperately seeking a touch from a seemingly distant God or crying out to him to draw near to you, can you instead imagine yourself already surrounded by or immersed in God, God in you and you in God? As a sponge soaked through by God, in a sense a part of and no longer wholly distinguishable from God.

What sort of images are you seeing in your mind as this metaphor is offered? What emotions is that image calling up within you?

Our aim isn't to establish theological doctrines here – we're just using our imagination to explore a symbolic image that might help us to conceive of or engage with God on a different level, beyond what we might normally do. Perhaps the sponge-in-ocean picture moves your centre of gravity somewhat from yourself towards one that is more creatively centred on allowing God to be God; for example, from *How do I know God is near me or will love me in a way that is meaningful to me?* to *If God is like an ocean all around and within me, he must be more immediately and continuously present than I could ever know or feel.*

Looking at God like this might also affect how we pray. Naturally we always hope for the results we want when we ask God for something. And yet maturity invites us to look beyond our desires towards an interest in what God's desires or intentions might be as well. We can be held back from trying this approach if we can't imagine a better outcome than the one we're asking for.

For instance, Psalm 91 appears to guarantee that no harm will ever befall those who love God, a kind of promise which I've heard recited many times. But if we look beyond the literal earthly meaning of praying for protection from snares, pestilence and sickness (vv. 3–13), other dimensions of spiritual truth and experience begin to emerge. As finite beings we instinctively feel that preserving our flesh and blood must be our greatest priority, but are these ultimately superseded by even greater measureless realities that also demand to be treasured and kept safe?

Just before Etty Hillesum, a Dutch Jewish author of religious diaries and letters, was taken to the death camps in 1943, she famously signposted that which lay beyond the clutches of evident evil, declaring: 'We safeguard that little piece of You, God in ourselves... and defend your dwelling place inside us to the last.'[80]

So instead of deciding what the best outcome should be as we pray (for ourselves or others) and only having faith for that, could faith be exercised by simply trusting in the inimitable wisdom of God to know and provide what's best? I wonder if choosing to look beyond our own immediate sense of self-preservation, interests or sense of what should happen enables us to perceive God's deeper purposes with greater clarity. Perhaps this is one way to interpret Paul's iconic pronouncement in Romans 8:28: 'And we know that in all things God works for the good of those who love him, who have been called according to his purpose.'

Looking beyond our normal image or expectation of God might allow us to move from a more transactional prayer (e.g. 'I can't see the way ahead and am frightened, so please to change my situation, God, or at least help me to know your presence') towards a more transformational approach (e.g. 'God, you already know all my needs, so I will just sit quietly with you, surrender my idea of what I think you should do, and without needing to use many words, soak in your ocean of love.')

'Hold on,' I hear you cry. 'I don't remember the Bible describing me as a sponge in the ocean!' And you'd be right. It's a metaphor. A bit like the one in Psalm 1 about a tree planted by streams of water. Water in the tree; the tree in water. Metaphors point to something beyond the literal, material or doctrinal, something that, without an imaginative picture to help us, can be hard to grasp, like the unity to which Jesus referred: 'On that day you will realise that I am in my Father, and you are in me, and I am in you' (John 14:20); 'That all of them may be one, Father, just as you are in me and I am in you. May they also be in us so that the world may believe that you have sent me' (John 17:21). Or as Paul writes: 'For you died, and your life is now hidden with Christ in God' (Colossians 3:3).

These verses offer us inspiration for connecting to God in our current life, but also a foretaste of what we may experience beyond death. Being open to refreshing our image of God, and so growing in our relationship with him as we travel the length of our earthly journey, is appropriate when we remember that we at present only have the capacity to 'see through a glass, darkly' (1 Corinthians 13:12, KJV). Resolving to look beyond what we've always known, assumed or experienced (both individually and communally) can offer an intriguing paradigm shift, deepening and enriching our walk in the here and now.

What's more, in Ephesians 2:6–7, Paul encourages us to join Christ in his nature in this current life and look from his viewpoint as we spiritually find ourselves seated with him in heavenly realms. This is a hard concept to grasp let alone apply. How can I possibly grasp what Christ's viewpoint in heavenly places might be?

Well, we could start by reading some of Jesus' parables, pronouncements and prophetic utterances with this in mind. If nothing else, it forces us to move beyond what I think about a particular scripture and prompts me to ask, 'What unique perspective that Jesus holds does it offer?' Let's move past theory quickly and go to something well-known, like the beatitudes (Matthew 5). These short but strangely mysterious statements might seem impenetrable, and there's no doubt they demand a certain Spirit-inspired wisdom. In choosing to sit with Jesus to perceive life from his vantage point, the attitudes and postures the beatitudes demand serious study. What concrete changes is he advocating? What priorities is he signposting? How are mourning, mercy and meekness being reframed?

Ah, so this is what looking at life and all human interaction through Jesus' eyes feels like! Perhaps there's always a deeper dimension of understanding to discover beyond what I've already grasped.

Looking beyond myself

Let's continue in this perspective and consider how I might perceive myself from Jesus' vantage point. One of the downsides of sticking with a self-centric perspective is that it produces a distorted view of ourselves. We worry about what our friend, our boss, and especially God thinks of us, and yet often that concern is firmly centred on our own limited understanding. We may veer between false humility, shamed guilt, overconfidence or avoid considering this angle altogether. But before we go all 'hair shirt and locusts' and assume we must always be beating our breasts, downplaying our worth so that we don't get too big-headed, I firmly believe that God wants us to love ourselves – no longer in an immature self-oriented way, but in a God-informed manner.

Bernard of Clairvaux, a Cistercian monk who lived in the twelfth century, certainly felt this was one of the many net results of growing up in Christ. He suggested that we begin, as children, with love of self for our own self's sake, and as new converts, graduate on to love of God, again for our own self's sake. But eventually we begin to love God for God's own sake (as one might love one's parent as an adult, perceiving their merits beyond what they can contribute to your life). And finally, in later stages of maturity, we find we are able to love ourselves as God does, at last understanding that fully loving God means we are able to love ourselves for his sake.[81] In other words, we learn to love ourselves from God's perspective.

Why is this evolution of love for self not only desirable but necessary? Because God has created us for love, to love extravagantly, without our defended-self getting in the way. This is presumably why he infers that 'loving our neighbour', in the greatest of all commandments (Matthew 22:36–40), must be informed by the extent to which we can love ourselves. Reflecting again on the dynamics of Trinity can be helpful here – the captivating image of the Godhead in which there is an even-handed and unequivocal exchange of love flowing in all three directions, so that all members feel equally known, loved and blessed.

Let's pause and examine what might get in the way of you loving yourself in a healthy, life-enhancing way? We touched on this in chapter 6, where we spoke about false forms of humility, but what would happen if you considered that both your love for God and for others might hinge on how freely you were able to love yourself? What might that change for you? What inner work might that flag up for you to do?

Looking beyond my perception of others

What might it mean for you to participate in God's love for others as you learn to love yourself? Far from making me self-involved, loving myself as God intends enables me to look beyond self towards the 'other', a fact that brings us neatly to how we might imagine or reimagine our relationships. This is easy enough, as Jesus observes, when thinking of people who love us and are therefore easy to love back (Matthew 5:46). It is much harder with people we don't particularly want to love or even those we might consider our enemy.

I wonder how you would define 'an enemy'. Cartography has frequently been used to depict relationships between countries, whether by the drawing or redrawing of boundaries or more literally by illustrating alliances geographically (e.g. the map on the next page).

Today, our personal 'maps' might categorise people we consider to be for or against us, informed by how we view or are treated by certain nations or by racial, religious or gender-related tribes. It's easy to identify someone as a potential enemy by this definition: those who hate me, show prejudice towards me or my kind, invade my country, murder my loved ones, the list goes on. But even outside of those

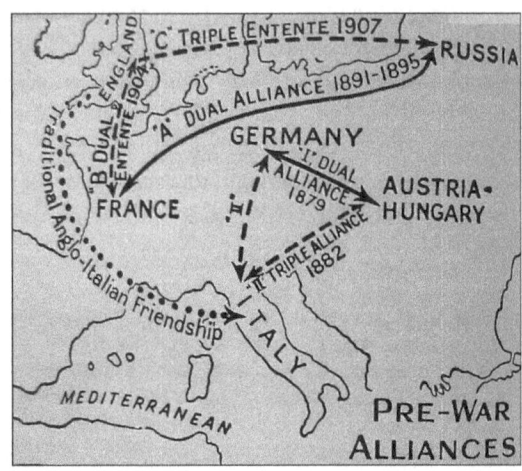

An early political map showing pre-World War I alliances

more obvious candidates, most of us quite instinctively, if somewhat subconsciously, can find ourselves categorising people as 'enemies' simply because they fail to meet our emotional needs in the way we feel they should be met. By this definition, almost anyone, including those in our families, communities or Christian circles, might well qualify.

Jesus knew a thing or two about having enemies – notably those who were out to get him as he regularly challenged the religious culture of that time. But unbelievably it appears that he held no feelings of enmity. Perhaps that's because he resolved to look beyond their impressions or reactions to him. Their rage and violent opposition provoked compassion instead of disgust, because Jesus could see where they were caught in their own pernicious cycles of sin and shame (Luke 23:34).

Much of Jesus' teaching encapsulated in the sermon on the mount encourages his disciples to look back and assess the reality of their lives, look within to discern their true attitudes and motives, and look beyond towards a greater kind of kingdom, one that runs on entirely different principles to the kingdoms of this world (Matthew 5—7). And when I look at all that Paul advocates in the famous 'love chapter' in 1 Corinthians 13, I wonder how much of this is even possible without reimagining our relationships through the eyes of mature love.

> Love is patient, love is kind. It does not envy, it does not boast, it is not proud... Love never fails.
> 1 CORINTHIANS 13:4, 8

This is an utterly compelling portrait of selfless love, but perhaps only realistically doable as we take our seat and look from the vantage point of being in heavenly places with Christ.

An invitation beckons for us to look beyond our default image of the person that we dislike (or who dislikes us) implying that we move on from feeling *I 'ought, should or must' love my enemies because Jesus commands it* to *I really desire to move beyond my self-oriented impulses towards authentic love for seeming enemies.* This mature view is nurtured as we allow our perspective to move from self-pleasing to God-pleasing (Matthew 5:48). Might this posture enable us to see and treat our enemies as those who are equally created and deeply loved by God? Might it also engender a better understanding or empathy for their struggles, however repugnant we find their outward expression – in short, to perceive an 'enemy' or unlovable person as a deeply flawed fellow human being just like me?

Let's test this principle by placing ourselves in the middle of an argument. Think back to a conflict you've had with someone recently. There you are, all fired up, defending your point of view, getting angry and frustrated that the other person isn't able or willing to see inside your head or heart – to perceive why this topic or your viewpoint is so significant to you. And now, press the pause button, freeze the action and ask yourself: how would the changes in perspective detailed above affect how I am perceiving, thinking and feeling about the other person in this situation? What alternative possibilities might open out if I took a God's-eye view of myself, them and the topic over which we are arguing?

Of course, all this depends on how fully I desire to embrace God's image within me, listening for the echoes of eternity and Trinity that the Holy Spirit mediates to and through me. Perhaps in this example I want to win the argument to augment my sense of self or to get revenge for all the ways I feel I am being misunderstood or mistreated. But the more I notice my own assumptions and desires and determine to think beyond them, the more my capacity grows to join with God in his loving purposes for both myself and the other person.

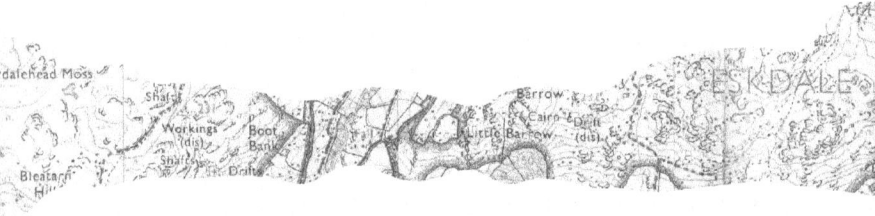

Looking beyond my faith map

Earlier we noted that the finite, defended-self wants a well-defined faith map that we can shape for ourselves. We want this because it keeps us feeling like we are in control, in the driving seat, even though we know we are dealing with a God who is infinitely greater than we are. But Jesus invites us in our humanity to look at our journey of faith from a much wider (and perhaps less controllable) spiritual perspective – to continue our pilgrimage beyond the familiar, what we know and can contain.

We see this in the way that the Bible is put together. Much in the Bible is well defined and has been formulated over the ages into doctrine and statements of belief, like the Nicene Creed agreed in AD381. These statements, and to some extent the scriptures from which they are derived, offer us a degree of certainty – something to hold on to.

However, the Bible is also full of truths, concepts and images that point beyond that which we can fully understand, grasp or even envisage; for example, many of the prophetic visions in the Old Testament (e.g.

Isaiah or Ezekiel) or the New Testament book of Revelation. What a timely reminder that our pursuit of certainty will always be thwarted by our finite capacity to engage with the quintessential 'otherness' of truth, dimensions that frustrate our vice-like grasp.

> As the heavens are higher than the earth,
>   so are my ways higher than your ways
>   and my thoughts than your thoughts.
> ISAIAH 55:9

In his Lent reflections on the Psalms, Patrick Woodhouse (former canon of Wells Cathedral) comments on this continuing pilgrimage to which we are all called in this regard:

> Every human being – even if they become deaf to it – is called to travel beyond what he or she knows, in search of a Reality that is unknown, but of which, because we are human, we have an intuitive sense. To be a Pilgrim is to go in search of this ultimate Reality, for in encountering it more fully we sense we will find our life.[82]

Entering a process through which we can enlarge our vision and begin to embrace a perspective that looks beyond the landscape we are used to travelling does not have to be abrupt or an impossible 'mountain to climb'. It can start with something relatively small and simple.

Widening out my map

Take my (Mary's) experience with my great-uncle Jim. The small town where I grew up was only two miles square. It felt safe and secure and represented my whole world emotionally and psychologically. I never considered how the world looked or might appear beyond that context and, in my childish state, I guess I wasn't really that interested either. Until the day Uncle Jim offered to take my brother and I up in his small four-seater plane. Having never been in any kind of airplane before,

I was enthralled by how quickly, as we lifted off the ground, the wider landscape spread out before me, situating the size and scope of my little town against the significantly larger backdrop of all the towns surrounding us. Much changed for me that day as my geographical horizons were exploded in an instant. I realised that it had strangely expanded my perspective on both my world and the wider world exponentially. Of course, today we'd simply use Google Earth to gain the same perspective.

Essentially, just as Uncle Jim introduced me to a bigger picture of a landscape I had always taken for granted, so we too are invited to explore a bigger picture of God and our Christian faith map, prompting ways of seeing the ordinary parts of our lives with fresh eyes.

Why don't we apply this to 'worship' to see what happens?

First, as I mention the act of worship, I wonder what instinctive images come to mind. Singing songs or hymns with sincere passion? Participation in weekly acts of confession, contrition or sacramental liturgy? Taking a vow to live a life of poverty or be devoted to full-time ministry? Thinking about how you might, in your own life, replicate Mary's extravagant act of devotion in breaking the alabaster jar of perfume over Jesus' feet?

These are some common ideas of worship, and of course you might have others. So far so good.

But let's extend the map a bit further and look beyond the usual or traditional. How might I also worship God by being the sort of employee at work who makes a deliberate point of practising integrity in all my business dealings (Proverbs 16:8)? Or by taking time to honour my own parents as they grow older (Ephesians 6:1) and endeavouring not to 'exasperate my children' (Ephesians 6:4) by taking my personal feelings of anger out on them? What would worship look like as a I resolve to honour God's work of creation through small acts of mindful stewardship (Deuteronomy 11:12)? Or act out of deep gratitude to God by deciding to welcome a refugee to live as part of my family (Leviticus 19:34)? Are these not also 'acts of worship'?

If I am committed to living in a consistently God-centric way, any surrender of my own immediate comfort, preference or inclination cultivates a different outlook, a different heart, a different expected outcome. This inevitably impacts what I think and do beyond my Christian community in the workplace or social action, for example. And it thus weaves worship into the very fabric of my life – above and beyond the formal communal moments I may experience on a Sunday (Micah 6:8).

On this basis we might expect our perception of other common landmarks on the Christian landscape to be multidimensional as well. So, let's consider 'mission', an activity of the earliest form of church, rightly and traditionally requiring some degree of verbal articulation about the good news of Christ. But according to LICC (referenced in the previous chapter), this is only one of six different ways we can authentically be involved in the mission of God to extend his kingdom. Other equally valid callings include modelling Godly character in all our human interactions, moulding culture to influence what happens in our families, workplaces or communities, and being a mouthpiece for truth and justice where we perceive its lack.[83]

Engaging therefore with all our usual landmarks of sacred places and rhythms of worship, mission, Christian community and ministry may start to look different when we give ourselves permission to look beyond our initial understandings of them. A reimagined landscape of faith means we might still expect to see God in all those places, but perhaps now we also able to perceive how God is still God beyond those borders. If nothing else, it opens up the possibility that we may run into him or notice his remarkable activity just as meaningfully elsewhere. As James Finley recognises: 'Sometimes you need a holy place to help you recognise the holiness of every place. You need a holy time to recognise the holiness of all time. You need to eat a holy meal to realise the holiness of all meals.'[84]

And that's the point. We've observed that whatever kind of map we hold, however evaluated and whatever navigational instruments we use, the sheer size and scope of God, God's love, God's plans and purposes, alongside the staggering dimensions of God's universe, will always be bigger than our capacity to crystalise or formulate. This is the inevitable consequence of following the God of the infinite, the God we only know because of what he's revealed to us. And that puts me firmly in my place when I am tempted to assume I know everything about Christian living.

Gazing God-wards

In an effort to graduate beyond our earth-bound perception, let's turn from our reflections *on* God to gaze more directly *towards* God. Like Copernicus and Galileo, who both observed evidence and exercised their imagination, let's attempt to acquire a different scale of worldview altogether, an out-of-this-world, cosmologically focused one. Training our gaze towards the heavens is the very opposite of the 'selection and emphasis' approach because now the picture is so gargantuan that it's hard even to work out what to focus on.

On Christmas Day 2022 I (Charles) was most excited about the launch of the James Webb Space Telescope (JWST). As we tucked into our turkey, I was furtively following its progress as it successfully set off towards its parking spot at a Lagrangian point beyond the moon. My excitement wasn't about the spectacle of the journey itself, but the potential that the JWST held to radically change our perspective on the universe – if it worked! And so far, it has not disappointed. Month by month new revelations about God's creation on a cosmic scale emerge from NASA's website, and the world's leading physicists are struggling to keep up.

It all points to a reality that stretches well beyond how I perceive the finite everyday world. As I look at the JWST images online and gaze through my own personal, somewhat smaller, telescope at the awesome features to be found even within our neighbourhood galaxy, it somehow reminds me of my true place in the universe. But rather than just feeling small or insignificant, I'm encouraged that there is much more to understand and experience about God when we endeavour to look beyond our own assumptions or horizons. If all creation is an expression of God, then I feel part of that expression, along with all of humanity (Psalm 19; Psalm 8; Romans 1).

Stargazing also helps me to appreciate Jesus as the transcendent Christ, the co-creator and sustainer of everything (John 1; Colossians 1) and this gazing at the 'cosmic Christ' helps me to go beyond my normal approaches to prayer. As I contemplate the Lord's glory, it brings me face to face with the reality that my defended-self is not all there is to me. In some hard-to-fathom way, I carry the image of God. And as we saw in chapter 6, it reminds me that I am certainly not at the centre of things. The vast universe of time and space that exists beyond my life or generation beckons me to extend the horizons of my imagination into what can only be described as unknown territory.

Embracing the transition

At this point our faith map ceases to be solely one that's carefully constructed from our tradition, beliefs or culture, because our map becomes the pattern and posture of Jesus Christ himself. In holding together the tension of human existence with a spiritual perspective, Jesus shows us where to look and how to live – the finite colliding with the infinite, that 'beyond' perspective informing our living in 'the now'.

Jesus began to answer the question 'Is this all there is?' in bringing the 'now' and 'not yet' spheres together through his post-resurrection appearances on the Emmaus Road, in the upper room and on the beach with Peter. At this point Jesus was somehow both the same and different. Even his closest friends didn't recognise him at first. He spoke, he ate, he bore marks of his violent death, but he also walked through walls, coming and going suddenly without warning or need for physical transportation. Jesus was a confusing pattern of the recognisable mixed in with the other-worldly, confirming the 'beyond realities' of which he had spoken so often. He was also a paradox of unimaginable proportions, which demanded that his disciples make a radical exchange of well-established authoritative perspectives for previously unthinkable new realities. Again and again, even before his resurrection, Jesus signalled this paradigm shift by using his famous refrain 'You have heard that it was said… [code for every Jewish listener to recall the unchanging truths of the Torah] but I tell you' (Matthew 5:38–48).

It seemed for the disciples that in many ways their old map had run out. To have any hope of navigating the new landscape they faced, they would have to get hold of a Jesus-shaped pattern beyond their old-school map of rules and rituals. They would need to learn to read the landscape and the signs of the times (Acts 2:19) by different means. And God sent his Holy Spirit to help them with this 'eternal perspective' – to enable them to navigate their present life and mission with an eye to the eternal realms that Jesus had made accessible.

God's Holy Spirit is also given to us as his followers in the 21st century as (among other things) a guide to help us to connect with the eternal God. As we have considered how we might look beyond our current image of God, of ourselves, of others and of the map of faith we have used thus far, my sense is that these all hinge to a great extent on learning to love God for God's sake. Not for what God can do for us but simply for who God is.

This takes us to the place within ourselves where we meet most deeply with God: heart to heart, soul to soul. Our critical analysis and epistemology (chapter 2), our discernment of feelings and surrendering of desires (chapter 7) have helped us to plot a course through our landscape of faith using our rational faculties and emotional responses. But we are also invited to change our perspective (chapter 6) by looking beyond these finite capacities to engage more deeply with our infinite God.

How then might we approach that? As we've seen, our rational thoughts and emotional responses normally dominate our minds with the self-concerned narratives of our defended-self if we let them. The discipline of Centring Prayer (see Appendix on p. 246) can help us to move beyond these. In Centring Prayer, we learn to let our thoughts and emotions rest. We gently but firmly refuse to let them define the boundaries of who we are, and don't give them the airtime to completely dominate our awareness. This is another way to 'take every thought captive' (2 Corinthians 10:5), adding to the process we explored in the previous chapter. It allows us to move beyond our thoughts and emotions into the inner space that silence affords, and to extend our awareness of the mystery of God we are groping our way towards.

And yet, even if we carve out islands of God-infused solitude and silence within our hectic everyday life so that we might feel close to God, we can remain self-centred. I long to experience the love of God; it is vital to my very existence ('As the deer pants for streams of water, so my soul pants for you, my God' – Psalm 42:1). But love flows in both directions. I naturally want to feel God's welcome invitation and slake my thirst with living water – that is loving God for my sake. But self-less love will also love God for God's sake, will welcome the lover of my soul with delight purely for who that lover is. In that sense, I do want to be the sponge, saturated with God, but that can only happen if I am myself submerged in the vast ocean that is God. And so Centring

Prayer provides me with an opportunity to look beyond my defended-self and exercise self-emptying love that looks only towards the other.

It seems to me that in the end, our defended-self will have to submit to the dust of death anyway, whereafter we will enjoy the fullness of being drawn into God's presence. And so, this practice allows us a foretaste perhaps, a glimpse of what's to come. And this is not solely a matter for our prayer-life. It undergirds and energises the embodiment of love that God intends for us to manifest in the here and now as we are invited to 'in humility value others above ourselves', looking to their interests in practical, everyday ways (Philippians 2:3–4).

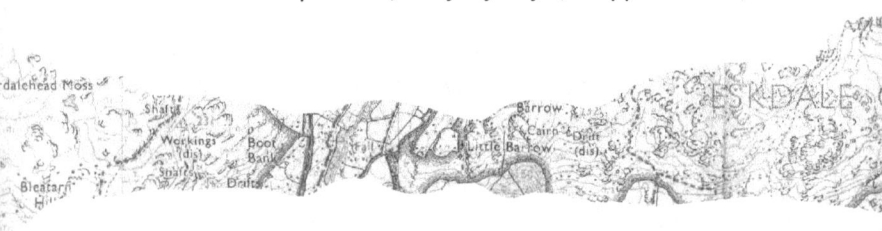

The ultimate pilgrimage

This leads us to the final landscape we have to traverse towards the end of our physical existence as we approach the afterlife. It is such a significant stage of our journey and yet one for which there is also no clear map. Despite the biblical imagery and promises we hold dear in Psalm 23, this last leg of our journey can naturally cause us to wobble. Even the concept of eternity, of time and space never ending, can evoke a strange feeling within us simply because we just can't imagine it. Our finite minds run out of capacity to process such an idea logically. But this is also where our spiritual practices can help us to in some ways make that leap, to explore the contours of our eternal nature, which Martin Laird suggests is like a 'an ocean of light'.[85]

When Bear Grylls leaves his hapless celebrities without map or compass, he still makes sure they know in which direction to proceed and how to work out what that is, sometimes with the obscurest of skills, like looking for moss on the side of a tree because it will grow mostly on the north face where it's cooler and moist. Navigating this stage of our journey can feel a bit like that for us.

I would like to feel similarly equipped as I begin to reach the end of my journey, because if I'm honest, I don't know what to expect about aging or what my last days on earth will entail. Many Christians find it hard to even consider slowing down or withdrawing from busy working lives, let alone think of retiring or being forced to let go of 'business as usual' through physical or mental incapacity of some sort.

Are there ways I might prepare? How could this apparently less-than-attractive stage of life also help me to grow spiritually in the now?

What living well can teach us about dying well

As it happens, simply following the natural human stages of aging, diminishing, weakening and surrendering can be enriching, if we have eyes to perceive and interpret those natural signs, like moss growing on the north face of a tree.

As Kathleen Dowling Singh suggests, aging offers specific opportunities to recognise how attached we have always been to beauty, recognition, respect, influence and bodies that function on command – in short, assumptions about what makes life worth living or how 'things should be'. Our sense of identity as we age is no longer so clear: who am I now without my strength, the roles I played in professional or social contexts, or other forms of validation and participation? Aging means that we may need help with the simplest most ignoble tasks and find ourselves at the mercy of others' kindness. Any kind of indignity feels undesirable, and the young struggle to imagine being in this state. We all love to feel special, but age levels that in many ways.[86]

I (Mary) was speaking to a friend as she prepared to retire after 35 years in the same profession and, not surprisingly, she felt terrified about her future, imagining how the loss of community, colleagues, connection and purpose would bear down on her, let alone having to navigate all those hours of what she assumed would be empty, directionless time. When asked what her fears were based on, she realised she was attached to a sense of control (which her job with its regular routine and familiarity provided for her) and also to feeling significant in her contributions to society. She was in effect asking herself, 'Is this all there is?' What could possibly be beyond my vision, my grasp that's worth going through a turbulent transition to get there?

We imagined together what might motivate a skydiver to throw themselves out of a plane travelling at 10,000 feet in the air? What could possibly get them over the threshold, especially on their maiden attempt, and how might they prepare for that seemingly kamikaze moment. And the only thing we could come up with was that their vision for the exhilaration of free-flight once in the air outweighed the gripping fear of casting themselves into that void. In other words, they were able to see beyond their natural desire for self-preservation to experience something of greater worth.

If only there was a satnav to help us navigate this bewildering stage of life, and that which lies beyond.

Interestingly, previous generations of cartographers have attempted to chart precisely that. Returning to the cartographical exhibition at the Bodleian we mentioned in chapter 1, one of the most interesting parts concerned how one might travel towards death and beyond, 'mapping the seemingly unmappable'. This was the exhibit commentary:

> How do you reach the afterlife without a map? Many of the world's cultures and belief systems use maps to guide the way and describe sacred topographies that are far beyond the terrestrial world we inhabit. Such maps can offer a graphic representation of the beginning of the world and its end, but what unites most of them is a belief that life is a journey that requires spiritual as well as geographical orientation. Many of

these maps when displayed in churches and temples encouraged the faithful in their spiritual pilgrimage through this world and into the next one. Death is not the end, but only one element in the individual's quest for salvation, enlightenment, rebirth or even oblivion.[87]

Humans have always been interested in figuring out what the afterlife might look like and how to 'get there'. These 'sacred topographies' pointed to hoped-for realities far beyond what could possibly be verified in any material sense. But their existence is an indication of our ongoing interest over the centuries, as well as demonstrating a creative use of our human powers of imagination.

The Bodleian exhibits included: a map depicting the Tibetan Wheel of Life, showing the cycle of transmigration and rebirth in the soul's quest for release (nirvana); a Jain map of the 16th–17th centuries drawn to show the realms where humanity dwells, beyond which lay the spiritual realms – an aide to help those following this ancient Indian religion navigate their way from one to the other; and even had a copy of Dante's Hell as described in *The Divine Comedy* (1308–20), showing Hell lying beneath Jerusalem, with Mount Purgatory at its antipodes.

These imaginative representations of death and the afterlife as they were understood at the time underline the fact that even a best guess about eternity could only ever represent an incomplete reflection of whatever God has ordained. The blank bits at the edges of many imaginary maps in film and literature are often denoted by the inscription 'Here be dragons'. Although this only seems to have appeared on one medieval map ('*Hic Sunt Dracones*' inscribed in Latin on the Lenox Globe, c. 1503–07). But it does give a nod to a sort of universal acknowledgement that there is a point beyond human understanding where our certainty and imagination give out, leaving only shadowy speculations about what life beyond our human senses or reason might contain.

I wonder whether what we most fear in death is the end of the 'me as I know myself to be'. This is a hard thing for anyone to get to grips with.

As Dowling Singh so aptly observes when representing the bewilderment people might feel as they face imminent death: 'But, I've never done this before…', 'I've never died before', 'What happens?', 'What do I do?'[88] About the outcome of our demise, she recognises:

> Our eyeglasses will be useless to anyone else. Someone will cut down the roses we planted and tended so carefully. Everything we are concerned about in this very moment will not matter at all: bills, quarrels, sensed inadequacies… fears, vanities, hopes… what to have for dinner. They will not matter at all. We leave self behind. Death is a letting go of this sense of self-reference.[89]

So perhaps in anticipation of death, our burning existential question might be: 'Who will I be then?'

My (Mary's) sister, who is a chaplain to the dying in hospices and hospitals, reports that many Christians nearing death feel an urgency about asking forgiveness from God to absolve them of guilt for unresolved situations. Some are possessed by a sudden desire to 'make things right' with an estranged friend or family member. These typical behaviours don't address what kind of form we might imagine we will take, but they do confirm how our sense of self continues to be intrinsically linked to our relationship with others, in the now as we begin to stare into the abyss of the beyond.

Taking our heads out of the sand

You might be surprised to learn just how many Christians keep their heads firmly in the sand and altogether avoid thinking about the end of their earthly existence. The prevailing narrative in Christian communities of the life we are promised beyond the grave can be severely tested when we are called upon to contemplate our own death or that of someone we love. I (Mary) have noticed through my own recent health scares that even facing the possibility of a terminal illness can turn a well-thought-through theology of a glorious future hope into a naked spirituality of fear and uncertainty. As it threatened to do for my friend Jess.

Jess was dying of cancer and was facing it with characteristic courage and acceptance, but she was deeply troubled about how to adequately prepare for her inevitable end. Around that time, I had begun having dreams about the house I grew up in, and I dreamt that I kept discovering new rooms in my house, rooms that hadn't been noticed before, but apparently had been there all along. There were rooms that had windows in unnoticed places which afforded huge panoramic views that seemed to spin off into eternity. As I stumbled around them in my dreams with an air of excitement and adventure, I began to feel less restricted and more peaceful. And upon waking, those images and feelings remained, seared on to my mind and heart.

So much so that in our final visits I shared my vivid dream-imaginings with Jess. I know that these kinds of dreams can often symbolise an expanding sense of our inner world as we mature spiritually, but their unusual theme and emphasis caused me to wonder whether another potential interpretation of unexplored spaces might be related to Jesus' promise that 'my Father's house has many rooms' (John 14:2).

On reflection, Jess decided that she might spend time, as her earthly time drew to a close, using her spiritual imagination to 'declutter her rooms' of both the trivial and the no-longer-as-important. By honestly identifying that which she was naturally inclined to cling on to, she resolved instead to surrender it, thus leaving space for furnishings of an eternal nature, such as love, creativity and beauty. It was, I suppose, a way of wiping the windows clean to enhance her view of the dimension beyond. We both hoped that by investing her imaginative energies in this way, these spaces, embedded deep in her soul and informed by her lifelong relationship with God, would eventually become familiar enough to feel recognisable and so wholly welcoming when she finally arrived in God's presence.

I deeply grieved the loss of my beautiful friend Jess when she died and have encountered the same overwhelming tsunami of feelings subsequently in losing my parents and other precious loved ones. Having spent some time volunteering in a local bereavement support group, I've come to realise that any experience of loss or bereavement can run a cannon ball through the most robust faith. Indeed, through our very being. This is partly because losing those with whom we are so intimately intertwined can profoundly challenge or compromise our own sense of being and purpose, leaving gaping holes, dangling ends and unanswerable questions.

Yet, the one thing that Jess and I discovered together was that to make a daily habit of surrendering what we cling to so tightly in this life seems to open up a mysterious portal in our thinking and feeling. While being fully grateful for and present to both the trivial and the significant in our present life, at the same time the spectre of a thoroughly different kind of landscape vies for our attention, a lighthouse ever beckoning us towards another vibrant shore.

I don't know if you've ever considered this but those who loved Jesus had to come to terms with two bouts of devastating loss in a very short time. Filled with despair after Jesus died, a seeming end of his story and thus their story with him signalled a first loss. Briefly reversed by the unexpected joy of having him back, the second act of letting him go was tied up in Jesus' return to his Father. Never mind that the gap between these two events was only a few weeks, spiritually it feels like it was a mile wide! Their first grief was doubtless based on despair coupled with a sense of finality, but the second, having perceived something beyond death, appears to have generated new-found purpose and energy. It seems that this glimpse of the beyond informed every part of the disciples' day-to-day reality from then onwards.

In life or death, God continues to hold all the mysteries of the universe. As I deliberately look beyond what I understand to be my life towards the mystery of my destiny in God, how can I let this inform how I live my life before I reach that final milestone?

Allowing eternity to inform the present

When the process that people go through in both loss and dying is examined in detail, we can see a number of parallels between this and that which is experienced as we travel through the successive stages of faith (see chapter 4). Confusion in transition, desperation to get back to any previous sense of normality, frustration with our own sense of powerlessness, inevitably resulting in common reactions of denial, anger, bargaining, depression and acceptance – all of which have been so ably documented by Elisabeth Kübler-Ross.[90] These are understandable responses of our defended-self to a situation in which it is clearly terminally threatened. Indeed, any kind of loss, whether that be involuntarily losing a significant relationship, role or job, dwelling place or community, can set off a similar chain reaction as we sense what we believe to be our fundamental identity, purpose or future to be in jeopardy.

But if we let go of what has driven us to take a defensive stance (our deep desires), we can also let go of what we are losing or have lost in our latter years and realise that our personal interior life is but a drop in the ocean of God's divine being. In spiritual terms, we may find we are now navigating towards a much larger reality, one which stretches away into eternal sensibilities, while still living in this finite reality. Much better that we cooperate in the present than continue to live in denial until one day life, or rather death, takes us by surprise and we are not ready. Or to put it another way through one sage's observation: 'Death is a mirror in which all of life is reflected.'[91]

I find this call to keep the end of my days in mind highly provocative, not in some sort of morbidly hopeless fashion, but rather as a prompt to allow the infinite to direct the priorities of the finite. We are, after all, a people with eternity set in our hearts (Ecclesiastes 3:11). And I suppose it is a comfort on one level that at least someone holds all the complexity, mystery and transitional turbulence of this dimension in their eternal hands.

But it does remind me of the immortal line uttered in the 1978 film *Superman*. Superman catches Lois Lane in mid-air as she falls from a stricken helicopter with the reassuring words 'Don't worry, I've got you.' But rather than this reassuring her, Lois Lane looks down at the distant street landscape below and exclaims in panic, 'Yes, but who's got *you*?'[92]

This may be a little like how we feel when we think about dying. We rightly predict that we are unlikely to feel in control, and we may struggle to fully embrace such an unnerving state. Even with a newly acquired taste for God to really be God, to rejoice in a God that stays 'just out of my reach', a God who has the right to surprise and confound me, I reckon it will still be very hard to completely trust someone's greater power over my life and death, to let go or endeavour to 'look beyond' all that I've known of my earthly existence, even while entrusting myself to those majestic, loving arms. This really is unmappable territory.

And so, let's end with some final questions to ponder.

Taking a long-term view

If you fast forward your way to the moment of your death, what does your own faith narrative include at that point? Not the narrative of your Christian community or friends and mentors, but yours. In other words, how do you imagine the end of your journey on earth might go?

And how do you feel about facing that? What might you need to adjust or inaugurate today in the light of that coming reality?

How could this longer-term perspective help you to grow in spiritual maturity in the present moment?

Whatever you feel at this moment, consider what it might be like to arrive at a destination that you were always meant to find. When you won't have to perceive through a glass darkly any longer, but instead have the full-on technicolour experience of gazing into the face of Christ. Knowing your God and yourself as you have always been known (1 Corinthians 13:12). What are your hopes for that final confirmation, the consummation of your faith journey? And lastly, how does that perspective motivate you to live your present life in Christ to the full?

Maybe there is understandable fear or anxiety as you anticipate the end. Or perhaps there is also a strange kind of curiosity or a sense of moving towards a greater existence. As those who had glimpsed Aslan's country or the Real Narnia kept advocating in C.S. Lewis' *The Last Battle*, we too are encouraged to 'Keep going – farther up and farther in!'[93]

Epilogue

We (Mary and Charles) wonder what you are thinking as we approach the end of our exploration together. Since our initial premise was that cartography represented a storied vehicle, we hope that using the map metaphor has helped you to examine your story in more visual and memorable ways. Like our friends on their day of pilgrimage in the Lake District, we all need the chance from time to time to step back, review the map we've been using either consciously or unconsciously and interpret the journey that map has facilitated. To critically evaluate where we are, how we got here, what it all means and where we hope to be going in the future, before our journey transitions into its final phase.

For it is in understanding the map we've been using that we discover our hidden assumptions about the way we want the world or our Christian journey to be. A complicated and lifelong pursuit indeed, but one that frees us to seek, recognise and accept God's version of these realities. It is in cultivating greater self-awareness that we are freed to move beyond our self-centric inner narratives, competing desires and besetting sins – elements of our being which otherwise could obstruct how we allow Christ to fully infuse our souls and empower us to become Christ to those around us. It is in identifying in which stage of faith we currently dwell that enables us to look beyond the dark valleys and difficulties towards their God-given purpose and value.

This is a posture or worldview open to anyone, regardless of where they are on their map – one that enables disciples of all kinds to see their journey not only as 'soul-saving', but as a series of 'soul-making' or 'soul-enriching' episodes. As our epistemological sources widen out, our desire for certainty expands to the hope and excitement of perceiving and engaging with infinite horizons of meaning and mystery.

We find ourselves worshipping both within but also beyond Christian communities and church-centric activity, through all of life. We seek God through contemplating earthly creation, cosmic dimensions, and the riches of solitude and silence. And we discover a selfless joy in connecting with the huge diversity of people on the earth that God has created.

Through this inner journey that invites our impoverished, finite self to join the self-emptying trinitarian dance, we discover the freedom to release the aroma of Christ into his world. And in that sense, we can retrieve some traditional landmarks of church and mission, and place them firmly back on to our faith map, but perhaps now tinged with a new perspective about their significance, provoking fresh motivation to make our contribution.

All this begins with noticing how you imagine God, yourself, the Christian journey and your own place in it. And then resolving to carry on reimagining all that until you need imagine no more. Because annoying signs of aging, distressing experiences of diminishment and weakness, crippling pain-filled illness, devastating and unwelcome bouts of loss, the finality of dying and death, though frightening and often ungovernable, do not represent the final word on the value or purpose of your life or mine. There are realities which far surpass even those seemingly life-defining experiences, things to come that are eminently, incomparably, infinitely beyond every stage or circumstance we will ever encounter. Realities which God has planned for those who are centred in him.

We have offered many ideas in the pages of this book but certainly don't claim to have the only or definitive perspective on what we assume the Christian journey to be. We understand that our knowledge, however well researched, is in the end limited and skewed, because we too are mindful that there will always be new pathways to discover on our faith maps. There are new pages to unfold, new revelations that throw shadows at old ones.

But we are also firmly committed to surrendering the idea that God should be there to serve our preferred agenda, theology or spiritual patterns. Isn't that something of what the concept of God represents – believing in a power or a being, however personal or impersonal, who exists *beyond* the understanding and authority of the human mind? Here too we see the value of simple imagining.

How then might *you* continue to reimagine the landscape of your faith as your journey unfolds? You might find encouragement from Paul's perspective:

> Now to him who is able to do immeasurably more than all we ask or imagine, according to his power that is at work within us, to him be glory in the church and in Christ Jesus throughout all generations, forever and ever! Amen.
> EPHESIANS 3:20–21

Appendix 1
Some key contributors to spiritual formation

Theology and spirituality

Sometimes these two words are used interchangeably, but although theology and spirituality are two sides of the same coin, they represent different but equally crucial aspects of faith.

On the one hand, Christian theology concerns the study of God, which demands that we learn how to discern, recognise and proclaim orthodox beliefs (an intrinsic part of any Christian epistemological pursuit – explained more fully in a minute). Theology also covers such areas as Christology (understanding how the life and atoning work of Jesus forms core Christian doctrines), ecclesiology (the purpose and nature of church life, church history), morality (how we discern right from wrong), and exegesis and hermeneutics (good interpretive and application principles).

Christian spirituality, on the other hand, is the common human experience of engaging with something greater than us, whom Christians see as the Trinitarian God (Father, Son and Holy Spirit). Spiritual thinking and engagement link our finite, physical, sensory experience as human beings with the infinite made known to us through Jesus Christ. And through this connection we find significance and purpose as part of the unfolding of the much wider life of the universe.

Spirituality, as it is understood and practised in the 21st century, may address holy living, supernatural phenomena, cultivating soul friends or mentors, and emotional or psychological development. Since modern theology has also begun to include pastoring, counselling and ministry training, we find the lines being increasingly blurred between these two disciplines, a Venn diagram of overlapping circles. As spirituality builds on, resides within and enhances frameworks of comprehensive theology, so it promotes substantial changes within the inner person.

Epistemology and psychology

A word on how epistemology fits into all the above. It's a word that we may not use very often, but it's an activity that we may engage in unconsciously every day. Simply put, it is the process by which we decide what we believe to be real or true. Epistemological enquiry involves weighing up and interpreting information, knowledge and wisdom that we receive through a variety of means to establish what we accept as truth or error. This process, whether formal or informal, conscious or subconscious, informs all our personal and communal religious, philosophical and political belief systems.

The ways in which psychological development contributes to our spiritual growth are possibly less familiar to many Christians. But when you consider that psychology is simply the study of how human beings work, mentally, emotionally and even physiologically (how the body influences and/or is influenced by our thoughts and emotions), it makes sense to actively engage with the wisdom offered by this field of study. Especially when we become aware how often we are acting out the dynamics of our psychological being every day through our beliefs, attitudes, behaviours and choices, whether intentionally or not. Certain dimensions of both psychology and epistemology are therefore always playing active roles in our spiritual formation, though not always visible or obvious to us.

The value of the imagination

As we are recommending the art of reimagining our landscapes of faith, it might be helpful to think about the use of imagination in general. Some might be suspicious of this most unique mental activity, because imagination can be considered childish – associated perhaps with the imaginary, as in dragons or fairies. But the human imagination is not only a great gift of God, it's also an aspect of being made in the image of God. Like an artist, musician or writer who begin their endeavours with a 'blank page', we see God's creative imagination at work when he created the universe from nothing.

We use our imagination every day in all sorts of ways, to conceive of things that could, but possibly do not yet, exist. We tell stories, make films, and construct new inventions and technologies to invite other people to experience what we have first imagined in our own heads. This is also an important part of map-making. And we use metaphors (figures of speech that evoke mental symbols or images) to help people better understand what we're trying to communicate. Try reading Jesus' parables, or indeed any novel or story, without 'seeing' images that they evoke on the inner screen of your mind.

How does using our imagination facilitate spiritual growth? Spiritual directors often find that disciples grow more significantly if they learn to notice the images that are present inside their minds and hearts and then reflect on how this affects their engagement with God. Not just in times of quiet meditation, but especially in the midst of the reality of their lives, both joyous and difficult.

For instance, we consistently employ our imaginations when visualising scenarios we fear, such as being attacked, suffering painful diseases or harm coming to loved ones. Most anxiety is based on these 'videos' which whirl around our heads, provoking emotional responses to situations which haven't even happened and may never happen. Of course, this influences our sense of need for God and what we bring to God in prayer. And it also takes imagination to put ourselves in someone else's shoes, to make empathy possible, to 'rejoice with those who rejoice; mourn with those who mourn' (Romans 12:15).

You will find that throughout this book we invite you to use your imagination in reflecting on where you find yourself on your spiritual journey. See Appendix 2 that follows.

Appendix 2
Sketching out your faith journey

LEGEND: some ideas for the landscape of your faith journey

GO	Embarking on your faith journey	⚠	The going gets tough
→	Finding the path	P	Taking a break
⚠	Discerning dangers	⚠	Falling over
T	Taking a wrong turn	⚠	Getting lost
⊙	Going round in circles	REDUCE SPEED NOW	Reflecting on your journey
Diversion	Getting distracted	GIVE WAY	Letting go

Appendix 3
Spiritual practices

Examen: noticing our inner narratives

Examen was introduced in the 16th century by St Ignatius of Loyola as part of his wider spiritual exercises, to grow self-awareness and reflect on how God might be moving in the course of everyday life. It has been used fruitfully by many Christians of various traditions over the centuries since.

It's best to begin using this practice at the end of the day to help you look back at what happened and how you responded both inside and out. Once you've become familiar with Examen, you can use it in shortened form to reflect on a particular experience or incident, shortly after it happens if necessary. Overall, regular use should help you to become more discerning about what's going on beneath the surface of your thoughts and emotions and to connect that with your spiritual and prayer life.

Examen can take many specific forms, and the following is tailored to help you work through the issues we are addressing in this book.

Stepping through Examen

Prepare
Take some slow, deep breaths to help you to relax and become 'present' in the moment. Begin by giving God thanks and ask him to highlight the things he wants you to notice as you pray and listen.

Review your day
Remember your day, reliving any significant moments and focusing on those that seem most important. Do any particular thoughts or emotions stand out?

Notice the movements within you and the actions you took
When did you give or receive love today? When might you have withheld love? What were you feeling at those different moments?

Notice the felt presence or absence of God
When did you feel most connected to God and when least? What was happening at those times?

Pray
Close by talking to God about what you have noticed and asking for God's help as you look forward to tomorrow. What did you learn about yourself… and God?

If you like using apps, you might try out *Reimagining the Examen* for a wider range of ways to use this reflective practice.

Welcoming Prayer: owning what we feel

Welcoming Prayer is a more recent spiritual practice than Examen and also comes in different forms. In chapter 7 we explore the use of this prayer in two parts, and we have indicated that division in the following.

Welcoming Prayer is best used to help you to recognise and handle negative emotions. By using it regularly you can learn to embrace what you feel rather than try to supress it (part 1), recognising that your emotions are a part of who you are; and then to engage with God by entrusting him with the underlying source of that emotion (part 2). In between these two parts, it's helpful for you to have recognised the underlying desire that's making you feel as you do, using the next practice, Self-Lectio.

Stepping through Welcoming Prayer

Part 1
Prepare
Take some slow, deep breaths to help you to relax and become 'present' in the moment. Begin by giving God thanks and remember his deep love for you as you work with this negative emotion.

Recognise and name the emotion
Take some time to reflect on the negative emotion that you are carrying and try to name it. It may be obvious, or you may simply feel a sense of unease that's harder to pin down. It can be helpful to ask yourself where in your body you are sensing that emotion. We often carry anger in our gut, fear as a tightness of chest or throat, and shame can cause us to hug ourselves, to look down and 'go in' on ourselves.

Welcome the emotion
Now this sounds a bit strange! Why would you want to welcome a bad feeling? But let's be clear here, we don't mean welcome the cause of you feeling bad but welcome the emotion itself. After all it's you that's feeling it, and in that sense it's a part of who you are. Instead of running

from that feeling, try meeting it face on. Offer it some hospitality and love rather than pushing it away or judging it to be unacceptable if that's what you might normally do.

Part 2
Surrender the desire behind that emotion to God
Once you have understood the unfulfilled desire that sits beneath your negative emotion, use this final step to surrender both the emotion and its underlying desire to God. You might find the following wording helpful:

> Loving God, thank you that you love me just as I am. *As I find my myself embraced by you, I let go of my shame and entrust my need for approval to you.*

> Loving God, thank you that you are with me. *As I sense your presence with me, I let go of my fear and entrust my need for security to you.*

> Loving God, thank you that you are in control. *As I sense your good purposes for me, I let go of my anger and entrust my need for control to you.*

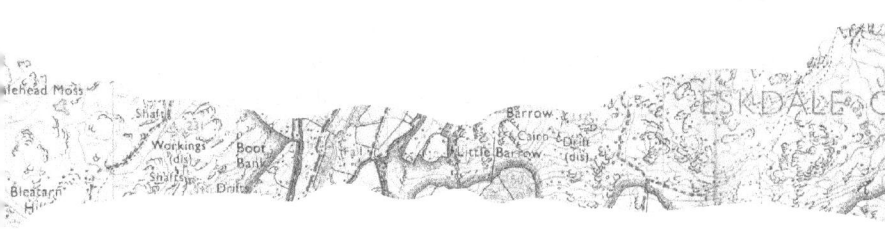

Lectio Divina and Self-Lectio: discerning our unfulfilled desires

Our next prayer practice takes us back to the sixth century, in which St Benedict introduced an approach to engaging with God as we read scripture reflectively. This practice, Lectio Divina, has been popularised through the app *Lectio 365* in recent years and in its original form includes four steps:

- **Reading** a passage slowly, perhaps out loud.
- **Reflecting** on anything that particularly struck you and reading that part again slowly.
- **Responding** to God by sharing your thoughts and feelings on this portion of scripture in prayer.
- **Resting** silently in God's presence.

Over the centuries, Lectio Divina has been adapted for use in different forms, for example, Visio Divina, in which the object of study is an inspiring image rather than words of scripture.

We encourage you to use Lectio Divina as you read the Bible, but for our purposes, we are going to use this 'Lectio' approach to help us engage with God as we reflect on the emotions and unfulfilled desires that motivate our thoughts and actions. Let's call this 'Self-Lectio', and in the steps that follow we assume that you are reflecting on a particular incident that has stirred some negative emotions in you. This form of reflection can help you with the process of noticing and surrendering your self-centredness and to entrust your legitimate needs to God.

The corresponding steps for this practice are as follows.

Stepping through a Self-Lectio

Prepare
Take some slow, deep breaths to help you to relax and become 'present' in the moment. Begin by giving God thanks and remember his deep love for you as you explore your inner self with God's help.

Read yourself in the moment: what happened and what were you feeling? Think back to the conversation or incident in question. Try to identify the most fundamental emotion. Brené Brown's *Atlas of the Heart* is very helpful in this regard.[94]

Reflect on what made you feel that way. Ask the Holy Spirit to help you discern any unfulfilled desire at the foundation of your emotion. In doing this, remember that:

- fear is often associated with an unfulfilled desire for safety or security
- shame is often associated with an unfulfilled desire for approval
- anger is often associated with an unfulfilled desire for a measure of control.

Of course, you can do the same with other emotions you might feel, such as sadness or disappointment.

Respond prayerfully. What do you want to say to God about that and what might God want to say to you? Talk with God about what you have noticed. If it's appropriate, you might also try Welcoming Prayer to help you to let go of any unfulfilled desires that you have identified.

Rest
Take some time now in an attitude of surrender simply to sit or stand in the presence of God, sharing silent fellowship and appreciating God's deep love for you and any others who may have been involved.

Centring Prayer: changing perspective

We'll spend more time introducing this prayer practice as it differs from what you may be used to, unless you are familiar with the contemplative tradition. Many ways of praying involve us voicing something to or listening for something from God. But what if we simply wanted to spend time with God? What if we spent time enjoying God's company in a wordless awareness of God's presence within and without us? A bit like two people sitting together on a park bench – saying nothing, but keenly aware of each other and sharing a close moment together.

Centring Prayer works in this space. It's a form of silent prayer in which we seek to quieten our scattered thoughts and desires in the still centre of the presence of God. Historically, Centring Prayer was brought to the attention of the modern church in the 1970s by a group of monks including Thomas Merton and Thomas Keating. But its roots go back many centuries before that to the anonymous writer of *The Cloud of Unknowing*[95] and the Benedictine monastic tradition in particular. While there is no record of Jesus practising Centring Prayer as such, he did encourage his disciples to do as he did and find a quiet place to pray. Some of the psalms also point us towards the value of quietening ourselves and silently waiting on God (e.g. Psalm 27; 132).

Centring Prayer helps us turn down the volume of our internal chatter and move our attention, our 'inner gaze', away from the demanding voice of our defended-self and towards an awareness of the presence of God. And by using this practice regularly in the quiet moment, we find our attention resting more naturally on God in the busyness of the day. In this way, Centring Payer can help our perspective on what happens to us in life to change its 'centre of gravity' from us to God.

On a practical note, most people find that it is very hard not to let your mind wander as you sit in silent prayer. That's okay. In the 21st century our attention has been kidnapped by the intrusive presence of constantly beckoning technology. Be kind to yourself! Whenever you find yourself distracted, simply return to a focus on God. You may find it helpful to choose a word or short phrase to use in these moments. Try something that has some clear devotional focus, such as *Jesus* or *love*, or it might be more a statement of intent such as *listen* or *behold*.

Stepping through Centring Prayer

Prepare
As you sit, take a few deep breaths. As you continue breathing slowly, perhaps offer a 'breath prayer': 'Our Father in heaven' on the in-breath and 'Hallowed be your name' on the out-breath.

Choose a sacred word
As you enter this time of silence, see if a word comes to mind. Mull it over – does it seem good to you? Choose your sacred word as the symbol of your invitation to God's presence and action within. Now that you have chosen a word, stay with it during this period of prayer. Use your word to direct the eyes of your heart towards God and to invite God's presence and action within.

Wait in the presence of God
Remain silently in this heart posture towards God. As you do that, inevitably thoughts, feelings and outside distractions will emerge. This is normal! Notice them, but don't engage them in conversation. Just gently return using your sacred word.

You might find this metaphor helpful. Imagine you are sitting on the bank of a slowly flowing river. On the river a number of boats are sailing past. And these boats represent your thoughts. You are tempted to jump on board and take the controls and sometimes you do. But once you realise where you are, you let go of the controls and return to the riverbank. You are content to sit quietly, letting each thought sail by.

Return
When you are ready to 'surface,' gently set your sacred word down and spend a few moments noticing what was going on within you as you spent that time in silent prayer.

Further resources

Top book recommendations

Brené Brown, *Atlas of the Heart: Mapping meaningful connection and the language of human experience* (Penguin Random House, 2021).

Janet O. Hagberg and Robert A. Guelich, *The Critical Journey: Stages in the life of faith* (Sheffield Publishing, 2005).

Alan Jamieson, *Chrysalis: The hidden transformation in the journey of faith* (Paternoster, 2008).

Peter Scazzero, *Emotionally Healthy Spirituality: It's impossible to be spiritually mature, while remaining emotionally immature* (Zondervan, 2014).

Curt Thompson, *The Soul of Shame: Retelling the stories we believe about ourselves* (IVP, 2015).

Other suggested reading

John Barton, *A History of the Bible: The book and its faiths* (Allen Lane, 2019).

David G. Benner, *Spirituality and the Awakening Self: The sacred journey of transformation* (Brazos Press, 2012).

Walter Brueggemann, *Spirituality of the Psalms* (Fortress Press, 2002).

Adele A. Calhoun, *Spiritual Disciplines Handbook: Practices that transform us* (IVP, 2015).

Joanna Collicutt, *The Psychology of Christian Character Formation* (SCM Press, 2015).

Kathleen Dowling Singh, *The Grace in Aging: Awaken as you grow older* (Wisdom Publications, 2014).

Kathleen Dowling Singh, *The Grace in Dying: A message of hope, comfort and spiritual transformation* (HarperCollins, 1998).

Peter Enns, *How the Bible Actually Works* (Hodder and Stoughton, 2019).

Kathy Escobar, *Faith Shift: Finding your way forward when everything you believe is coming apart* (Convergent Books, 2014)

James W. Fowler, *Stages of Faith: The psychology of human development and the quest for meaning* (Harper and Row, 1981).

Richard Foster, *Streams of Living Water: Essential practices from the six great traditions of Christian faith* (HarperCollins, 2001).

Simon Garfield, *On the Map: Why the world looks the way it does* (Profile Books, 2013).

Thomas H. Green, *When the Well Runs Dry: Prayer beyond the beginnings* (Ave Maria Press, 1979).

John M. Hull, *What Prevents Christian Adults from Learning?* (SCM Press, 1985).

Alan Jamieson, *Journeying in Faith: In and beyond the tough places* (SPCK, 2004).

Alan Jones, *Soul Making: The desert way of spirituality* (Harper and Row, 1985).

Kieran Kavanaugh and Otilio Rodriguez (trans), *The Collected Works of Saint John of the Cross* (ICS Publications, 1991).

Martin Laird, *An Ocean of Light: Contemplation, transformation, liberation* (Oxford University Press, 2019).

Sandra M. Levy, *Imagination and the Journey of Faith* (Eerdmans, 2008).

Gregory Mayers, *Listen to the Desert: Secrets of spiritual maturity from the Desert Fathers and Mothers* (Burns and Oates, 1997).

Brian D. McLaren, *Faith After Doubt: Why your beliefs stopped working and what to do about it* (Hodder and Stoughton, 2021).

Thomas Merton, *New Seeds of Contemplation* (New Directions Books, 1961).

Michael Mitton, *Travellers of the Heart: Exploring new pathways on our spiritual journey* (BRF Ministries, 2013).

Gary Moon and David Benner (eds), *Spiritual Direction and the Care of Souls: A guide to Christian approaches and practices* (IVP, 2004).

Kevin O'Brien, *The Ignatian Adventure: Experiencing the spiritual exercises of Saint Ignatius in daily life* (Loyola Press, 2011).

Jenna Riemersma, *Altogether You: Experiencing personal and spiritual transformation with Internal Family Systems therapy* (Pivotal Press, 2020).

Don Riso and Russ Hudson, *The Wisdom of the Enneagram* (Random House, 1999).
Richard Rohr, *Falling Upward: A spirituality for the two halves of life* (Jossey-Bass, 2011).
Philip Sheldrake, *Befriending Our Desires* (Liturgical Press, 2016).
F. LeRon Shults and Steven J. Sandage, *Transforming Spirituality: Integrating theology and psychology* (Baker Academic, 2006).
Gordon T. Smith, *Transforming Conversion: Rethinking the language and contours of Christian initiation* (Baker Academic, 2010).
Jo Swinney, *Through the Dark Woods: A young woman's journey out of depression* (Monarch Books, 2006).
St Teresa of Ávila, *The Interior Castle*, trans. M. Starr (Riverhead Books, 2003).
Mark E. Thibodeaux, *Reimagining the Ignatian Examen: Fresh ways to pray from your day* (Loyola Press, 2015). Also comes as an app.
Curt Thompson, *Anatomy of the Soul: Surprising connections between neuroscience and spiritual practices that can transform your life* (Tyndale House, 2010).
Curt Thompson, *The Soul of Desire: Discovering the neuroscience of longing, beauty, and community* (IVP, 2021).
Bessel Van der Kolk, *The Body Keeps the Score: Brain, mind, and body in the healing of trauma* (Allen Lane, 2014).
Dallas Willard, *Renovation of the Heart: Putting on the character of Christ* (Nav Press, 2002).
Philip Yancey, *Reaching for the Invisible God* (Zondervan, 2000).
Philip Yancey, *The Bible Jesus Read: Why the Old Testament matters* (Zondervan, 1999).

Helpful podcasts

Unlocking Us with Brené Brown
Emotionally Healthy Leader with Peter Scazzero
Soul + Practice: Raw Conversations and Real Practices with Kathy Escobar and Phyllis Mathis
Turning to the Mystics with James Finley and Kirsten Oates
Mid-Faith Crisis with Nick Page and Joe Davis

Notes

1 For more information on spiritual direction and accompaniment, see the London Centre for Spiritual Direction: **lcsd.org.uk**
2 Philip Yancey, *The Jesus I Never Knew* (Marshall Pickering, 1995), p. 75.
3 For a taste of what we learned at this exhibition, see Jerry Brotton and Nick Millea, *Fifty Maps and the Stories They Tell* (Bodleian Library, 2019).
4 'Talking Maps', Bodleian Library exhibition, July 2019–March 2020.
5 Simon Garfield, *On the Map: Why the world looks the way it does* (Profile Books, 2013), p. 13.
6 Royal Museums Greenwich, 'What is the Prime Meridian – and why is it in Greenwich?', **rmg.co.uk/stories/topics/what-prime-meridian-why-it-greenwich**
7 **en.wikipedia.org/wiki/Mappa_mundi**
8 E. Louise Adnams, 'Pilgrimage: A paradigm for spiritual formation', *McMaster Journal of Theology and Ministry*, 12 (2010–11), pp. 132–65.
9 C.S. Lewis, *The Magician's Nephew* (The Bodley Head, 1955).
10 Richard Reddie, 'The church: enslaver or liberator', **bbc.co.uk/history/british/abolition/church_and_slavery_article_01.shtml**
11 Peter Enns, *How the Bible Actually Works* (Hodder and Stoughton, 2019), p. 5.
12 For much more on this and other crucial background knowledge, see John Barton, *A History of the Bible: The book and its faiths* (Allen Lane, 2019), ch. 1.
13 Barton, *A History of the Bible*, ch. 8.
14 **traumaresearchuk.org/ras-reticular-activating-system**.
15 Curt Thompson, *The Soul of Shame: Retelling the stories we believe about ourselves* (IVP, 2015), pp. 136–38.
16 Darryl Dash, 'Be careful about calling somebody a heretic', 2 June 2021, **ca.thegospelcoalition.org/columns/straight-paths/be-careful-about-calling-somebody-a-heretic**
17 Kathleen Dowling Singh, *The Grace in Aging: Awaken as you grow older* (Wisdom Publications, 2014), p. 44.
18 For a discussion of how conversion has been understood historically, see Gordon T. Smith, *Transforming Conversion: Rethinking the language and contours of Christian initiation* (Baker Academic, 2010).

19 Sheldon Sorge, in David L. Bartlett and Barbara Brown Taylor (eds), *Feasting on the Word*, Year C, Vol. 2 (Westminster John Knox Press, 2009), p. 294.
20 Richard Foster, *Streams of Living Water: Essential practices from the six great traditions of Christian faith* (HarperCollins, 2001).
21 Charlie Mackesy, *The Boy, the Mole, the Fox and the Horse* (Ebury Press, 2022).
22 Curt Thompson, *Anatomy of the Soul: Surprising connections between neuroscience and spiritual practices that can transform your life* (Tyndale House, 2010), ch. 3.
23 Richard Rohr, *Immortal Diamond: The search for our true self* (Wiley, 2013), p. 45.
24 Brené Brown, *I Thought It Was Just Me (But It Isn't): Making the journey from 'What will people think?' to 'I am enough'* (Avery, 2007); Thompson, *The Soul of Shame*.
25 Thompson, *The Soul of Shame*, p. 103.
26 Thomas Keating, *Invitation to Love: The way of Christian contemplation*, 20th Anniversary Edition (Bloomsbury, 2012), ch. 1.
27 Philip Sheldrake, *Befriending our Desires* (Liturgical Press, 2016), Introduction.
28 For more on conflicting parts of our inner self, see Jenna Riemersma, *Altogether You: Experiencing personal and spiritual transformation with Internal Family Systems therapy* (Pivotal Press, 2020).
29 We are of course much more nuanced than this as human beings and carry many more 'flavours' of desire and emotions, but we have chosen to focus on three core ones for simplicity here.
30 Don Riso and Russ Hudson, *The Wisdom of the Enneagram* (Random House, 1999), p. 49.
31 Adele Calhoun, Doug Calhoun, Clare Loughrige and Scott Loughrige, *Spiritual Rhythms for the Enneagram: A handbook for harmony and transformation* (IVP, 2019), p. 15.
32 Sebastian Münster, *Tabula Novarum Insularum* (1540).
33 David G. Benner, *Spirituality and the Awakening Self: The sacred journey of transformation* (Brazos Press, 2012).
34 Peter Scazzero, *Emotionally Healthy Spirituality: It's impossible to be spiritually mature, while remaining emotionally immature* (Zondervan, 2014).
35 F. LeRon Shults and Steven J. Sandage, *Transforming Spirituality: Integrating theology and psychology* (Baker Academic, 2006), pp. 215–16.

36 Janet O. Hagberg and Robert A. Guelich, *The Critical Journey: Stages in the life of faith* (Sheffield Publishing, 2005).
37 Scazzero, *Emotionally Healthy Spirituality*, pp. 7–21.
38 Shults and Sandage, *Transforming Spirituality*, p. 213.
39 For example, Teresa of Ávila describes the progression of 'rooms' one travels through in the process of spiritual formation. She also uses the metaphor of a caterpillar transforming into a butterfly. See St Teresa of Ávila, *The Interior Castle*, trans. M. Starr (Riverhead Books, 2003), chs 1, 2.
40 Walter Brueggemann, *Spirituality of the Psalms* (Fortress Press, 2002).
41 John M. Hull, *What Prevents Christian Adults from Learning?* (SCM Press, 1985), p. 127.
42 Dallas Willard, *Renovation of the Heart: Putting on the character of Christ* (Nav Press, 2002), p. 238.
43 Dick Van Dyke, *Keep Moving: And other tips and truths about living well longer* (Hachette Books, 2016).
44 Thomas H. Green, *When the Well Runs Dry: Prayer beyond the beginnings* (Ave Maria Press, 1979), p. 97.
45 Philip Yancey, *Reaching for the Invisible God* (Zondervan, 2000), p. 52.
46 Alan Jamieson, *Journeying in Faith: In and beyond the tough places* (SPCK, 2004); *Chrysalis: The hidden transformation in the journey of faith* (Paternoster, 2008).
47 Ajani Bazile-Dutes, '25 reasons why people stopped believing in God', BuzzFeed, 28 April 2019, **buzzfeed.com/ajanibazile/reasons-people-stopped-believing-in-god**
48 Kathy Escobar, *Faith Shift: Finding your way forward when everything you believe is coming apart* (Convergent Books, 2014), pp. 66–67.
49 Richard Rohr, 'Admitting our powerlessness', Center for Action and Contemplation daily meditations, 26 March 2023, **cac.org/daily-meditations/admitting-our-powerlessness-2023-03-26**
50 Brueggemann, *Spirituality of the Psalms*, p. 27.
51 Hagberg and Guelich, *The Critical Journey*, ch. 7.
52 Harvey Edser, 'Coping with our faith crises', The Evangelical Liberal, 11 August 2016, **evangelicalliberal.wordpress.com/2016/08/11/coping-with-our-faith-crises**.
53 See suggested reading, Kieran Kavanaugh and Otilio Rodriguez (trans), *The Collected Works of Saint John of the Cross* (ICS Publications, 1991); Teresa of Ávila, *The Interior Castle*; Gregory Mayers, *Listen to the Desert: Secrets of spiritual maturity from the Desert Fathers and Mothers* (Burns and Oates, 1997).

54 Jo Swinney, *Through the Dark Woods: A young woman's journey out of depression* (Monarch Books, 2006), p. 29.
55 Gordon Lynch, *Losing My Religion: Moving on from evangelical faith* (Darton, Longman and Todd, 2003), p. 20.
56 Dan Allender and Tremper Longman, *The Cry of the Soul: How our emotions reveal our deepest questions about God* (Longman Tremper, 1994), pp. 24–25.
57 Kavanaugh and Rodriguez (trans), *The Collected Works of Saint John of the Cross*, p. 376.
58 Chris Armstrong, 'C.S. Lewis's dark night of the soul', Grateful to the dead: A church historian's playground, 24 August 2011, **gratefultothedead.com/2011/08/24/c-s-lewiss-dark-night-of-the-soul**
59 St John of the Cross, as quoted by James Finley, *Turning to the Mystics*, CAC Podcast, season 3, session 17, 2021.
60 Thomas Merton, as quoted by Finley, *Turning to the Mystics*, season 1, session 6, 2020.
61 Martin Laird, *A Sunlit Absence: Silence, awareness and contemplation* (Oxford University Press, 2011), p. 62.
62 Peter Scazzero also points out that recognising we are not the centre of the universe through this sort of internal Copernican Revolution is key to mature relationships with our spouse, friend, child or colleague. Scazzero, *Emotionally Healthy Spirituality*, p. 181.
63 Alan Cowell, 'After 350 years Vatican says Galileo was right: it moves', *New York Times*, 31 October 1992, section 1, p. 1.
64 Joseph Luft, *The Johari Window: A graphic model of awareness in interpersonal relations* (Luft and Ingham, 1961).
65 Brené Brown, *Atlas of the Heart: Mapping meaningful connection and the language of human experience* (Penguin Random House, 2021), p. 158.
66 Morgan Freeman playing God in *Bruce Almighty* (Universal Pictures, 2003).
67 Thompson, *Anatomy of the Soul*, p. 133.
68 Martin Laird, *An Ocean of Light: Contemplation, transformation, liberation* (Oxford University Press, 2019), p. 88.
69 Ronald Cole-Turner, *Feasting on the Word*, Year B, Vol. 2, ed. David Bartlett and Barbara Brown Taylor (Westminster John Knox Press, 2003), p. 420.
70 Adele A. Calhoun, *Spiritual Disciplines Handbook: Practices that transform us* (IVP, 2015), p. 20.

71 Lisa Pauwels, Sima Chalavi and Stephan P. Swinnen, 'Aging and brain plasticity', *Aging*, 10(8), 2018, pp. 1789–90.
72 'Effects of trauma', **mind.org.uk/information-support/types-of-mental-health-problems/trauma/effects-of-trauma**
73 Brian McLaren, *Naked Spirituality: A life with God in twelve simple words* (Hodder and Stoughton, 2010), p. 239.
74 Richard Rohr, *Breathing under Water: Spirituality and the twelve steps* (SPCK, 2018).
75 Mark Greene, *Fruitfulness on the Frontline: Making a difference where you are* (IVP, 2014), p. 38.
76 Herbert Alphonso, *Discovering your Personal Vocation: The search for meaning through the spiritual exercises* (Paulist Press, 2001), p. 21.
77 This quote is attributed to Paula D'Arcy, but we cannot find the source of it.
78 Charles Hippsley and Mary Hippsley, *Growing on the Frontline: Grow more like Jesus where you are* (London Institute for Contemporary Christianity, 2022), p. 62.
79 Br. Geoffrey Tristram, 'Pilgrimage: a journey within', **ssje.org/2018/11/16/pilgrimage**
80 Etty Hillesum quoted in Patrick Woodhouse, *Life in the Psalms: Contemporary meaning in ancient texts* (Bloomsbury, 2015), p. 229.
81 Richard J. Foster and James Bryan Smith, *Devotional Classics: Selected readings for individuals and groups* (HarperCollins, 1993), pp. 41–47.
82 Woodhouse, *Life in the Psalms*.
83 Greene, *Fruitfulness on the Frontline*, p. 38.
84 Finley, *Turning to the Mystics*, season 3, session 17, 2021.
85 Laird, *An Ocean of Light*, ch. 5.
86 Dowling Singh, *The Grace in Aging*, pp. 53–54, 96–97.
87 'Talking maps', Bodleian Library exhibition, July 2019–March 2020.
88 Kathleen Dowling Singh, *The Grace in Dying: A message of hope, comfort and spiritual transformation* (HarperCollins, 1998), p. 180.
89 Dowling Singh, *The Grace in Aging*, pp. 96–97.
90 Elisabeth Kübler-Ross, *On Death and Dying: What the dying have to teach doctors, nurses, clergy and their own families* (Routledge, 2009).
91 Sogyal Rinpoche, *The Tibetan Book of Living and Dying* (Harper San Francisco, 1992), p. 107
92 Christopher Reeve playing Superman, *Superman* (Warner Bros. Pictures, 1978).
93 C.S. Lewis, *The Last Battle* (HarperCollins, 1998), pp. 209, 212, 213.

94 Brown, *Atlas of the Heart*.
95 You can find a good modern translation of this by Carmen Acevedo Butcher, *The Cloud of Unknowing: A new translation* (Shambhala Pocket Library, 2018).